The Tightwad Gazette II

The Tightwad Gazette II

Promoting Thrift as a Viable Alternative Lifestyle

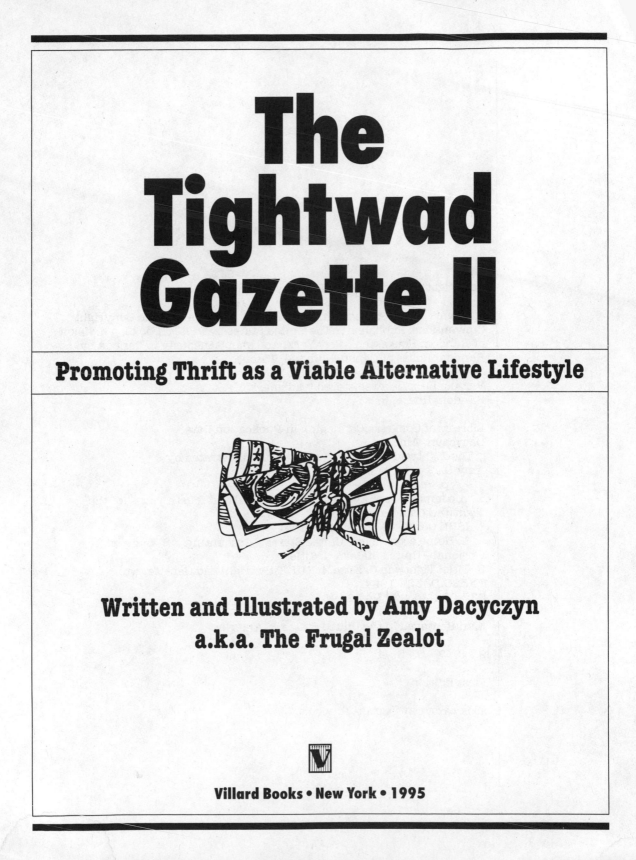

Written and Illustrated by Amy Dacyczyn
a.k.a. The Frugal Zealot

Villard Books • New York • 1995

Library of Congress Cataloging-in-Publication Data
Dacyczyn, Amy.
   The Tightwad Gazette II / written and illustrated by
Amy Dacyczyn.—1st ed.
        p.   cm.
   "A compilation of articles from the third and fourth years [of the
Tightwad Gazette newsletter]"—Introd.
      ISBN 0-679-75078-9 (acid-free)
      1. Home economics—United States—Accounting.   2. Budgets,
Personal—United States.   I. Title.
II. Title: Tightwad Gazette 2.   III. Title: Tightwad Gazette two.
TX326.D332   1994
332.024—dc20   94-12490

Manufactured in the United States of America

9 8 7 6 5 4 3 2

First Edition

BOOK LAYOUT BY BARBARA M. MARKS

A Word of Caution

Tightwads are by nature unconventional. We push the normal limits to make things last longer. We reuse things in unusual ways. We experiment constantly to find new, cheaper ways to do almost everything. Because this book draws upon the experiences of tightwads throughout the country, there is a chance we will inadvertently publish information that is technically illegal or not safe. On the other hand, all of the information in this book was previously published in a newsletter that was read by tens of thousands of people. Whenever any reader pointed out a concern, I thoroughly researched the question and then made a judgment as to the validity of the concern. These judgments are all incorporated in this book.

Based on this, to the best of my knowledge, all of the ideas in this book are legal. Likewise I believe all the ideas meet a reasonable level of safety. I pointed out any significant hazard I was aware of, but I did not point out safety concerns if the hazard was extremely remote. For example, when I suggested turning out the lights to save electricity, I did not warn you about the hazard of stumbling over your toddler's pull toy in the darkness.

You must exercise your personal judgment when using ideas in this book and take reasonable precautions.

Introduction

I know what you're thinking. "*The Tightwad Gazette II* . . . isn't that kind of like *Rocky II*?"

Interpretation: "All of the good ideas were used up in the original work. The sequel gets the leftovers." There are exceptions to this rule: The nine *Little House* books and the three *Godfather* movies come to mind. I believe you'll consider this *Tightwad* sequel an exception, too.

My new book is a compilation of about 80 percent of the articles from the third and fourth years of the *Tightwad Gazette* newsletter; my first book contained articles from the first two years. Although much of the work has the same character, there are a few differences, which resulted from changes in my life and in the outside world.

When I began my newsletter in June 1990, I had no journalism experience. I had a high-school-English background and had written reams of letters to grandmothers. I naïvely believed that if I could find a few thousand subscribers, between what I knew and what they knew we would never run out of ideas. Nine months later I had 1,700 subscribers. Since it was still hard to fill the "reader correspondence" page with good information from the very thin file of letters I received, the material continued to consist mostly of my own ideas, based on my own experience. At this time I was wearing all the hats in running the business. Jim, my husband, still worked for the Navy, and his long commute kept him away for twelve hours a day.

As we neared the close of the first year, the newsletter received extraordinary national publicity. A local reporter sold our story to *Parade* magazine, then we were featured as the sole guests on *Donahue*. At the time our business mushroomed to 40,000 subscribers, I was about to give birth to twins, my fifth and sixth children. Life became chaotic, despite the best efforts of my husband, who retired from the military and immediately stepped in to manage our business. At this point, the operation had a flock of "employees" (any friend or acquaintance who was willing to lend a hand) and was still run from the front parlor of our house. Our yard perpetually resembled a used-car lot.

Toward the end of the second year I was unhappy about the quality of our family life—we were eating too many macaroni-and-cheese dinners at 8:00 P.M.—and the conditions under which we were operating our business made it difficult to produce my best work. I was fast approaching burnout. One night Jim and I collapsed on the couch, each holding a sleeping baby, and one of us (I don't recall which) said, "We both need a clone."

My clone turned out to be Brad Lemley, the very same writer who had sold our story to *Parade* and the namesake of my youngest son. Brad said the story he wrote about us for *Parade* had influenced him more than any story he had ever written. He became a card-carrying tightwad. We stayed in touch over the following year as an unexpected friendship grew out of the way in which we had changed each other's lives. Brad offered continuing support and encouragement and endless hours of over-the-phone idea-bouncing. Two years ago, he confided that he wanted to quit his newspaper job. He knew I needed help. In order to supplement his other writing, he needed two days of employment a week. I hired him on the spot. Imagine this: A real writer—someone who has written for national magazines and (golly!) has a college education—wants to work for the *Tightwad Gazette!*

Our plan was that Brad would help only with research, editing, and letter reading. I wanted to retain sole responsibility for the creative writing. But then, one day while I was banging my head against a computer screen to come up with a clever headline, he said, "What about 'Chalk Is Cheap'?" It was perfect. Over time our collaborative effort has evolved into a

joined-at-the-hip writing style. We literally sit side-by-side, sharing one computer keyboard, often laughing until the tears come. I usually write the basic articles alone, then we refine them together.

When we discussed a potential clone for Jim, a perfect-but-unavailable candidate came to mind: Elaine Briggs, the owner of a small computer store, a friend, and a longtime subscriber. Word of our search traveled through the grapevine. Then one day Elaine appeared on our doorstep, announcing she *was* available and applying for the job. Elaine possesses exceptional business and computer skills, which keep our business running like clockwork. Most important, she brought to the job an unspoken understanding that her job is to make my job easier. With the addition of a capable manager, Jim could really "retire" to the full-time job of managing our household. We now eat real meals at reasonable times. We moved our business out of our front parlor, moving all the employees, mailings, noisy equipment, and the used-car lot to a ranch house four miles away. I still work out of my home office.

In addition to these two clones, we have six more full- and part-time workers. They sort incoming mail, fill orders, send out the monthly mailing, do bookkeeping, run errands, and occasionally offer creative headlines and article ideas. They've become our closest friends and extended family, with whom we've shared tightwad practical jokes, rubber-band shootouts, "pizza Fridays," and ruthless croquet games.

So, getting back to what I said

about sequels, *The Tightwad Gazette* is no longer a one-woman operation. This book has subtle differences that make it even more useful than before. Since I've had more free time to research, I've written a higher number of in-depth articles based on the expert opinions of others.

You'll also find much more participation from readers. For the past two years, I have had enough time to read some of the mountain of reader letters I received during the overload days, and many became the basis for articles. Previously when I asked readers for ideas on a specific subject, I would get only a handful of replies. Now up to 250 people respond when I ask for information. My network of newsletter readers (now about 50,000—not including the huge number of cheapies who read other people's *Gazettes*) is a frugal-ingenuity resource unparalleled anywhere in journalism. I've found that someone out there knows the answer to any tight-waddery question. If I'm wrong about anything, someone out there will let me know.

One feature this book has in common with the first is its "loose" structure. Because the material first appeared in a loosely structured newsletter, trying to shoehorn these articles and illustrations into a highly structured format would result in an organizational nightmare. Even more important, the looser structure makes the *Tightwad* books more readable. Most readers of the first book reported that it was fun to read. One reader offered the most astute observation. She found that this loose structure forced her to read the whole book rather than simply skip to chapters she thought would be relevant. As a result, she gained a broader range of information.

As you read this book, remember that the material first appeared in a newsletter, and that the very purpose of a newsletter is to address a need that is not met by the mainstream media. Traditional financial and consumer writers offer safe, halfway advice: They'll tell you how to feed a family of four for $84 a week (when it can be done for half that amount). The same writers tell you it's becoming increasingly difficult, if not impossible, for families to make ends meet. In fact, by adhering to this halfway advice, many families would not make ends meet. The *Tightwad Gazette* newsletter came about as a reaction to this traditional advice and the widespread belief that, financially speaking, life in the nineties is impossible. I knew that people could achieve the "impossible" with a little discipline and a willingness to do things that mainstream thinkers deem too extreme.

If you do not have difficulty making ends meet, you'll find that some of the material in the book does not apply to you. But you will find fresh ideas for saving money. Even if you do have trouble making ends meet, some of my ideas may seem too radical to you. It was never my intention to write about ideas that were 100 percent acceptable to mainstream America. This book explores the boundaries, and my intent is to present options, not to suggest that every idea is appropriate for everyone.

Finally, this is not only a financial textbook, it is also a celebration of the frugal life. While most of the articles contain practical information, some are there simply to express what I have found: that tightwaddery is about not hardship and deprivation, but fun and creativity.

The Tightwad Gazette II

A READER'S GUIDE TO *THE TIGHTWAD GAZETTE*

A hardworking math instructor stood before a blackboard, demonstrating how to multiply large numbers. After she completed the third problem, a student raised his hand and said, "I suppose a few kids might need to know that 37 times 79 equals 2,923, that 16 times 81 equals 1,296, and that 46 times 59 equals 2,714, but I don't. I need to know what 83 times 22 equals. You're just not giving me answers that help me."

Obviously, the student didn't understand the instructor's teaching strategy. When she first began teaching multiplication to the class, she had students memorize multiplication tables. When they had mastered those, she proceeded to teach them how to use them to multiply larger numbers.

Because of the infinite number of combinations that could be multiplied, it wasn't practical to have students memorize beyond 12 times 12. Likewise, the teacher could not predict the multiplication answers her students might need to know in the future. So the instructor's purpose was to teach the *process* of multiplying by demonstrating specific examples. Once the students mastered the process, they would be able to solve every multiplication problem they encountered for the rest of their lives.

Teaching people how to save money through creative use of their resources is much like teaching multiplication.

A few problems are common to most people and can be solved with resources that are common to most households. For example,

page 93's "Budget Bug Busting" presents seven inexpensive bug killers that can be made of stuff found in any household.

But in most cases, each of us is presented with unique problems, which we must solve with our own unique supply of resources. An example of this is the story on page 118 about how Jim made a sled for our twins using scrap lumber and old skis.

When you multiply the number of possible problems by the number of possible resources, the solutions are infinite.

Like the math instructor, I am from time to time confronted by readers who are frustrated that space was devoted to an idea or article that wasn't useful to them. In many cases, readers fail to see that he or she benefits from learning the process or from having a process they already know reinforced.

For example, when I wrote about making a Frankenstein Halloween mask from dryer-lint mâché, I thought a few readers might attempt to make a Frankenstein Halloween mask from dryer-lint mâché. Some might be inspired to make Halloween masks from other inexpensive materials. Others might be inspired to make other projects from dryer-lint mâché. Most would learn a larger concept—that wonderful things can be made from the humblest of materials. A few readers, unfortunately, would not see any point in it at all.

The desire for "relevant tips" rather than "process" leads to a common observation among either older or single readers: that there are too many children's articles that "don't apply to me." Elaine, my business manager and an early subscriber, was the first to bring this up.

On the average, 12.9 percent of the total column space has been devoted to ideas relating to children of various ages. A high percentage of my readers have children, so to me this does not seem to be overdoing it.

No periodical is able to hit every reader right between the eyes with every article; that's the nature of publishing. In fact, many of the specific subjects that I write about are not relevant to *my* life. The mail-order prescription-drug article, the storage article, and the inexpensive travel-lodging article are a few of those that are not relevant to me.

But in each of these articles, the process—digging for the least expensive option—*is* relevant to me. And every once in a while I know that the lessons are getting through when a reader takes it upon herself to solve a problem. In a recent letter, Katherine Richardson Kenward of Homewood, Illinois, said she almost wrote to ask me if ground turkey at $1.18 per pound (the best price in her area) was a better deal than whole turkey at 49¢ per pound. But inspired by my many examples of nitpicky calculations, she decided

to figure it out herself. She cooked up a whole turkey, deboned it, and weighed the meat. She learned that whole-turkey meat was 82¢ per pound. And she could make broth from the bones to boot.

When I decided to write about frugality, I made a conscious decision to approach the subject in a unique way. Some of my predecessors wrote about frugality as a collection of tips. But, like answers to multiplication problems, random tips are hard to remember and have limited application. Other predecessors wrote about frugality as a philosophy or process. Again, like learning about multiplication, general processes are hard to grasp and retain unless they are taught through specific examples.

So I've always worked for a balance of specific examples and process/philosophy. This way, even if the example isn't useful to every reader, the larger idea is reinforced.

Furthermore, tips alone are boring, as is process alone, but the combination tends to be far more interesting.

Finally: Sometimes, it's surprising to see what turns out to be relevant after all. We ran an article about making a hat by draping and molding sheets of newspaper over a kid's head, winding masking tape around the crown, and crumpling the paper up to form the brim. Elaine (a.k.a. Little Miss It-Doesn't-Relate-to-Me-I'm-Single) was so taken with my daughter's hat that she asked me to make her one, paper plume and all.

THE TIGHTWAD-PER-CAPITA SURVEY

Did you ever wonder if frugality is more acceptable in some parts of the country than in others?

We wondered if that could be figured based on our mailing list. Since our publicity has had an even distribution throughout the country via *Parade* magazine, *Donahue,* and several other national programs and publications, the notion didn't seem far-fetched.

We broke down our mailing list of everyone who had ever subscribed (over 100,000) and compared those numbers to the 1990 census. After a couple of hours of tedious work with a calculator, I came up with figures for how many subscribers we have per 100,000 people in each state.

Obviously, the Maine figure, and perhaps the New Hampshire and Vermont figures, reflects more local media coverage. Aside from that, we are generally more popular in the North than in the South. Beyond that, I don't see an obvious

TIGHTWAD GAZETTE SUBSCRIBERS PER 100,000

State	Value	State	Value	State	Value
Maine	215.05	Rhode Island	50.03	New Mexico	36.36
New Hampshire	86.81	Iowa	49.46	New Jersey	36.15
Vermont	81.90	Ohio	48.08	Tennessee	34.31
Alaska	69.44	Missouri	46.26	Indiana	30.96
Wyoming	66.14	Montana	44.80	South Carolina	30.95
Washington	62.46	Illinois	44.68	Alabama	30.05
Nebraska	59.10	Pennsylvania	44.44	New York	30.03
Delaware	58.38	Georgia	43.80	California	28.67
Wisconsin	58.24	Virginia	41.53	Arkansas	28.50
Connecticut	57.60	North Carolina	40.57	West Virginia	26.54
Oregon	57.11	Maryland	40.00	Kentucky	26.38
Colorado	54.53	Michigan	39.59	Oklahoma	25.02
Minnesota	52.99	Florida	39.51	Louisiana	23.22
Idaho	52.55	Texas	38.57	South Dakota	22.84
Kansas	52.55	North Dakota	38.04	Washington, D.C.	22.74
Utah	52.47	Arizona	37.76	Mississippi	20.83
Massachusetts	51.92	Nevada	36.64	Hawaii	18.68

pattern. Why are we three times more popular in Alaska than in Mississippi? Beats me. Perhaps these figures demonstrate the popularity of *The Tightwad Gazette,* not a state's overall frugality.

In any case, to me by far the most revealing figure is that Washington, D.C., has the third fewest tightwads per 100,000.

POSTAL PRESCRIPTIONS

According to Joe and Dr. Theresa Graedon, who write a syndicated column called "People's Pharmacy," over the last decade prescription-drug prices rose at triple the inflation rate, which made the drug industry the most profitable in the nation.

You can combat these price increases by purchasing drugs through mail-order pharmacies.

Local pharmacies argue that they offer better service, but mail-order pharmacies also keep records of the drugs you have bought from them and have staff pharmacists available to answer questions.

As always, we ask you to compare for yourself. All of these companies will quote prices on the phone. And remember, ask your doctor to write "substitutions permitted" on your prescription so that you can get the generic equivalent. By law, these must be as good as the name brand and are often exactly the same medicine, made by the same company that makes the name brand.

I compared prices of several mail-order pharmacies with a large chain pharmacy in our area.

For the purposes of comparison, I requested the prices of four "maintenance" medications, the sort taken over a long period of time for chronic conditions. These were: Zantac, 150 milligrams, used to treat ulcers; Prozac, 20 milligrams, an antidepressant; Micronase, 5 milligrams, for diabetes; and Tenormin, 50 milligrams, for high blood pressure. All medications compared were in 100-tablet quantities.

Generally, a drug prescribed for a one-time use should be purchased locally, since you probably can't wait a week to receive it through the mail.

Below are prices for the

	Action	AARP	Family	Medi-Mail	America's	Local Chain
Zantac	$123.39	$126.85	$137.40	$138.95	$142.98	$148.21
Prozac	$162.99	$171.35	$182.97	$180.95	$187.98	$209.56
Micronase	$ 41.39	$ 41.60	$ 42.86*	$ 43.95	$ 50.00	$ 50.46
Tenormin	$ 73.39*	$ 69.95*	$ 75.24*	$ 76.95*	$ 77.79*	$ 78.69*

pharmacies I compared. (Ordering information follows.) Asterisks indicate that these companies offer a generic or alternative drug that is significantly cheaper.

The local chain pharmacy offers a 10 percent discount to senior citizens, which is not reflected in the prices listed. If you factor in this discount and the shipping-and-handling charge, the local chain pharmacy's prices become competitive with some, but not all, of the mail-order prices.

Action Mail Order Drug
P.O. Box 787
Waterville, ME 04903-0787
(800) 452-1976
Requirements: The written prescription must be mailed or the doctor must call.
Shipping and handling: 75¢ per order.
(Thanks to reader Kathryn Buck of Brunswick, Maine, for sending us information on Action Drug.)

AARP Pharmacy Service
P.O. Box 30047
Reno, NV 89520-3047
(800) 477-7407
Requirements: The written prescription must be mailed or the doctor must call. Anyone can use this service; you don't need to be a member of the AARP.
Shipping and handling: $1 per order.
Note: There are 13 AARP Pharmacy Service centers; call 1-800-456-2277 for the one nearest you.

Family Pharmaceuticals
P.O. Box 1288
Mt. Pleasant, SC 29465
(800) 922-3444
Requirements: The written pre-

scription must be mailed or the doctor must call.
Shipping and handling: $1.50 per order.

Medi-Mail, Inc.
P.O. Box 98520
Las Vegas, NV 89193-8520
(800) 331-1458
Requirements: The written prescription must be mailed or the doctor must call.
Shipping and handling: $1.48 per order.

America's Pharmacy
6109 Willowmere Drive
Des Moines, IA 50321
(515) 243-6447
Requirements: For the first order, you must mail in the prescription. For subsequent orders, your physician may call.
Shipping and handling: $1.40 per order.

PIZZA FOR PENNIES

Jim can make two cheese pizzas for under $1 each in less than 20 minutes of hands-on time. How?

Our pizza dough recipe comes from a wonderful cookbook called *The Food Processor Bread Book* by the editors of Consumer Guide, published by Simon & Schuster. Unfortunately, it is out of print, but you may be able to get it from your library, through an inter-library loan, or from a used bookstore.

Bread dough made in a food processor requires no hand kneading. (A food processor is, in my opinion, a valuable tightwad tool.)

THICK AND CHEWY PIZZA DOUGH

½ to ¾ cup warm water (105 to
    115 degrees F.)
1 package (1 tablespoon) dry
    yeast
1 teaspoon sugar
2 cups flour
1 tablespoon vegetable oil
½ teaspoon salt

Combine ¼ cup of the water
with the yeast and sugar.
Stir to dissolve the yeast,
and let stand until bub-
bly, about five min-
utes.

Put the flour,
oil, and salt
into a food
processor,
and process
about five seconds with a steel
blade.

Add the yeast mixture to the
flour mixture, and process about
10 seconds, or until blended.

Turn on the processor and drizzle just enough of the remaining
water through the feed tube so the
dough forms a ball that cleans the
sides of the bowl. Process so that
the ball turns around about 25
times.

Put the dough ball onto a 14-
inch greased pizza pan or large
cookie sheet. Cover with plastic
wrap or a bowl, and let stand 10
minutes.

Pat the dough out so that it covers the pan, leaving a ridge on the
edges. (Or, if you're feeling really
adventurous, spin the dough in
the air a few times.) Spread with
pizza sauce, and add cheese and
toppings.

Bake at 425 degrees for 15 to
20 minutes, or until the crust is
golden and the cheese is bubbly.

We use the following recipe for
homemade spaghetti/pizza sauce.
We grow our own tomatoes and
peppers, buy spices cheap from a
health-food store, and buy tomato
paste on sale, so the cost is only
about 40¢ per quart.

If you have to buy the produce,
this recipe probably wouldn't beat
double-coupon-purchased sauce.
But even if you can't garden, you
might have a friend or relative
who has surplus tomatoes. And
top-quality produce isn't needed;
we have purchased pepper seconds from a grower.

We have experimented with
making tomato paste, but the required time to cook tomatoes down
to paste thickness did not seem
economical. Adding tomato paste
to the sauce lessens the cooking
time significantly.

Because you make large quantities at a time, this recipe is also a
time saver compared to making
sauce from scratch every time you
need it.

SPAGHETTI/PIZZA SAUCE

12 onions
6 green peppers
1½ cups vegetable oil
1½ teaspoons black pepper
36 tomatoes, skinned
4 cloves garlic, minced
3 tablespoons salt
4 tablespoons sugar
2 tablespoons each: oregano,
    sweet basil, and thyme
12 bay leaves
5 12-ounce cans tomato paste

Grind (as you would with a meat
grinder) onions and peppers, and
simmer in vegetable oil. Add black
pepper.

In a *large* pot place tomatoes, garlic, salt, sugar, herbs, and onion-pepper mixture. Bring to a good rolling boil. Add tomato paste last, one can at a time. Pour into canning jars and process in a pressure cooker for 25 minutes. Or sauce can be frozen. Makes 7 quarts.

WHAT TO DO WITH . . .

As you read these, keep in mind: You don't have to save every toilet-paper tube in the hope of finding a use for it, but if you have a need and a toilet-paper tube works, why not use it? The point is that you should look to the available materials you have before you spend money.

For example: Recently, I was framing several photographs with old wooden frames. I had everything but those tiny brads or diamond-shaped things used to hold the backing in the frame. The project lay unfinished for several days while I waited until I could get to the store. In the meantime, I spotted my huge collection of used X-Acto blades, which are too dull for doing paste-ups but fine for rougher cutting. These worked perfectly—even better than the brads—for securing my pictures in the frames.

The benefit of reusing things goes beyond monetary savings. In this case, even if I waited until I was running other errands, a special trip to a frame shop or hardware store might have required 15 to 30 minutes, depending on how many stores I needed to visit. It always amazes me that people don't think shopping is time-consuming.

Bread Bags. Use to make jump ropes by splitting the bag down the side seams to make a long piece of plastic. Braid three lengths together. When you get to an end of plastic, wrap another  bag end around the first. Stagger joinings to prevent a clump. Make handles from duct tape. (Jean Trocchia, Vermilion, Ohio.)

Burned Cookies. Use a coarse grater to scrape off the burned bottom of the cookie. This works much faster and better than using a knife.

Six-Pack Plastic Rings. Use to make a volleyball net. Tie them together with twist ties. During the winter months let kids use a balloon for indoor volleyball. (Denise Muhlbauer, Carroll, Iowa.)

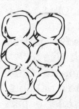

Bread Tabs. Use for stitch counters on knitting needles. Or use as a divider for index cards. Secure with tape on both sides. Use a permanent marker. (Dolly-Ellen Walters, Eagle River, Alaska.)

The Serrated Edge on Wax-Paper Box. Make a picture frame hanger. Cut into small sections, and bend into

needed shape. Nail onto a frame with two tiny nails. The serrated edge already has holes for nailing. (Jadie Henton, Lynnwood, Washington.)

Old Blue Jeans. Make coin purses out of the pockets for kids. Re-

move two pockets from pants, sew a zipper across the top, and stitch the sides together. (Laurel Craven, Fort Worth, Texas.)

Old Shower Curtains. Make baby bibs. Clean and sterilize. Sew on bias tape for neck strings. Fold up bottom, sew to make a food-catcher pocket. (Sheryl-Anne Tumlin-Welch, Akron, Ohio.)

Magazine Stamps from Junk Mail. Use to make a piñata. Glue stamps to a balloon, and use toilet-paper tubes to make legs and head. (Sandra Sterner, Pittsburgh, Pennsylvania.)

Worn Tube Socks. If the toes wear out, first turn them inside out, cut off worn toe, and resew on a curve. Same sock, just shorter. (Judy O'Boyle, Kalispell, Montana.)

Old Credit Cards. Make several guitar picks from one card. Make

softer picks from milk-jug plastic or plastic lids. (Rebecca Bryant, Russell Springs, Kentucky.)

Margarine Containers. Using a paper punch, make holes in the lid. This makes a great shaker container for cinnamon sugar to sprinkle on toast.

Milk Jugs. Use to get free hot water. Paint jugs a dark color, fill

with water, and let them sit in the hot sun. (Linda Louden, Sierra Vista, Arizona.)

Film Canisters. Poke holes in the bottoms to make salt and pepper shakers for lunch boxes or camping trips.

Junk Mail. Save any large colored pieces of paper, such as the plain back of a brochure, for future art projects.

TO WASH, TO WAX, OR TO RUST

A friend told me his theory that waxing your car frequently would prevent rust. This seemed like worthy subject matter for *The Tightwad Gazette,* because rust kills cars, and new cars cost money. To check out his theory we devised the following test:

Ten years ago we bought three 1985 Plymouth Horizons. Car #1 was washed and waxed regularly. Car #2 was washed only. Car #3 was neither washed nor waxed.

Over the last decade we have taken great pains to insure that all three cars received equal exposure to the elements.

Today, cars #1 and #2 both have bodies in approximately the same good condition. Car #3, however, sits today a rusted-out hulk, a mere memory of its former self.

Our test results demonstrate conclusively that car washing by itself will greatly reduce a tendency to rust.

Only kiddin', folks.

There's a far tightwaddier way to gather information. Cite the research done by publications with more resources than we have.

In 1984, *Consumer Reports* took a survey (they didn't do the which-of-these-three-cars-will-rust-to-oblivion test either) of 3,303 car owners whose cars were at least eight years old or had traveled at least 100,000 miles.

Of snow-belt cars, 25 percent of those washed infrequently suffered significant rust, while only 8 percent of those washed frequently suffered severe rust problems.

But *CR* also discovered that of the frequently washed group, those that were also waxed often were not better off in terms of keeping rust at bay.

The *CR* engineers say that's because rust usually starts on the inside of the body. So keep your car washed, and be especially careful to rinse road salt off of the underbody and from under the fenders. An easy time to do this is when you are changing your oil: With the front wheels on ramps, the underbody is accessible for thorough squirting.

And, if you have time, a nice wax job looks good.

FIRE AND ICE

Dear Amy,

I put three pieces of charcoal in my refrigerator and three in my freezer. They are great at absorbing unwanted odors. After a month, I replace them with fresh ones and return the old ones to the bag for burning on the grill.

—Irene Hartley
Fowler, Ohio

TRASH 'N' TREASURE

Dear Amy,

Twice a year our church has a clothing exchange. One day, everyone may bring any clothes, toys, housewares, etc. that they don't need, and the next day they may come back and take anything they do need. No money changes hands; it's purely stewardship. On the first day, anyone who helps sort clothes (an all-day job) gets to take home things to try on that day; it's our "payment."

—Mary T. Lichlyter
Colorado Springs, Colorado

PICKLE-JUICE REUSE

Dear Amy,

I save the liquid from a jar of pickles when the pickles are gone. Then I buy a cucumber, slice it thin, and pack the slices back down in the pickle jar with its liquid. Cover, refrigerate for four days, and you have a jar of pickles for the cost of one cucumber.

—Claire Morgret
Elida, Ohio

CALCULATING YOUR C.P.M.

I've finally done something I've been meaning to do for years. I have always wanted to work out *and* write down the costs of various ingredients that I use frequently in baking so that I can easily calculate the savings of baking from scratch.

So here's my chart. I weighed a cup of each ingredient. From that, and the price per pound, I calculated the cost per cup. A cup has 16 tablespoons, and a tablespoon has 3 teaspoons, so I calculated those two quantities and rounded the cost to the nearest ⅒th for easy addition.

The important information here is the volume-to-weight equivalences. If your prices vary from mine (as they almost certainly will) you can use these equivalences to make your own equa-tions. Then you, too, will be able to compute your C.P.M. (Cost Per Muffin).

The chart has two references to milk: dry milk powder for when you add it in dry form to your recipe, and liquid milk for when you add milk made from dry milk powder to your recipe. If you (heaven forbid!) use whole milk in your baking, the cost will be about 50% more, or 13½¢ per cup if you purchase milk at $2.19 per gallon.

The chart does not include the cost of eggs. If you pay 89¢ for a dozen, then one egg costs 7½¢.

For those who don't know . . . Soy flour makes a terrific substitu-tion for eggs in baking, meatloafs, etc. A heaping tablespoon of soy flour and a tablespoon of water equals an egg. Once baked, there is no taste or texture difference in the final product. Look for it at natural-food stores.

Ingredient	Price Per Pound	Weight Per Cup	Price Per Cup	Price Per Tablespoon	Price Per Teaspoon
Flour	$ .16	6 oz.	6¢	⅗₀¢	⅒¢
Oatmeal	.40	4 oz.	10¢	⁶⁄₁₀¢	²⁄₁₀¢
Cornmeal	.30	6 oz.	11¢	⁷⁄₁₀¢	²⁄₁₀¢
Soy Flour	1.00	4 oz.	25¢	1⁵⁄₁₀¢	⁵⁄₁₀¢
Sugar	.35	8 oz.	18¢	1¹⁄₁₀¢	⁴⁄₁₀¢
Brown Sugar	.38	7 oz.	17¢	1¢	³⁄₁₀¢
Dry Milk Powder	1.74	3 oz.	33¢	2¢	⁷⁄₁₀¢
Liquid Milk	.18	8 oz.	9¢	⁶⁄₁₀¢	²⁄₁₀¢
Margarine	.40	8 oz.	20¢	1³⁄₁₀¢	⁴⁄₁₀¢
Shortening	.66	8 oz.	33¢	2¢	⁷⁄₁₀¢
Corn Oil	.52	8 oz.	26¢	1⁶⁄₁₀¢	⁵⁄₁₀¢
Cocoa	1.15	4 oz.	29¢	1⁸⁄₁₀¢	⁶⁄₁₀¢
Baking Powder	.91	8 oz.	45¢	2⁸⁄₁₀¢	⁹⁄₁₀¢
Baking Soda	.33	8 oz.	17¢	1¹⁄₁₀¢	³⁄₁₀¢
Cream of Tartar	1.80	8 oz.	90¢	5⁶⁄₁₀¢	1⁸⁄₁₀¢
Salt	.29	10 oz.	18¢	1¹⁄₁₀¢	⁴⁄₁₀¢
Raisins	1.05	4 oz.	26¢	1⁶⁄₁₀¢	⁵⁄₁₀¢
Coconut	1.15	2 oz.	14¢	⁹⁄₁₀¢	³⁄₁₀¢

HOW TO DISSECT A PAIR OF PANTY HOSE

Hortense DuVall of Clinton, Maryland, swears by a product called Hosiery Mate, which the maker claims more than doubles hosiery life. The directions say that you should rinse between wearings and it will strengthen the fibers to prevent snags and runs. A 16-fluid-ounce bottle for $3.50 is good for 60 rinses. I am not familiar with Hosiery Mate, but because it costs less than a pair of hose, it does seem that it would save you money.

When it's time to retire a pair of hose, don't throw it away. Cut it up for other uses:

Use the elastic for a bungee cord or to replace stretched-out elastic in pajamas, or cover with cloth to make a headband.

Segments can be tied off at the bottom, attached to a trellis, and used as slings to support cantaloupe, eggplant, and other heavy fruits. This is useful in gardens with limited space where produce must be grown vertically. (Jill Finch, Irving, Texas.)

Cut into loops to make filler for stuffed animals.

Put onions into one leg of clean panty hose. Tie a knot between each one. Snip onions off as needed. No mess. (Kathy Takvam, Silver Bay, Minnesota.)

Lengths of panty hose can be used to tie many things. Because they're soft and elastic, they're perfect for tying up tomato vines.

Cut off the bad leg and wear the remaining good one-legged panty hose with another pair of one-legged panty hose. (Amazingly, some people have not heard of this oldest of tightwad tricks.)

Put human hair (obtained in quantity from a barber) or dog hair into tied-off sections and place them around your garden. The scent keeps deer away.

Cut in a spiral to make a thin strip that can be crocheted to make bracelets, headbands, rope—even a bikini. (Lorelle Becton, Philadelphia, Pennsylvania.)

Cut off and wear over your head for a bank-robber or monster Halloween mask.

Lop off the toes. Put a "toe" on each foot before you put on a new pair to keep the toes from wearing through.

NEW LIFE FOR OLD CARTRIDGES

Computers sometimes remind me of Barbie dolls: The expense isn't in the toy itself, but in the accessories.

Software, CD-ROM drives, modems, and other computer stuff all cost money, but for us, and probably many computer users, the biggest ongoing expense is supplying the printer with new cartridge-type ribbons. Both daisy-wheel and dot-matrix printers use them. Prices range from $3 to $32, with the average around $8.

Fortunately, there is an alternative to simply tossing and replacing cartridges. They can be reused.

Because of the great number of ribbon types, manufacturers, and distributors, it wasn't easy to compare costs. In some cases, it can be cheaper to buy a new ribbon than reuse an old one. This is especially true of one-time film ribbons, which cannot be reinked. This article, therefore, addresses reuse of the more common fabric ribbons.

There are two ways to squeeze more use out of a ribbon cartridge: re-inking and reloading.

RE-INKING (three methods)

1. Pry open your cartridge with a knife (test this on an old cartridge to see whether it can be opened and closed without damage), and drip a specially formulated ink directly onto the ribbon coil. This ink, called Ribbon Re-new, is sold by V-Tech Inc., 2223 Rebecca, Hatfield, PA, 19440, (215) 822-2989. V-Tech says if left overnight, the ink's wicking action will thoroughly coat the ribbon. One $4.95 bottle will re-ink a ribbon up to 30 times. The instructions recommend using 20 drops of ink, but reader David W. Carnell of Wilmington, North Carolina, found that only 10 drops work fine.

2. Re-ink your ribbon on a re-inking machine. These devices run the ribbon around an ink-filled spool.

The least expensive one we found is the EZEE Inker, a hand-cranked model offered for $39.50 plus $4.00 shipping by Borg Industries, Ltd., P.O. Box 508, Janesville, IA, 50647, (800) 553-2404. Borg sells motorized models too.

The most popular motorized re-inker among our readers was the MacInker, which sells for $69.95 plus $6 shipping by Computer Friends, 14250 N.W. Science Park Dr., Portland, OR, 97229, (503) 626-2291.

We bought a similar motorized machine from V-Tech for $63 (call them for shipping costs) and found it easy to use. The ribbon must run at a constant speed around the ink spool for at least fifteen minutes to get even coating, so we recommend the motorized version for all but the most patient.

Remember:

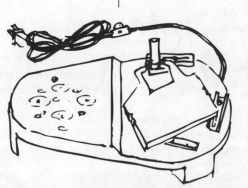

You must use a lot of ribbons for a re-inker to pay for itself quickly (unless you are one of the poor slobs who has to buy those $32 cartridges).

3. If you are not the do-it-yourself type, mail your old cartridges to a professional re-inking company. The typical cost might be $3 per ribbon.

A note of caution: A reader who runs a computer-maintenance shop says that you must use specially formulated ink, like the kind sold by the companies listed here, or your printhead could be damaged. He also warns that if you let your ribbon get too worn, a pin from your dot-matrix printhead can catch in the frayed fibers and bend, so keep an eye on the ribbon's condition.

RELOADING (two methods)

1. You can pop a new ribbon into your old cartridge. V-Tech sells these, along with instructions, for about one quarter the cost of a new cartridge. Company president Gene Beals told us the process can be a bit messy, but what the heck—you end up with an essentially new cartridge (ready for a new succession of re-inkings).

2. You can send your old ribbons to a reloading company, but the savings drop off dramatically. One such company is Best Impressions, 1480 N. Cave Creek Rd., Suite 18, Phoenix, AZ, 85032, (800) 798-2345, which reloads ribbons for about 30 percent less than the price of their new ones.

Again, there are no cut-and-dried answers. You need to check all of the options and see what makes the most sense for you.

MAKING A SOLAR BOX COOKER

Across America, tightwads crank up their stoves to cook supper on hot summer days. As their utility bills roll in, they broil along with their chickens and mutter, "There must be a better way."

There is.

Solar cookers have been around for decades. But many of the early designs were expensive and needed almost constant tending. Then in 1976, Barbara Kerr, a Phoenix social worker and backyard tinkerer, fiddled with various solar-oven designs and came up with one that could be constructed in a couple of hours with common household materials and tools.

Her new design can reach 275 degrees F., hot enough to cook food or kill germs in water. It can cook almost anything that can be cooked in a conventional oven or on a stovetop. It can bake bread, roast chicken, cook stew, and steam rice, beans, potatoes, and other vegetables. The cooking time is about twice as long as by conventional methods, but there is less labor because there is no need for stirring or basting.

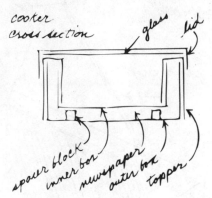

cooker cross section

glass

lid

spacer block

inner box

newspaper

outer box

topper

We got a set of plans and built one. Basically, you cover the bottom of a big box with insulating material such as crumpled newspaper. Put six small spacer blocks on the bottom of the box, and set a smaller box inside the big one. Fill the space between the sides of the two boxes with more crumpled newspaper. If your boxes have flaps, use these to fold over and cover the insulated space. Or you can make "toppers," which are pieces of cardboard folded over the top of the insulated space; they cover the inside of the inside box and outside the outside box and are tied with string at the corners. Line the inner box and inside of the topper sides with aluminum foil adhered with nontoxic glue, so that the entire inside of the cooker is lined. Set a piece of glass over the oven. Make a cardboard lid that has a large, foil-lined reflector flap cut out of it that can be adjusted to catch the sun.

When building the oven, maintain the basic design, but modify to take advantage of materials you have on hand. In your resourcefulness, avoid using materials that might give off toxic fumes when heated, such as Styrofoam pellets and duct tape.

Your biggest expense will be the glass, so if you have a piece on hand—perhaps from an old storm window—try using that. We used old curtain rods for reflector-flap props. If you already have a dark, lidded pot, you'll want to make your cooker deep enough to accommodate that.

The ideal solar cooker is made to specific proportions. The inner box should be at least 18 inches by 22 inches, rectangular, and as shallow as possible while still being deeper than your pot. The ideal space between the inner and outer boxes is 1 to 2 inches.

Solar cookers can be used six months of the year in northern climates and year-round in tropical climates. (No one can accuse us of printing ideas that work best only in our geographic area.)

We have done some experimenting and like the idea, although this design seems a bit awkward. Because the oven lid and glass are not attached, it's a little clumsy to get food in and out.

reflector flap

reflector flap prop

lid
glass
aluminum foil

We plan to build a wooden oven with a hinged top and glass. However, I recommend trying this cardboard version first.

Some general tips:

Use covered pots with tight-fitting lids, except for breads, cakes, and cookies. The pots should be made of thin metal and be painted black. These can be set on a black tray to absorb more heat. Use flat black latex paint.

The golden rule of solar cooking is, "Get the food in early; don't worry about overcooking."

To keep foods hot after you lose the sun, add several bricks or large stones when you start cooking. These will help hold heat. To maximize heat retention, close the reflective lid and cover with a blanket.

Many foods can be cooked without moving the box to follow the sun. Just aim the cooker so that halfway through the cooking time the sun will be right in front of the cooker. For large quantities of food, or on partly cloudy days, you may have to move the cooker once or twice.

To bake cakes or bread, preheat the cooker for at least a half hour before adding the food.

I've tried to give you enough information to make a solar cooker on your own. However, you may feel you need additional resources. Kits and ready-made solar box cookers are available from these two sources:

Kerr Enterprises
P.O. Box 27417
Tempe, AZ 85285
(602) 968-3068
Plans for a cardboard model

cost $2.85. Plans for a wooden model are $5.10. Kits cost $55 to $69. Ready-made boxes cost $72 to $85. Shipping is extra.

Solar Box Cookers International
1724 11th St.
Sacramento, CA 95814
(916) 444-6616
Plans for a cardboard model cost $5. A foldable, portable box with polyester window costs $50. Add 10 percent shipping for each item. SBCI's programs spread cookers throughout the Third World, where they can help sterilize water and stop deforestation caused by cutting wood for cooking fires.

Reader Michele Cahill of Carmichael, California, who cooks most of her meals in the cooker and "can't praise this idea enough," sent us the following list of cookbooks. All prices include postage and handling:

Eleanor's Solar Cookbook
by Cemese Publishers
7028 Leesburg
Stockton, CA, 95207
Cost is $10.

Solar Cooking Naturally
(Michele's favorite)
Sun Life Energy
745 Mountain Shadows
Sedona, AZ 86336
(602) 282-1344
Cost is $11.50.

Solar Box Cooking
by Sacramento Municipal Utility District
P.O. Box 15830
Sacramento, CA 95852-1830
(916) 732-5130
Cost is $5.

"HELP! MY FAMILY WON'T TRY STORE BRANDS."

Tell them this story:

As a teenager, Jim learned a valuable lesson about brand loyalty when he worked at Oxford Pickle Company for a few months in the mid sixties. He personally oversaw the filling of jars of many pickle brands. Typically, after the workers had filled the order for Oxford's pickles, they would stop the line and switch the jars with labels for Cain's, Finast, or other name or store brands. The jar style, label, and retail price changed, but the vat of pickles was the same.

The practice remains the same today, according to our interviews with several supermarket executives and the Private Label Manufacturers' Association.

Although some stores have their own packaging plants, many store brands are packaged by name-brand manufacturers. For example, Safeway's store-brand green beans are packaged by Del Monte as well as 15 other companies. Safeway's store-brand cereal is made by Malt-O-Meal and Ralston Purina.

Does this mean that store brands and name brands are identical? Not necessarily. It all depends on the specifications each supermarket chain gives its suppliers. Most large supermarket chains specify that their store brands must be as good or better than the leading name brand.

If the products are of the same quality, why are name brands more expensive? Name-brand prices are inflated because of advertising costs, more complex packaging, the expense of handling coupons and refunds, and the "slotting fees" manufacturers must pay supermarkets to reserve a certain amount of shelf space.

Test marketing also makes name brands expensive. For example, in the 1970s, name-brand manufacturers spent big bucks to convince Americans to eat that weird, sour-milk stuff called yogurt. Only after the market was established did store-brand yogurt appear.

Are store brands always cheaper? On the average, store brands cost about 15 percent less, but that gap varies widely. With some products, such as baby food, the store brand and name brand cost almost the same. Other store-brand items, such as vitamins, toothbrushes, and English muffins, cost, on average, more than 30 percent less than name brands.

Who buys store brands? Almost everyone. A recent Gallup poll showed that 84 percent of those earning under $25,000 bought store brands. The figure was 90 percent for those earning $25,000 to $45,000, and 87 percent for those earning over $45,000.

What if you've tried store brands and really don't like them? Since each store sets its own specifications, you might try switching stores until you find store brands that suit you. If you can't switch stores, complain. It may also be that your store has improved its store-brand products since you last tried them. Supermarkets across the country have made dramatic improvements in store-brand quality in the last decade, and consumers are responding: 33

percent of respondents told Gallup they are buying more store brands now than they did a year ago.

Finally, remember that preference is an acquired thing. How do we know what a Cheerio is supposed to taste like, anyway? If you've eaten only General Mills Cheerios since you were a kid, then store-brand toasted-oat cereal might not taste right to you. Consider that if you had been raised on the store-brand version you might very well hold the unshakable conviction that General Mills Cheerios taste inferior.

AMAZING DISH-COVERY

Dear Amy,

The other day I read the directions on my box of dishwasher detergent. I was curious to see how much powder they recommend using, since in the past I simply filled the dispenser in the machine without thinking. It said to "Follow manufacturer's instructions, or use one tablespoon of powder." Talk about feeling stupid. By blindly filling the dispenser, I used about 6 tablespoons of powder. Now I use just 1 tablespoon, and the results are the same.

—Karen S. Phillips
Louisville, Kentucky

FREE WHEELER

Dear Amy,

I found a $39 designer stroller in the trash by the mall. One wheel was cracked. I popped it in the trunk and called the manufacturer's 800 number when I got home. For $2.50 and a little

cleaning up, I now have a new stroller from a reputable manufacturer. I got the number from the free *Consumer's Resource Handbook.* For a copy, write to Consumer Information Center, Pueblo, CO 81009.

—Dawn Ward
Jackson Heights, New York

(Most major manufacturers have toll-free numbers. Another way to find them is by calling toll-free information at [800] 555-1212. FZ)

DRYER STRAITS

Dear Amy,

I am a retired appliance repairman (42 years). In that time I have fixed a lot of appliances that did not need a repairman.

Example: Your electric dryer runs but won't heat. Check to make sure both 30-amp. fuses or circuit breakers are okay. If one is out, the dryer could run but not heat, since it takes 220 volts to make the heating element work, but only 110 volts for the motor.

If it runs with heat but takes a long time to dry, check the vent pipe for lint.

—Tom Farmer
Monroe, Michigan

CHEAP-SCAPE

Dear Amy,

My training in school was in landscape architecture. I have come up with some ideas for inexpensive but effective ways to have a beautiful landscape:

1. Use what you have! If you

have too many rocks, edge with the larger ones, accent with the huge ones, and pound the little ones into a garden path.

2. Use native plants if you can. They will likely grow regardless of what you do to them. Some Forest Service areas permit harvesting plants by permit from public lands at very low cost.

3. Many plants are free! If you can learn to be patient, plant ground covers many times farther apart than the nursery suggests, then break off pieces as the plants grow, and fill in between the older plants. Ask friends for "shoots" from their plants that you like, take them home, and start new plants from them. Libraries have good books on propagating this way.

—Grant Collier
   Flagstaff, Arizona

DO SWEAT THE SMALL STUFF

Which is cheaper to use—cloth or paper napkins? To research this pressing and complex question, I laboriously and tediously calculated . . .

(Across the country, thousands of readers' eyes glaze over and they think, "Egad! Another endless cost analysis that will yield a minuscule saving! What is it with this woman? This ranks up there with her riveting conclusion that using baking soda and cream of tartar is marginally cheaper than using baking powder, or that boiling water in the microwave versus on the stove may use an extra

fraction of a penny's worth of energy, or that a ½-inch-by-1-yard hunk of duct tape is 3.2¢ cheaper than the same amount of clear tape. Get a life!")

So why should you sweat the small stuff? And why should I devote so much space to it in the newsletter? Because the small stuff is the essence of the tightwad life. Because it's where the action is! Because I'll run out of stuff to write about without it! Because:

1. There are more small strategies than big strategies. Think about it. How many ways are there to immediately save a huge wad of money? Five? Maybe ten? And of those that come to mind, how many are commonly known? Take prepaying your mortgage. Seems like every week I hear a TV financial reporter do a story on that idea. But there are thousands of small things you can do to shave a few cents off that most people don't know about.

2. There are more *opportunities* to use small strategies than big ones. How often do you buy a car? You do the small stuff every day, and the savings accumulate. If you discover that your dishwasher cleans just as well with 1 tablespoon of detergent as when you blithely dumped in 6 tablespoons, the cumulative savings over your lifetime is substantial. Once you figure something out, you *own* that information for the rest of your life.

3. Similarly, the time investment in figuring out this minuscule stuff actually yields a high "hourly wage." It might take you a total of five hours to make up a price book for comparison grocery shopping, but after several years of supermarket excursions, you may dis-

idea that might save you only 50¢ a month, that's important, too. I'm allowing you to decide whether doing that marginal-savings activity is worth it to you.

6. It's fun. If you are a real, genetically programmed, dyed-in-the-wool tightwad, you just love this stuff. So if your eyes didn't glaze over at the mention of another tedious calculation, if they actually widened with eager anticipation, let's forge ahead into the dark continent of napkin calculation:

Naturally, I could never wash a full load of cloth napkins, since I have only 30, but I figured the cumulative effect would eventually result in an extra load of laundry. So the best way to calculate it was as if I were washing a full load of napkins.

How many in a load? Theorizing that the material in cloth napkins was about the same type and thickness as in twin sheets, I used sheets as a basis for calculation. I figured out how many napkins equaled a sheet by comparing them two ways—by weight and by square inches (factoring in sheet hems; the napkin hems were negligible). I averaged those two napkins-in-a-sheet numbers and multiplied that by 8, which is the number of sheets I can wash in a single load. I concluded I could wash 200 napkins in a single load.

I didn't factor in the cost of pur-

cover that your hourly "pay" for those five hours was over $1,000.

4. It's good training. It keeps you in the habit of thinking frugally, so that when one of those big financial decisions come along, you naturally attack it with a tightwad mind-set. You may find what I have found: that keeping my mathematical muscles toned by computing scotch-tape economies helps me make the right choices for life insurance.

5. Like most frugal writers, I could just throw one-liner tips at you, without showing how I arrived at those conclusions. But you need to know how I figured something out, because the variables in your situation are probably different. (Or—gasp!—I might even make a mistake.) And when I show you an chasing the napkins. All that I have were either homemade, given to me, purchased at yard sales, or are more than 12 years old and still going strong.

Figuring that it costs 12½¢ for detergent and about 4¢ for electricity to run a cold-wash cycle (based on information in a brochure from the electric company), I can wash 200 napkins for 16½¢. I hang my laundry to dry, but if I had to use my dryer, I would have to add 44¢ (for 60 minutes of dryer time to dry the eight sheets) to the total cost. If I had to pay for water (we have a well), I would have to figure that in. If I had to use a pay machine, the cost would be higher.

The cheapest paper napkins cost 50¢ per 120, or ⁴⁰⁄₁₀₀ of a cent each. Washing and machine-drying cloth napkins cost ³⁰⁄₁₀₀ of a cent each. Washing and air-drying cloth napkins cost ⁸⁄₁₀₀ of a cent each.

If a family of four uses 12 napkins per day (one at each meal), paper napkins would cost $17.52 per year versus air-dried cloth napkins at $3.50 per year. So cloth napkins could save about $14 per year, or $140 per 10 years, or $1,400 per 100 years, or . . .

This trivial bit of information is yours to do with as you will.

DIALING FOR (INSURANCE) DOLLARS

Large, boring books have been written about the controversy over which kind of life insurance is better: cash-value or term.

Cash-value (which comes in several mutations: whole life, adjustable life, universal life, and variable life) is a combination of investment and insurance. Because it performs these two functions—*and* because insurance agents rack up five to ten times more in commissions selling this kind as opposed to term—it's expensive. Term, on the other hand, is pure insurance; it has no cash value. It costs more as you get older, but is far cheaper than cash-value insurance, at least until you reach retirement age.

Basically, I have come to the conclusion that for relatively well-off people, cash-value is a good deal because it offers attractive tax breaks. Others—generally, the young and not-rich—should get term. But the subject is much more complex than this and beyond the capacity of this newsletter, so plunge into one of those books. (One that is not so boring is *Winning the Insurance Game* by Ralph Nader.)

If you've decided on term, the next step is finding the least expensive policy. Start by calling: Insurance Information, Inc.
23 Route 134
South Dennis, MA 02660
(800) 472-5800

As far as we can determine, this is the only truly independent source of information on term life-insurance rates (unlike other nationwide insurance price-quote services, this one does not *sell* insurance). This company is recommended in two excellent books: *Scrooge Investing* by Mark Skousen and *Smart Money,* by Ken and Daria Dolan.

We called company founder Milton Brown (if you want to talk with him personally, call [508] 394-9117). He told us that the first step is to call. If you are not ready for a quote but just want more information, his company will send you a packet.

If you want a quote, you give your credit-card number, your age, the amount of insurance coverage wanted, and some other general information. Insurance Information runs this through a data base of about 250 companies. They deduct a $50 fee from your credit-card account and send you information on the five least expensive companies that they find. The search includes only companies that are rated "A" or better by A. M. Best, a firm that tracks the financial health of insurance companies. You can take this information to your insurance agent, or in some cases you can call the insurer directly to buy a policy, thus saving commission fees.

If you already have a policy, and Insurance Information cannot find one that saves you at least $50, they will send you the information they have found and will not charge you (Brown says of the 25,000 or so customers he serves annually, he only has to do this less than 1 percent of the time). In other words, if they can only save you $49 or less, you get the information free.

MIDNIGHT MAGIC

What can you do outside, on a late August night, with someone you love, that's free, fun, requires lying on a blanket, and if everything goes right, you see shooting stars?

Okay, name two things.

The second one is watching the Perseid meteor shower, which occurs annually from August 10–14, peaking on August 12.

Some visible meteors—also known, inaccurately, as shooting stars—fall every night, and there are about 15 recognized "showers" each year. But the Perseid shower has the advantage of happening in warm weather, and it's the biggest, with about 60 meteors visible hourly.

We watched the Perseid shower last year, and it's hard to say which was more exciting, the streaking lights in the sky or the kids' delight at this rare chance to be up in the middle of the night.

The best viewing time is after midnight, so check the weather forecast, lay out your blankets in advance, and set the alarm to wake the kids (this means no funny business).

BREAKFAST BREAKTHROUGH

I leaped a major hurdle in my development as a tightwad when I stopped going nuts for "bar-gains" (Wow! Double coupons will save me a buck on that box of Cheerios!). Instead I began comparing the cost of foods by the portion.

The breakfast-portion comparison below provides an excellent example of how much one can save by thinking this way.

When I began to compare breakfast costs, I ignored the 1-ounce-per-portion suggestion on the sides of cereal boxes and actually weighed the amount I thought I would eat. Therefore, I compared 2 ounces of cereal to two 4-inch pancakes, and so on. This works better than comparing by weight only, because most people eat a bowlful or plateful, not a certain weight.

In most cases, I basically compared a portion of grain-based starch. Clearly, it's a tad unfair to compare frozen breakfasts, which also contain meat, but I wanted to include them in the study—and besides, how much can that microscopic sausage be worth, anyway?

Obviously, all of these breakfasts would be supplemented with juice, fruit, jam, sugar, milk, syrup, and so on.

After I worked out my comparison, I rationalized that scratch breakfasts use some energy in cooking (a penny or so per serving), so I decided cold cereal would be a good value if I could get it for 7¢ or less per ounce (or about 14¢ a serving). So I went to the double-coupon store with a calculator in one hand and a fistful of coupons in the other and stood in the aisle with scores of cereals stacked to the ceiling and found almost none that were cheap enough. As a result, we eat very little cold cereal.

People buy convenience breakfast foods because they think they're too busy to make scratch breakfasts. We're busy too. When we're truly short on time we rely on "fast" scratch foods such as oatmeal or a pan of corn bread.

When we have a bit more time, we make things like whole-grain

---

2 ounces cornmeal (to make
    cornmeal mush)=4¢
2 ounces bulk-purchased
    oatmeal=5¢
2 4-inch scratch pancakes=6¢
2 scratch muffins=7¢
2 4-inch scratch waffles=8¢
2 pieces of french toast=8¢
2 oatmeal-raisin scones=8¢
2 2-inch squares corn
    bread=8¢
2 ounces store-brand
    oatmeal=9¢
2 4-inch Bisquick
    pancakes=10¢
1 egg and 1 slice of toast=11¢
2 ounces Quaker oatmeal=15¢
2 store-brand English
    muffins=16¢
2 ounces store-brand toasted-
    oat cereal=20¢
2 ounces Cream of Wheat=21¢
2 Eggo waffles=36¢
2 ounces Cap'n Crunch=41¢
2 ounces Froot Loops=42¢
2 store-brand doughnuts=43¢
Carnation Instant
    Breakfast=43¢
2 4-inch pancakes from store
    batter=49¢
2 bakery-made cinnamon
    rolls=51¢
2 Pop-Tarts=82¢
Great Starts microwaveable
    breakfast=$1.49

---

pancakes, waffles, and muffins. If your kitchen is well organized, with your baking utensils and ingredients in one place, you can get a double batch of muffins into the oven in less than 20 minutes. (Then, take your shower while they're baking.) We always make extra and freeze the surplus for days when we don't even have time to make oatmeal.

Most of our breakfasts cost 10¢ or less per serving. If a family of four chooses breakfasts that cost 10¢ per serving over breakfasts that cost 25¢ per serving, it will save $219 a year.

THE FRAME GAME

If you wanted to drop a wad of dough, acquiring ready-framed art would be easy—too easy. But like soup that tastes better when it has simmered all day, your home will feel more personal and to your liking if you take more time and acquire decorative items slowly.

Plus, you'll save your wad.

Relax with your blank walls. Work with the best that you have now. Think of the art, the frame, and where you hang them as fluid, changing as you find things you like better.

When I gathered the stuff I wanted to frame and my collection of frames—mostly found in the attic when we bought the house—I discovered only one obvious match of frame and art. So I looked harder for solutions. Here are a few I used or have learned of:

FRAME SOLUTIONS

Look closely at the yard-sale frames that have been overlooked because of what's in them—like the framed, mildewed print I bought for 50¢. I discarded the print and put a picture of my great grandmother in the nice, old, wood frame.

Clean up older, varnished wood frames with a little denatured alcohol and linseed oil. The alcohol is a mild solvent that will redistribute the finish to minimize scratches.

Spray-paint frames with a paint you already have. I had several with odd colors that I painted with gloss-black paint. This allows you to group together frames of different sizes and styles in a single display.

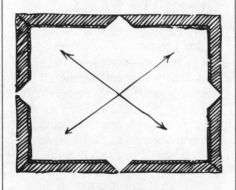

Cut down a large wooden frame to make a matching pair of smaller ones. Jim did this to an old 20-inch by 32-inch frame that I couldn't imagine ever finding art to fit. Don't cut down a frame that has antique value or that you care greatly about. This risky process requires skill and proper mitering tools. Or, as in my case, a husband with modest skills, Mickey Mouse tools, and great patience.

Reconsider those old, hopelessly chipped, ornate gold frames. These are made of gold-painted plaster molded onto a wood frame. The plaster will soak

off, and the underlying frame may be attractive enough to refinish. Or it could be downright ugly, so only attempt this with a free frame. Don't soak frames in your bathtub and wash the plaster down the drain. You can buy a lot of frames for the cost of hiring a plumber.

When you disassemble an old frame, carefully save all of the parts (wire, eye screws, nails, backing, etc.) for reuse.

MATTING SOLUTIONS

A mat is a border between the artwork and the frame. Generally it is cut to fit the art, but a mat also allows you to resize art to fit an existing frame, without actually cutting the art. By floating the window over a larger piece of art, you can find a new, smaller composition.

At Vesper George School of Art in Boston, I learned that the ideal mat should have a beveled, cut-out window for the art to show through. The sides and the top should be of equal measure, and the bottom should be slightly wider (by about ½ inch). But being a purist gets expensive. You can break the rules as long as the results are pleasing to you.

mat

Without going to a frame shop, there's almost no way to get that beveled cut. Instead use a utility or X-Acto knife when cutting a (non-beveled) mat. A drawing board and a T square can help to get things square. However, you can simply trace your frame on your mat and measure from those lines.

If you don't have mat board, cut the mat from very stiff paper, such as the inside of a brochure cover.

Skip the window. Trim your artwork and put it on top of a mat. Or use any piece of solid-colored or white paper backed with a heavier piece of cardboard. Sometimes the back side of the old art that was originally in the frame will do.

Spray-paint gray (not corrugated) cardboard to make a mat. Reader Tamar Fleishman of Baltimore, Maryland, suggests using the cardboard from a panty hose package. I tried this and found that even mat-finish paint didn't result in a completely even coat, but the glass hid the slight variation. Cut your window before painting.

Make a mat by covering cardboard with a solid-colored or small-patterned scrap of fabric. I made two fabric-covered mats: One scrap was from an old skirt, one was from the cotton couch-cushion covers I saved when I replaced them. I picked sections with little wear, and again, any imperfection was hidden by the glass.

Fabric can be folded around a precut mat and attached to the back side with a hot-glue gun. Instead, I coated one side of a mat with my handy and familiar one-coat rubber cement, which dries tacky. I pressed the glued side against the wrong side of the fabric. Using an X-Acto knife, I cut the fabric as shown so that I could fold it over and adhere it to the mat's back side.

Then, to give my artwork a visual breather from the fabric pattern, I made a smaller, heavy-paper mat so that it would create a quarter-inch inner border. This worked very well with a black-and-white photo and a black frame.

You can also make fabric frames by taking this method a step further: Use stiffer cardboard.

GLASS SOLUTIONS

If the frame you're using doesn't have glass, reuse other glass you already have.

mat   fabric

I cut down large chunks of broken glass and old storm-window glass for frames.

Start with a clean, nonrusty glass cutter—if yours is rusty, buy another and store it in mineral oil. Using a straight edge, score the glass heavily just once. Bear down hard; you should be able to see the line clearly and hear the scoring process.

Tap the scored line with the opposite end of the glass cutter. If this does not snap the glass, hang the glass over a tabletop with the scored line facing upward. Line up the score with the table's edge. Apply quick pressure downward on the overhanging glass. Wear gloves and protective eyewear.

ARTWORK SOLUTIONS

Now . . . what to frame? I like "real art," but I seldom like it enough to pay real-art prices, so I compromise.

Examples of nonreal but frameable art abound—like the art on calenders and note cards. I received two cards from the same series, from different people. These went in a pair of matched frames. Also, scrutinize magazines with elegant photos that could be cut out and framed. Sometimes the labels from cans and packages have vintage-looking art.

Look for items with a more personal interest. Our attic yielded some interesting old newspapers I plan to frame. Other old finds might include a section of lace or a quilted square.

Family photographs are excellent sources of inexpensive, personal art. Pictures of ancestors are more interesting than the steady stream of student portraits. (And your kids will forever cringe at toothless smiles, acne, and outdated haircuts. Dead people can't complain.)

Create your own artwork to fit the odd-size frame. You may feel you are not artistic enough to paint a picture. Try creating arrangements of pressed flowers. Take up calligraphy or cross-stitch.

Frame your child's art. Once under glass, you'll be amazed at how their brightly colored efforts resemble modern art. I've heard of one family that had a permanent "kid's art" frame and continually put new examples of children's work in this place of honor.

If you have a really wonderful antique frame and absolutely cannot find the right art for it, pop in a mirror.

FINAL NOTES

If you're unable to handle any one aspect of the framing process, ask whether your local frame shop would cut a mat, cut a piece of glass, or cut down a frame for you. You can still save some of the material and labor costs. The do-it-yourself frame shops save a little money if you want a highly professional job.

Successful framing is marriage of art, mat, and frame. I experiment until I find a combination that I like, but before assembling it permanently and hanging, I leave it out a few days. Then, if I still like it, I finish the job.

A SMARTER STARTER

Save money—and avoid the charcoal-lighter-fluid taste. Next time you barbecue, use this free, easily made charcoal lighter.

Make holes around the bottom of a clean gallon can with a triangle-punch can opener. Then remove both of the can's ends. Use a nail or drill to punch holes on either side of the top, and attach a handle made of coat-hanger wire.

Remove the grill, and set the can in the barbecue. Put one or two sheets of loosely wadded newspaper (use the black-and-white sheets, since colors can release chemicals) in the bottom. Fill the can with briquets. Light the newspaper from the bottom through one of the punched holes. If you will need more briquets for your barbecue, pile them around the outside of the can.

When the coals are glowing, use tongs or a hot pad to lift the can from the barbecue. The lit coals will spread the fire to the surrounding ones.

We tried this, and it worked like a charm.

Gardener's Supply Company, an otherwise marvelous organization, sells a metal tube that does this job for $15.95.

According to the brochure from my electric company, most ovens cost about 28¢ to operate per hour. Charcoal briquets, when purchased at a wholesale store, cost about 10¢ per dozen. If you use the briquets conservatively—say, two dozen per meal, barbecuing chicken will cost the same, or less, than baking it in the oven.

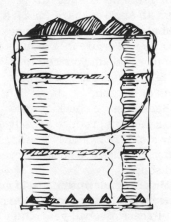

GARDENING ALTERNATIVES

Growing fruits and vegetables isn't a viable option for everyone. But during the harvest season there *are* ways to get produce cheaply.

Reader Lucille Ross of Springfield, Oregon, says her county has a "gleaner association." For $6 a month and two days of work a year, she can get free fruit, veggies, and nuts as well as bread from a local bakery. Check with your local county extension office to see if there is one in your community. You may need to meet income restrictions.

Some farmers throw away their seconds because supermarkets won't take them. Ask around to see if you can find a grower who is willing to sell these for a reduced price.

One man I met recently told me that surplus vegetables from a farmer's market are sold at auction in his area. He buys vegetables there more cheaply than he can grow them.

Check out the "U-Pick" places in your area. We can get "drops" from an apple orchard for $2 a bushel. In Maine this summer strawberries were 99¢ a quart if you picked them yourself and $2.89 per quart if you bought them at a stand.

Remember to check out the marked-down produce at your grocery store. The slightly gone fruits and vegetables are good for breads and soups.

Make friends with an avid gardener who always grows a surplus just in case of a bad year. Offer to help in the garden or to barter. Although most gardeners won't bring it to you, they are happy to share the surplus if you pick it yourself.

Cathy Millet, a reader from Bangor, Maine (a big city for these parts), was so successful in getting produce from alternative sources that she was able to freeze, can, and dry fruits and vegetables, even though she doesn't garden.

Always do your homework, though. Often there is little or no cost savings when you preserve produce that you have purchased.

NO PLAIN, NO GAIN

Dear Amy,

I laugh at the commercial extolling the virtues of "Top Job with ammonia." Why not just use plain ammonia and save yourself the expense?

I also laugh at all the expensive baby powders proclaiming their "100% cornstarch" contents. I buy regular cornstarch at the grocery store for a third of the cost and pour it into an old baby-powder container.

—Paula Ramm
  Hoffman Estates, Illinois

(You can mix a cup of ammonia to a gallon of water for a strong cleaner. Use less ammonia when a milder cleaner is needed. Never mix ammonia with bleach. FZ)

THICK TRICK

Dear Amy,

Don't cook down tomatoes to get thick sauce. Once they are prepared and ready to cook, just put

them in the refrigerator overnight. In the morning, use your
turkey baster to remove the clear
liquid that has floated to the top.
Voilà!

—Elaine Stalder
  Harrisburg, Oregon

LATE RATE

Dear Amy,

Resist the temptation to renew
magazine subscriptions whenever
they happen to expire. Many magazines offer special holiday gift
rates. So I just call or write and
give my husband a gift of a re-
newed subscription, and he does
the same for me. I recently saved
half the regular subscription rate
on a popular golf magazine my
husband enjoys!

—Carole Kline
  Columbia, Maryland

CHEAP SHOTS

Dear Amy,

Our local health department
gives free immunizations to anyone in our county. There are no income requirements. We filled out a
couple of short forms, got shots,
and were on our way in less than
15 minutes. No waiting room full
of sick people, and best of all, it
was free! I don't know if it is like
this everywhere, but for anyone
with kids, it is definitely worth
looking into.

—Lisa Thompson
  Shelburne, Indiana

GAS VERSUS ELECTRIC

When the day comes to spend big
bucks for a new water heater,
clothes dryer, or range, many of
us simply go with what's familiar:
If we're accustomed to gas, that's
what we get; ditto for electric.

But there's a better way to
make the choice.

Linda Watkins of Crofton,
Maryland, sent me a fact sheet
put together by the Baltimore Gas
and Electric company. The company gathered information from a
variety of sources to compile a
"Cost of Operation" chart for home
appliances. It's incredibly detailed.
Did you know the average video-
game system (not counting the
TV) uses 9¢ worth of electricity a
month?

I found the most interesting
comparison to be the approximate
operating cost per month for gas
versus electric appliances. These
costs are based on the national average of 9¢ per kilowatt-hour for
electricity and 50¢ per therm for
natural gas:

- Gas range/oven: $1.85
- Electric range/oven: $10.98

- Gas water heater: $14.32
- Electric water heater: $39.99
  (Based on a 30-gallon heater
  serving a family of four.)

- Gas clothes dryer: $2.00
- Electric clothes dryer: $9.90

These figures are averages and
won't apply in all situations. But
they do underscore a general rule
that's good to remember: It is almost always a bad idea to make
heat with electricity. Electricity is
an expensive and precious source

of energy that should be used for what it's best at: tasks such as lighting and powering computers and small motors.

Of course, there are several variables you must take into account before chucking out your electrical collection. Gas may be relatively expensive in your area (if you are not on a natural-gas pipeline and must use bottled propane, your operating cost will almost certainly be greater than for natural gas), while electricity may be fairly cheap. And gas appliances require gas lines and venting; this adds to the installation cost. If there is still some life left in your electrical appliances, *figure out the payback cost* before getting rid of them.

For example: You sell your old electric range for $50. A new gas range, including taxes, delivery fees, and installation, costs $600. If a gas range saves $9.13 per month, it would take five years to make up your $550 out-of-pocket cost. You may decide that this is too long to make it worth the hassle of swapping for gas.

On the other hand, if you *need* a new stove, you'll find that gas ranges cost an average of $150 more than electrics, so you would make up the extra cost of the gas version in just 16 months.

Individual appliances also vary in efficiency, which is why it's essential to check the yellow "Energyguide" label on new appliances to see how they stack up. The figures above are intended to inspire you to compare between the Energyguides on gas and electric appliances—not just between those on electric appliances.

AVOIDING COUCH OUCH

Eleven years ago, Jim and I shopped intensively for a couch. We salivated over trendy, sand-colored, upholstered couches for several days before we came to our senses. Finally, one of us said, "This is nuts. The first time a toddler attacks one of these with a ballpoint pen, we're sunk."

So we opted for a different sort of couch. Though it wasn't my first choice aesthetically, we have never regretted the purchase.

We rationalized that the furniture style sometimes referred to as "crate furniture," manufactured by companies such as Cargo or This End Up, would withstand the toddler onslaught better than any upholstered couch. The style basically is a sturdy, exposed wooden frame with back, seat, and arm cushions. Usually viewed in a small mall store, crowded together with crate chairs, crate coffee tables, crate bookcases, and crate bunk beds, it tends to look a bit heavy. But as a single piece in our living room, the couch looks fine.

We found that this style offered many advantages:

1. An ink blotch, or any other damage, could easily be hidden by flipping the cushion over. (It was actually me, with a pen in my back pocket, who committed the first ink transgression.) Although upholstered couches have flippable seat cushions, the rest of the couch is vulnerable.

2. This kind of furniture is ordered to the customer's specifications, not picked out from a showroom floor. This allowed us to get precisely the dark shade for the cushion covers that we felt would hide dirt and blemishes best—such as a navy blue (ink-colored) fabric.

3. When the covers get dirty on both sides, they are removable for cleaning. Although the manufacturer recommended dry cleaning, we learned we could wash them in cold water in our washing machine. the savings on the dry-cleaning bill more than offset any possible acceleration of fabric wear.

4. Kid grime could be washed off the wooden frame with Murphy's Oil Soap. Should the frame sustain any damage, we could easily sand out dents, scuff marks, or crayon doodlings and refinish.

5. When the covers wore out completely, we could buy new ones from the manufacturer for much less than we could hire someone to make them for us. (With my limited sewing skills, I figure I could make them myself and save about $1 per hour of work.) The manufacturer also sold replacement foam-rubber cushions.

With six active kids, our couch sees constant use; it's our most commonly sat upon piece of furniture. As a result, we wear out the covers every four years. After eight years we replaced the three foam seat cushions. With each re-

placement, we have an instant new couch. Aside from the financial savings, I feel a lot better about bagging up old seat covers to save for scraps and zipper scavenging rather than putting a beat-up couch out on the curb.

When we replaced covers the first time, we noticed this manufacturer had one disadvantage: It changes its fabric selection periodically, and our fabric had been discontinued. We realized that if we wanted to replace a single cover sometime in the future, it might not be possible. And now, having gone through two complete sets of covers (seats, backs, and arms), we realize that the seat covers wear out twice as fast as the back and arm covers.

But a solution was at hand. Shortly after we bought our third set of covers, the manufacturer sent us a $50 coupon good toward the purchase or more of their stuff. I suspect they wanted us to buy another big piece of furniture.

Instead, I brilliantly applied the coupon toward the purchase of three more seat covers of the same color as the set we just bought. We plan to rotate the two sets of seat covers so that each set wears at the same slower rate as the arm and back covers. By doing this, we hope to extend the life expectancy of the entire set of covers from four years to eight years for little extra cost.

Now, let's suppose that you don't have the least inclination to buy a crate-style couch. What can you learn here?

First, whenever you acquire furniture, remember that the concept of a couch or chair with an exposed wooden frame and removable cushions, regardless of the style, makes sense. Other companies make wood-framed furniture. (I don't own any stock in Cargo, and there may be more reasonably priced manufacturers in today's marketplace.) We own an antique Morris chair, an oak armchair with cushions, that has the same advantage. Many current designs could be easily duplicated if someone had the right woodworking skills, a table saw, and a cheap source of materials.

Second, if you do have an upholstered couch and you have it reupholstered, remember that if one of your lovely new seat covers were to be damaged, you might not be able to find the same fabric again. Even if you do find it, dye lots vary—and couch fabric changes due to even the slightest wear, so a new cushion may not look right. So consider having at least one extra seat cover made at the same time. Then rotate the covers. If one is damaged, you'll still have a complete, matching set. If none is damaged, you will at least extend the life of the seat covers—and you might double the life of the whole reupholstery job.

BRINGING UP BABY— CHEAP

As soon as our fourth child outgrew them, I gave away and yard-saled most of the baby things I thought I would never need again.

Enter surprise twins. Suddenly, I had to come up with twice as much as I had just unloaded. So I employed all the baby-stuff tactics I had learned with the first four. Amazingly, when the twins reached their first birthday, I calculated that, aside from food and doctor bills, we had spent less than $100 on them.

Here are our basic strategies:

1. Buy used. When no longer needed, well-maintained items can be resold for the same price as you paid.

2. Subtly steer well-meaning relatives and friends from giving you cute outfits that will fit and/or look new for five minutes. Encourage practical gifts.

3. Borrow. Most people *don't* sell their stuff right away.

4. Graciously accept all the secondhand things people give you. Keep what you can use, pass on what you can't. This ensures a steady flow of used things.

5. Put off necessary purchases until you can find the items cheap. Avoid unnecessary items (this point covers

a lot of ground). Make substitutions, either short- or long-term, to achieve both objectives.

Although you have to acquire some things, often some items can substitute for others, at least temporarily. Here are some ideas:

Baby Shampoo. Use regular shampoo. Simply be careful to keep it out of baby's eyes.

Baby Tub. Wash infant in sink, or hold carefully in a bathtub filled with 2 inches of water.

Baby Wipes. Use old washcloths or cut-up old diapers.

Bottles. Babies can be nursed until a year old (or longer) and then taught to drink from a regular cup, without ever using a bottle.

Car Seat. There is absolutely no substitute for this. Some hospitals rent them for a nominal fee, say $1 per month, but in the long run it would be cheaper to buy a new one. A rental can serve until you find a used one.

Changing Table. Use a towel on a bed or bureau top—with baby-changing items in a nearby shoe box. I never owned a changing table.

Cloth Diapers, Rubber Pants, and Pins. Of the $100 we spent, $65 went to these. Rubber pants can sometimes be bought used, but diapers and pins generally cannot. We never use disposables, even for traveling. Sharon Fluet of Charlotte, North Carolina, says she discovered that cloth diapers could be used even in day-care centers. She says the directors of two separate centers told her that cloth diapers were permissible if she provided an adequate supply of diapers, pins, and plastic pants, provided an airtight container for the used diapers, and took the used diapers home daily. As she put it, "It can't hurt to ask!"

Clothes. If you don't get bag upon bag of free things from friends and relatives, you can find used things by the ton at yard sales, thrift and consignment shops. As long as babies have one good-looking public outfit, what they wear at home doesn't matter. In a pinch, pajamas can be worn in the daytime, and daytime clothes can be worn to bed. In warm weather, babies only need diapers and a shirt.

Crib. Use bedding in a bureau drawer on the floor for an infant. Put bedding in a playpen for an older child.

Crib Bumpers. Make a towel roll if you worry about bumped heads.

Diaper Bag. Use any sturdy bag: a duffel bag or backpack, for example. I often simply toss diapers, a bread bag (for wet diapers), and a wet washcloth in a Baggie into a plastic grocery bag for short trips.

Diaper Bucket. Real ones close securely to contain odors. But you can use a 5-gallon bucket that originally contained laundry detergent or drywall compound. Don't leave a bucket of water accessible to a small child.

Diaper Stuff. Shortening substitutes for petroleum jelly, and cornstarch substitutes for powders, but neither is necessary for every change. Some people swear by Desitin for diaper rash, but I remain unconvinced that it speeds healing. I use ointments and powders so sparingly that I never used up the samples I got in the hospital. When a rash is present I have found it's best to bathe the baby and put on a diaper without rubber pants to allow the skin to breathe. I also change the baby more often.

Eating Utensils. Babies will eat food served on adult plates with an adult-size spoon. Warming dishes and suction-bottomed bowls are not needed.

Formula. If at all possible, breast-feed. Formula can cost up to $800 per year and is inferior to breast milk.

Gate. Confine baby in playpen or crib, or close doors. If you need a gate for one doorway only, you can make one that hinges on the door casing.

High Chair. Use a baby swing, walker, or stroller, or hold the baby in your lap while feeding. Or buy the kind of seat that attaches to a tabletop for much less than a high chair.

Mobile. Babies soon tire of these and other entertainment devices. Instead, hold and entertain the baby yourself. The housework can wait a few years.

Pacifiers. All my babies thought these were projectiles.

Playpen. Use a crib or a baby-proofed room with doors or baby gates.

Shoes. Unnecessary (and perhaps even harmful) until the child begins to walk. Use socks and booties in cool weather.

Store-Bought Baby Food. As long as the babies are on breast milk or formula, they are getting adequate nutrition. So the timing (at six months or so) and variety of solid foods is not critical. For about $8, you can buy a hand-cranked device that grinds all sorts of foods to baby-food consistency, but it isn't needed. Feed them cooked cereals, mashed potatoes, or applesauce. Foods such as salt-free canned green beans, spaghetti, and bananas can be mashed with a fork.

Stroller. Use a baby backpack.

36

Toys. Babies are happiest with pot lids and measuring spoons, and they are given more toys than they need.

Walker. Some doctors don't like these because of the potential hazard of kids toppling on stairs or thresholds and because they feel it can slow development. But my kids were happier in a walker than in a playpen and safer than on the floor. All walked between 9 and 12 months of age. Walkers aren't essential, but they substitute for many other things.

Wind-up Swing. All of my babies tired of this within a few weeks. Some babies hate it from the start. Buy only if used.

It goes without saying to always think about safety. Older used equipment, homemade toys, and unconventional substitutes may not meet with current safety guidelines. So educate yourself and use your head.

FROM READERS

We asked readers for their best frugal repair tips. Here are the best.

The Plastic-Stuff Fix. Melvin Tremper of Topsham, Maine, has a plastic "welding" technique that he's used to repair laundry baskets and other plastic items. First, he uses his hot-glue gun to seal the crack. Then, with more hot glue, he reinforces the repair with the flat plastic tabs used to close bread bags. He says since the tabs come in different colors, if you save them up, your collection should have some that match the object you are fixing.

Great minds think alike; before reading this, I attempted to fix the hole my dish drainer's foot had poked through its rubber mat using this exact same technique: I hot-glued a bread tab to both sides of the hole. However, the water and weight won out. I've put a juice lid over the hole until I can figure out something else.

Shower-Curtain Fixes. To save a favorite shower curtain that was tearing at the hanger holes, Shirley Jacobs of Tucson, Arizona, painted metal washers a complementary color and affixed them with Goop glue. Other possible hole reinforcers are plastic washers and various kinds of scrap plastic (from milk jugs, plastic lids, etc.) cut into washer shapes. Joy Ramler of Greenville, South Carolina, saved her shower curtain by folding down the top, then sewing buttonholes through the doubled material about a half inch below the old holes.

The Laundry-Basket "Mesh" Fix. A plastic laundry basket that has a tear in its light mesh "weave" can be fixed by applying duct tape to the inside *and* outside of the torn area. The tape sticks to itself and holds the tear tightly.

We noticed that our upstairs tub/shower curtain's end holes tore, while the middle ones held, so when we needed a new curtain for our downstairs shower stall, we just cut out the upstairs curtain's center section to use downstairs and bought a new curtain for upstairs.

I've wondered if hot glue could be used to fix shower curtains. I have used it to successfully repair the side seam that always splits in babies' rubber pants. So far, it seems to be holding up to washing.

Sneaker Fixes. The weak spot in running shoes is always where the upper is glued to the sole. I gave up on duct-tape repair and am experimenting with hot glue. This works better with porous materials such as suede and canvas rather than vinyl. Jane Ann Sayers of Elizabeth, Illinois, put inner-tube cutouts inside her tennis shoes after she had worn a hole in the sole.

The Car-Top Fix. When the vinyl top on the 1975 Oldsmobile that belongs to Tom Hoy of Scotland, South Dakota, began to tear due to time and moisture penetration, he sealed it with three coats of urethane finish. Not only did this seal the cracks, it gave the top a glossy finish that repels water. A new top would have cost $200.

Refrigerator-Door Fixes. Jean Fountain of Iowa City, Iowa, says that when the door handle of her refrigerator broke, she replaced it with a bolted-on leather-belt section. When that eventually broke, her husband removed the chrome oven-door handle from an old cookstove, sawed it to length,

drilled it, and bolted it to the refrigerator. A new handle would have cost $58.

My grandmother's refrigerator repair illustrates the same concept: Do a quick fix until you can get a permanent one. When the door catch failed, she hooked one end of a bungee cord to the handle and the other to a hook on the wall behind the fridge. This held her over until a visiting handy relative took the door apart and fixed it for her.

The Toilet-Flapper-Chain Fix. Dick Bauer of Hartford, Wisconsin, used 25-pound test, braided, nylon fishing line to replace his toilet's broken flapper chain.

The Screen-Door Fix. Tracy Creager of Kettering, Ohio, also used fishing line—in this case, to "sew" a patch of screen material into a hole in her screen door. "It may not look as nice as a new screen, but it keeps the bugs out," she writes.

The Washer-Tub Fix. Kenneth Rondeau of Manchester, New Hampshire, had a ⅛-inch hole in the tub of his 14-year-old washing machine that seemed unfixable—until an appliance repairman told him about "metal-repair epoxy putty." He followed the package directions and reports that the $2.95 repair has lasted four months.

The Zipper Fix. Joanna Garber Miller of Jarrettsville, Maryland, writes that when she found the zipper on her consignment-shop jeans would not stay up, she threaded a paper clip to the top of her zipper pull. Then she opened the upper loop of the clip to make a hook to loop over the jean-button's shank. She always makes sure that the open side of the paper clip is directed toward the inside of the fly, so it does not peek out.

The When-You-Can't Fix. Finally, keep in mind that you need not always repair something if you can find a workable substitute. The gas gauge on my friend's car broke two years ago and would have cost over $200 to fix. He simply got into the habit of resetting his trip odometer every time he filled up with gas. He calculated his car's mileage and discovered it went 400 miles on a tankful. So now he fills the tank every time the odometer hits 350. He has no need for the gauge.

THE PIZZA PLAN

Dear Amy,

I, too, am the mother of pizza fiends and have resorted to clever ways of satisfying appetites without going broke. I make pizza crusts four to six at a time, then

"par" bake for 8 minutes at 350 degrees, cool and stack in a large freezer bag. I go to a local dairy that has a cheese outlet and pay $1.59 for ends of mozzarella or provolone—this amounts to a savings of over $1.00 over grocery-store brands. I buy at least 5 pounds at a time, go home, get out the food processor, grate it all, and spread it on baking pans to freeze. Then I put it in Ziploc bags and use as it is needed. It keeps for months and cooks up beautifully.

—Sarah Severns
  Kensington, Ohio

OBEY OR PAY

Dear Amy,

Saving tip: Always obey the speed limit! Not only will this save you gas, stress, wear and tear on tires, brakes, etc., and reduce the chance of costly accidents, but a speeding ticket can be a penny-pincher's disaster! I should know: I got one, and now our auto insurance is going through the roof. "Bad driver" surcharges stay with you three to five years, and we're talking hundreds of dollars per year (not to mention the fine!).

—Alida Snow and Phil Carey
  Bath, Maine

TANKS FOR NOTHING

Dear Amy,

I know a man who is a plumber and therefore has access to old hot-water heaters as he replaces them for people. He has taken several of them and hooked them up in a series at the side of his house out of sight. All water coming into his home from the city supply is routed through these old heaters before it gets to his faucets indoors. He always has a supply of 300-plus gallons of fresh water on hand for emergencies. Here in California we are cautioned to have enough water for our family's use for 72 hours.

—Laurine Jones
  Moraga, California

NOT FOR HAIR ONLY

Dear Amy,

I have used Breck Shampoo (full-strength) to remove grease, blood, grass stains, ink, etc. for at least 20 years. I have even used it to soak clothes (charred black from fighting a fire) overnight and then washed as usual and *no stains.* I buy a 16-ounce bottle for 99¢ less 50¢ to 60¢ with a double coupon. No more expensive prestain treatments for me.

—Barbara Blau
  Bartow, Florida

COOL AT SCHOOL

Dear Amy,

My children felt deprived because other children were bringing box drinks or "Squeeze-Its" in their lunch boxes. In their school, thermoses are considered "uncool."

I found some colored cosmetic squeeze bottles on sale and bought some. They're the kind sold to use in travel for shampoo, etc. They have a pull-out, push-in top and are leakproof.

I started filling the bottles with juice, milk, or water and putting them in lunch boxes. I told my children they had their own reusable "Squeeze-Its." They haven't complained since.

The amazing thing is that their friends have started doing the same thing, and now it has spread through the school. My children feel like they started something.

—Deanna Beutler
  Littleton, Colorado

RAGS TO RINSES

Dear Amy,

I restore limp but otherwise good-condition yard-sale clothing with a light rinse of starch. Makes it "new" looking.

—Alice Strong
  El Monte, California

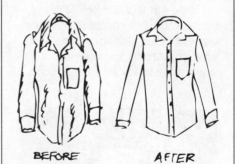

BEFORE   AFTER

WRITE MAKES RIGHT

Dear Amy,

Keeping a record of monthly expenses is the best thing for reforming a spendthrift! It worked for me, and my husband (a firm believer in frugality) and I are thrilled! It makes me think about each expense.

For example, generally, after I pay our bills on the 15th of the month, I have $300 left over to get us through to the next paycheck. After just two weeks of recording and considering expenses, I paid our bills on May 15 and had over $1,300 left over. What a testimony to the practice of disciplined record-keeping!

—Kirsten Melton
Pleasant Hill, California

A LOFTY IDEA

Dear Amy,

I have noticed that the kids can get very excited over simple things. A prime example was a small backyard tree house I built in a willow tree. All I did was take a pallet and rest it into the crotch of the tree. I nailed it for security and put a piece of scrap plywood on top. My older boys almost lived there during the summer. Every day I had to go out and see what "improvements" they had made.

—Conrad Potemra
Poolesville, Maryland

(Conrad goes on to describe a sandbox he made from a used tractor tire—he set the tire on its side and enlarged the opening with a jig saw—and a swingset he made from old telephone poles. FZ)

ACTIVE AND PASSIVE TIGHTWADDERY

Three years ago, Neal, then five, tousle-haired and sleepy-eyed, stumbled into the kitchen and asked me for help with a stubborn blue-jean snap. As I stooped to fasten it, I had to chuckle to myself.

In what seemed like a previous life, I had patched the jeans with my whole-knee-patch technique I wrote about in the first book—a method where I patched pants by sewing on a large piece of good denim scavenged from the cut-off leg of another pair of jeans.

But Neal's pants had developed holes in the patches months ago, and not only did I lack the time to repair them, but I seriously wondered if I would *ever* have time to patch pants again.

These pants, previously worn by two cousins, a sister, and a brother, revealed as rich a history as any archaeologist could hope to find. And they demonstrate the two types of frugality—passive and active.

When most people think of thriftiness, all those active images come to mind. They imagine patching pants, baking bread, hanging laundry, and rebuilding car engines. It all sounds like so much hard work.

But most of frugality is about the passive stuff—it's not what we do, it's what we don't do. It's about letting pants go unpatched.

This idea is surprisingly difficult to get across. When photographers from the media come here, they want to take pictures of active frugality. After the first couple of shoots, we ran out of new examples of active frugality with sufficient "visual interest" to show them. As a result, I've hung laundry on my attic clothesline for a dozen photographers.

But it always bothered me to do this, because I was afraid I was actually scaring people away from frugality—making it seem like it took tons of time and effort.

Instead, we suggested they shoot what we *don't* do. We told them they could set up the video camera across the street from McDonald's, and we'd pile all the kids in our Chevy Suburban and zzzooommm by. Or we could go to the supermarket, and they could position their cameras looking down the potato-chip aisle and capture that split second as we bypassed it.

The photographers looked at us like we'd been eating too many bread-crumb cookies and sent us back to the attic to hang our laundry.

The frugal lifestyle encompasses both modes, and they are equally valid. However, each of us will make different choices based on what we like to do, what quality issues are important to us, and how much time and energy we have. Let's look at these factors, one by one.

I would much rather be working in the garden, with dirt squishing up between my toes, than buying cases of vegetables at the warehouse store. Because I like gardening, we employ active frugality to get our vegetables.

Conversely, I don't enjoy sewing enough to whip up matching Easter outfits for all eight members of my family (I am in awe of readers who send me snapshots documenting such fashion feats). So I get nice clothes in the passive mode—by picking up things as I happen to see them while doing my regular shopping at yard sales.

When it comes to quality issues, I like to have nice-looking antique furniture. So I am willing to spend hours refinishing a chair. On the other hand, eating exquisitely prepared meals every day is low on my quality list, so we eat simply prepared, sometimes humdrum scratch foods rather than fussed-over dishes.

But I have learned that the most important factor in the active/passive question does seem to be time.

Within weeks of being notified we were going to be on the cover of *Parade* magazine, my obstetrician saw two blobs on the ultrasound screen and said, "Uh oh!"

We experienced the most wonderful/horrible year you could imagine. The number of our offspring increased by 50 percent as our fledgling business went from 1,500 subscribers to over 50,000. All that active-frugality stuff got tossed out the window.

Jim stopped baking bread and began buying it at the bakery thrift store. We postponed do-it-yourself renovations. I wrote letters less frequently.

I prefer to do active-frugality humdinger birthday parties that would blow any Hallmark-accessorized extravaganza right out of the water. That year, the kids were lucky just to pick the color of the frosting on a sheet cake.

Gradually our lives have begun to fall into place again. We hired a business manager and bought a separate building for our employees, while I still work from home. I hired additional research and support help to work directly on the newsletter. As a result, Jim has been able to fully retire from the workaday world. He now runs the home and takes care of the children.

We've found time for those active things again. Jim dug out his bread recipes, and I actually patched a pair of pants. The first time I went hunting in the attic for a piece of denim with a suitable shade-of-fade match, I found a cutoff pant leg with one of those holey whole-knee patches and chuckled to myself again.

BUY ALL THAT YOU CAN BUY—FROM THE ARMY

The focal point of the Second Annual *Tightwad Gazette* Barbecue and Croquet Tournament was a canopied smorgasbord table, which ranks as one of Jim's finest near-freebie achievements. He constructed it from a military-surplus parachute, a center pole, a 6-foot-diameter cable spool, tent stakes, and small poles cut from our woods.

The men in attendance—cowed and flustered by my no-mercy croquet style—huddled under it and made admiring comments. Although partly motivated by their fear of another game with me, they also gathered there out of sheer awe for Jim's creation.

"Sure, great," you mutter. "Her husband was in the Navy. Where do mere civilians get this stuff?"

Any civilians—or military personnel—over age 18 can buy surplus at military auctions.

We spoke with Lee Rude and Dale Guiou, who run the Defense Reutilization and Marketing Office (DRMO) at the Brunswick, Maine, Naval Air Station, and with Jim, the scrounging chief of our tightwad estate, who has been to these auctions both in Norfolk, Virginia, and Brunswick.

Military auctions sell anything that the Defense Department no longer needs. Once it has been offered to, and rejected by, other federal, state, and local government agencies, military surplus goes on the block.

The major exceptions are weapons and jeeps (sorry, the old "$50 surplus jeep" is a myth: The Department of Transportation won't allow military jeeps to be sold because they cannot be licensed for public road use). And generally, items worth more than about $10,000 are sold through a nationwide "sealed bid" auction, which your local DRMO can also tell you about.

To find an auction, first locate the DRMO office nearest you. There are 142 of them around the world—including three right here in little old Maine. If there is a military base of any size near you, call base information and ask for the DRMO office. The people there will tell you when the next auction is. To get a complete list of stuff to be auctioned, ask to be put on their mailing list.

Typical items offered include chairs, couches, desks, bookcases, lawn mowers, bush hogs, garden tractors, refrigerators, stoves, computers, sound equipment, pickup trucks, and boats. Sometimes there's even stuff for kids, as the bases cycle toys, cribs, high chairs, and other items through their day-care centers.

Clothing—mostly uni-forms—is generally sold by the crateload, and consequently usually bought by surplus stores rather than by individuals.

Along with this mundane stuff there is also a wide selection of exotica to excite the backyard tinkerer. Oddments Jim has seen include 55-gallon drums full of skis, broken-down tractors, barrels of outdated lubricants, automatic barnacle-scrapers, snowmobiles, ejectable fuel tanks from aircraft (these make great floats for docks), even the landing parachutes from an *Apollo* space capsule.

If you know what you're doing, these auctions can be a source of income. Guiou said one lady bought a gadget with the intriguing title of "titillating machine," for $85. "She had done her homework," he said. "It turns out this thing was part of a heating system for a large warehouse. She sold it for somewhere around $10,000."

While the Defense Department is to be commended for holding these auctions (it beats throwing the stuff away, right?), the items for sale can give you a disturbing peek at Taxes Down the Drain. Example: The Navy phases in—and phases out—an expensive new gun so rapidly that the expensive new gun-adjusting tools, in their perfect, watertight cases, never get used and get sold at auction. Jim says at the auction he attended, people bought these, threw away the tools, and kept the nice boxes.

There's a two-day inspection period before the auction. It's important to inspect stuff for two reasons:

1. Many items, especially those with motors, are probably busted, otherwise, another government agency would have snatched them. Inspection will tell you whether they can be fixed.

2. Items are not displayed on the auction block on the day of sale; the auctioneer will say only, "What am I bid for lot twenty-seven?" If you haven't inspected lot 27, you'll be stuck.

The government's goal is to get back 5 percent of its purchase price (hmmmm . . . 5 percent of a $600 toilet seat is . . .). At the last auction he organized, Rude says he got a 12 percent return.

Once you buy your titillating machine, automatic barnacle-scraper, or any other goody, you have five days to remove it.

Military auctions are like most other types of auctions: Some stuff goes cheaply, some seems moderate, and some overpriced. You must regard auction-going as a form of entertainment, with a great buy as a lucky by-product.

(Incidentally, the men at our barbecue learned there was no reason to fear my croquet prowess. The neat aspect of this game is that even a ten-year-old beginner can—and did—beat the likes of me.)

TRANSMISSION CONTROL

Dear Amy,

Last week, the transmission went out on my eight-year-old Subaru GL station wagon. I took it to my local mechanic, who is very good and trustworthy. He called back and told me that the only used transmission he could find would cost me $600. . . . I immediately began calling salvage yards in the area and in ten minutes located a transmission for my car, in a town 40 miles away, for $200.

My mechanic wasn't surprised. He said, "I don't have time to call around . . . and I don't have time to drive 40 miles." I drove the 40 miles, picked up the transmission, and had it installed in my car. I saved $400.

—Angie Lockhart
  Eudora, Kansas

RUGS AND HUGS

Dear Amy,

My carpet needed cleaning. I rented the steam cleaner ($19) and bought liquid carpet cleaner ($5) and defoamer ($5). My two neighbors are elderly widows.

After I finished my carpets I had solution left, so I offered to clean their carpets. They were so pleased, and I was glad to do it. Each offered me $10. So my $30 went down to $10. My carpets were clean, and I felt good to do a favor. Both told me it would have cost $40 to have their carpets cleaned professionally.

—Susan Pannutti
 Hillsville, Pennsylvania

LIPSTICK TRICK

Dear Amy,
 I found a way to use that last stub of lipstick to make lip gloss. Put the lipstick stub with an equal amount of petroleum jelly in a small dish. Melt in a microwave about one minute, stirring a couple of times with a small stick. Keep in a small container. It works as well as the store-bought kind.

—Mary Steiner
 Greenfield, Massachusetts

A PAIR OF REPAIRS

Dear Amy,
 My husband just repaired our VCR tape player. It would start and then kick off . . . a small rubber band that ran to the counter had worn out and snapped. He put in a new plain brown rubber band that we get every morning on our newspaper. The last time this happened, about a year ago, he repaired it the same way.
 The silverware basket in my dishwasher is plastic. One of the crosspieces in the bottom broke out, and the silverware handles

would fall through. So I took a plastic trash-bag tie—the jagged slip-through type—and slipped it through both sides of the open space and strapped it tight. This has lasted at least two years.

—Shireen Eddings
 Glendale, Arizona

WATT A SAVINGS!

Dear Amy,
 Before beginning a tightwad regime, our yearly cost for electricity was $1,443.64. After:
 1. Air-drying all of our clothes instead of using the dryer,
 2. Using the air conditioner only when the internal temperature of the house went over 85, and
 3. Being vigilant about turning off lights, our yearly bill decreased to $609.58—we saved $934.06!

—Kerry and Vernon Bassett
 Clarksville, Georgia

SOLAR CLEANER

Dear Amy,
 To clean gunky grills and oven racks: On a hot, sunny day place them in a dark plastic trash bag. Pour a cup of ammonia into the bag, seal with a twist tie, and leave out to cook in the sun. At the end of the day take out the grills and wash under hose water. Most of the crud will wipe off.

—Marian Hukle
 Tonganoxie, Kansas

The Tightwad A to Z

A is for apple-oatmeal bars. The recipe is from *Stories and Recipes of the Great Depression* by Rita Van Amber (Van Amber Publishers, P.O. Box 267, Menomonie, WI 54751):

1 cup oatmeal
$\frac{1}{2}$ teaspoon salt
$\frac{1}{2}$ cup butter
1 cup flour
$\frac{1}{2}$ teaspoon cinnamon
$2\frac{1}{2}$ cups chopped apples
$\frac{1}{2}$ cup sugar

Combine the first five ingredients, and pat half into an 8-inch-by-8-inch pan. Layer on apples and sugar. Crumble remaining mixture on top. Bake 35 minutes at 350 degrees.

B is for barbed-wire wreath, which I saw in a (trash-picked) *Country Living* magazine. You don't have to buy craft materials to make one, but even better, you have an incentive to finally remove that camou-

flaged barbed-wire booby trap in the woods that you stumbled over in a slapstick-in-real-life style, tearing a hole in this year's jeans.

C is for credit-card insurance, which you don't need. Federal law protects you in case of loss or theft of credit cards. If you notify the issuing company immediately, you don't have to pay anything. Even if you don't make the notification immediately, your maximum liability is $50 per card on charges made after the loss or theft.

D is for defrost. Do it when the ice buildup in your freezer reaches $\frac{1}{4}$-inch deep; doing it more or less often wastes energy.

E is for egg-carton bats, a Halloween decoration. Use a three-egg-cup section. Cut

off the outer third of the end cups. String a rubber band, fastened by a small nail or pin, through the top of the middle one to make the bat fly. Paint the whole thing black, and paint, draw, or glue on eyes. (Beth Vipperman, Fort Lauderdale, Florida.)

F is for film, which can be purchased cheaply in one of two ways: Buy outdated rolls from a photo shop, freeze, and thaw when needed, which we've done with great success, or get it by mail from a discount developer. Both Clark and York Color Labs sell three rolls of 100-speed, 36-exposure, 35mm film for about $6.10. We've also been happy with mail-order film developing.

G is for grocery-store scale, a great tool for saving on produce. When buying produce sold by the bag or piece instead of by the pound, weigh several to determine the heaviest. If a "5-pound" bag of fruit weighs 5½ pounds, you get that ½ pound free.

H is for hangers: classic tightwad raw material. Years ago I made a new "fastener" for an overall strap with coat-hanger wire. Using two pairs of pliers, the task required 45 while-watching-TV minutes, but I get a rush each time the overalls get passed down to another kid and I see my creation again. A new set of fasteners costs $2.50. Another way to get cheap sewing notions is by scavenging from yard-sale clothes.

I is for ice-cream sandwich, which the ice cream truck sold for

50¢, which the Navy commissary sold for 12½¢, and which we sold for 25¢ to our kids whenever the truck came by.

J is for the jar into which we put the ice-cream sand wich profits, along with deposit money from cans that we picked up along the side of the road, for a fund to go to the carnival.

K is for kaput, which is what an item must be, absolutely, before a tightwad will consider throwing it away.

L is for labeling. Put the family member's name on a glass, mug, towel, or other frequently washed item. Make the user responsible for deciding when the item needs cleaning, thus eliminating unnecessary washings. Reader Rosanne Dobbin of New York City suggests giving each family member a "unique" cloth napkin holder, so that the napkins can be used for more than one meal. Although paper napkins can also be reused, cloth napkins look better the second, third, or fourth time around.

M is for milk-crate toddler swing. Jim made one by cutting away two places for feet to come through. He then tied the crate securely to an existing swing. Once toddler Brad is belted in, it's impossible for him to fall out (his twin sister, Laura, doesn't like it). Milk crates are the property of the dairy, regardless of how you came by them, and therefore should be returned. This crate belonged to a dairy that went out of business years ago. If you don't have a "legal" milk crate, you can also make a toddler swing by scavenging the seat from a kaput indoor wind-up baby swing. (Since the elements will weather the seat, you shouldn't use one from a good swing.)

N is for nuts. I figure you'd have to be nuts to pay $4 a pound for something that only adds a bit of crunch to a cookie. At best, they are a healthful extravagance. Instead, I buy bulk, shelled sunflower seeds from a local health-food store. On sale, they are 89¢ a pound.

O is for oil-and-filter change. The cheapest local garages charge $15. Buying oil on sale for under $1, and filters for under $3, Jim can do a change for $7 in 15 minutes.

P is for poison-ivy relief. Once when severely afflicted, I was driven to a spending frenzy and bought every cream on the market. None worked. More recently I accidentally discovered, and later read in *The Doctor's Book of Home Remedies* by Rodale Press, that very hot water can provide relief. Submerse the rash in the hottest tap water you can stand. For the first few minutes the itching will intensify greatly. When the itching subsides you will be itch-free for a sufficient amount of time to, say, fall asleep.

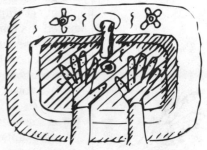

Q is for quote: "That most of us are considered poor is no disgrace, but does us credit; for, as the mind is weakened by luxurious living, so it is strengthened by a frugal life." Minucius Felix, third century A.D.

R is for rubber spatula. It always astounds me that some people don't use this elementary kitchen utensil. Using one, you can rescue a half muffin's worth of batter or enough peanut butter to make a couple more sandwiches.

S is for stamps, which you can buy by mail instead of wasting gas driving to the post office. The Postal Service pays postage both ways. Request a "stamps by mail" envelope from your local post office.

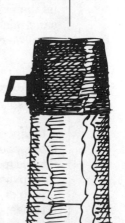

T is for thermos, which we religiously fill with ice water to take in the car every time we drive anywhere. When the kids claim they are dying of thirst and must have a soda, we practice frugal rehydration.

U is for user's manuals. If you have a tool or appliance problem, check these first to save time and/or repair costs. Jim spent an hour trying to figure out the reason for the oil leak from the top of the gearbox on his Rototiller. Completely stumped, he finally consulted the manual and learned that it was *supposed* to leak—it's the overflow feature. You should keep all your manuals and warranties together in a file folder.

V is for vegetable storage. Root vegetables, like carrots and parsnips, can be stored in a cool, dark place in 5-gallon buckets of sand. Layer vegetables flat so that they don't touch each other. Scott and Helen Nearing, famous Maine environmentalists, stored vegetables in layers of leaves. We didn't grow carrots before because they grew poorly in our native Massachusetts and because they are inexpensive to buy. Mystified, our new Maine neighbors showed us their fine carrot crops and this sand-bucket method of preservation. We converted.

W is for whipped topping. Here's an inexpensive and relatively healthy recipe:

1 teaspoon unflavored gelatin
2 teaspoons cold water
3 tablespoons boiling water
$^1/_2$ cup ice water
$^1/_2$ cup dry milk powder
3 tablespoons sugar
3 tablespoons oil

Chill a small bowl. Soften gelatin in the cold water, then add the boiling water, stirring until the gelatin is completely dissolved. Cool until tepid. Place the ice water and milk powder in the chilled bowl. Beat at high speed until it forms peaks. While still beating, add the sugar, then the oil and the gelatin. Place in the freezer for about 15 minutes, then transfer to the refrigerator. Stir before using. Makes 2 cups for about 27¢.

X is for xenoJell-Ophobia. An irrational fear that strange convenience foods like Jell-O Pudding Snack Paks will invade your happy tightwad home. (Bet you were wondering what I'd come up with for *X*.)

Y is for yeast, one of the best bulk-buy deals. It costs $2.56 a pound when purchased in bulk from our health-food store, versus $23.29 per pound purchased in individual packets  in the supermarket. Bulk-purchased yeast is usually sold in 1–2-pound bags. If you are afraid you won't use it all up before it goes bad, split the bag, and the cost, with a friend. Even if you *give away* half of it, you'll still save money.

Z is for zero, my favorite price.

THE SUPERMARKET VERSUS THE STOCK MARKET

I have gotten a few letters from people who feel it's time for the newsletter to "graduate" to the big leagues, to discuss a really important, more intellectual topic: investing. They want my views on mutual funds, CDs, T-bills, IRAs, REITs, DRIPs, and so on.

They don't intend to be critical, but reading between the lines, the implication is that the information in the newsletter to date is unimportant, penny-ante, "women's" stuff.

I'm not closing out the option; I may write about investing in the future. But at the moment I have no plans to do so. Here's why:

1. I'm not qualified. Frankly, I sometimes wonder if anyone is. Experts seldom agree on even basic points. Examples: Charles Givens thinks whole-life insurance is always a rip-off. Some experts recommend prepaying your mortgage, but conflicting articles say the money could be better used for investing. These two issues, although somewhat complex, look like child's play compared to other areas of investing; among mutual funds alone there are over 3,000 to choose from.

2. The "right" investment changes constantly. When we were saving for this house, our CDs performed better than our mutual funds. Since then, the trend has reversed. Lately the two have just about evened out, and who knows what will happen next month? I much prefer the "timeless" quality of frugality. People tell me they save the *Gazette* in a three-ring

binder. The information in a two-year-old issue is still applicable.

3. Investing information is available in other places. *Money, Fortune, The Wall Street Journal, Barron's,* and countless other periodicals obsessively track every hiccup of the Dow Jones average. You can get it straight from the horse's mouth for free at the library.

4. Compared to investing, tightwaddery is more tangible. It's simple; I don't need to be a rocket scientist to track grocery prices in my price book. It's predictable; I know if I install a low-flow shower head I'll save money on my energy bill. It's quantifiable; I can always figure out something with a calculator, such as the cost of flushing the toilet. It's testable; I can put Desitin on one side and nothing on the other to see if it heals diaper rash faster (it didn't on my kids).

5. Most people need to do a more basic type of investing first. They

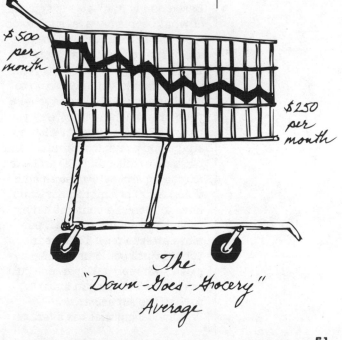

$500 per month

$250 per month

The "Down-Goes-Grocery" Average

should put money into tools and maintenance that will save money, and they should pay off debts. It's nuts to be squirreling money away in a retirement account, but have credit-card debt and no extra money to buy a freezer.

6. Even if you make a killing on your investments, you'll blow it all unless you have learned how to conduct your personal financial life. It would be the same as getting a raise and never feeling it because your poor spending habits absorb the financial gain. Almost all of the financial giants, from J. D. Rockefeller to J. Paul Getty to Sam Walton, were tightwads *before* they made their money. That's how they got it to invest, and that's how they hung on to it.

But here's the clincher, the climax, the triple-whammy:

7. Tightwaddery gives you a great financial return for a similar investment of time.

Suppose you learn to save $250 a month on your grocery bill. Based on my mail, this is typical of what people have learned to do from the newsletter, and many are surprised by how easy it is. This works out to $3,000 a year.

What would you have to do to get that same $250 by improving your investment ability? Say you have $25,000 to invest. With no study, you could drop it into a simple, safe credit-union CD and earn maybe 5 percent. To net an additional $250 per month, you would have to increase your return by at least 16 percent (to net 12 percent more after taxes). This means your return would have to be at least a whopping 21 percent, just to equal what you can learn to save at the supermarket.

Considering that the average

mutual fund lost money in the first six months of this year, anyone whose investments are doing this well is a financial wizard, is probably devoting a great deal of time to study, and/or is extremely lucky.

The supermarket doesn't require a huge amount of money, time, or luck. And it's safe (providing you can squeak by those Jell-O Pudding Snack Paks).

In short, there's nothing wrong with learning about investing—particularly if you own your home, are debt-free, have a financial surplus, and have mastered all the principles of penny-pinching. But in my experience, very few people have all of these bases covered. Until you do, it's incorrect to assume that investing is a superior pursuit to tightwaddery.

As long as the newsstands and airwaves are crowded with information about investing, I'm going to stick with what I write about best.

A BETTER BREAKFAST

Listen up, all you despisers of hot cereals! So you hate the pasty consistency of oatmeal? Try this hot-breakfast idea recently passed on to me by a friend.

Serve hot rice with milk and sugar. It was so successful, it became an instant addition to our breakfast repertoire. We tried it plain with brown sugar, and with cinnamon and raisins.

We buy store-brand, white, long-grain enriched rice in 5-pound bags for 27¢ per pound. At about 4¢ a serving, this is as cheap as cornmeal mush, which was the cheapest breakfast we found in our "Breakfast Breakthrough" survey on page 24. And who could liken the consistency of cooked rice to that beige slime?

Rice, cooked from scratch, is quick to prepare. And leftover rice steams well, making an even easier breakfast.

THIS SPUD'S FOR YOU

One of our favorite cheap-and-easy meals is baked potatoes topped with chopped, steamed broccoli, cheese sauce, and a sprinkle of bacon bits. I can feed my entire family for less than a dollar with this complete, balanced dish.

In the fall, we get a 50-pound bag of potatoes from a local, independent market for $3.99. Stored in a cool, dry place, they last into the spring. Although we live in potato country now, even when we lived in Virginia we could get 50 pounds for $4.99.

Again, if this is more than you can use, *cooperate.* Split the cost with one or more friends. We frequently sell a small quantity of bulk goods at cost to singles, couples, and smaller families.

For the rest of the year, we buy 10-pound bags for around $1.50. This means that a large potato costs us an average of 3¢ to 5¢.

We grow and freeze the broccoli, so it is practically free.

We buy and freeze bacon when it is a loss-leader sale item at about 89¢ a pound. To get enough for one meal, I saw off about 1 inch from the end of the frozen slab with my multipurpose Ginsu knife (also cuts through nails and beer cans! Somebody gave it to me—I swear I didn't succumb to one of those TV ads). Bacon should not be considered a protein. Use it sparingly, and think of it as a condiment.

The cheese sauce is simple (no, don't buy Cheez Whiz and nuke it in the microwave). Melt 2 tablespoons of butter in a saucepan. Blend in 2 tablespoons of flour. Combine it with 1 cup of milk, and salt and pepper to taste. Cook until sauce thickens. Add a half-cup of grated cheddar cheese and cook until smooth. You can freeze any surplus. (Cooks of any experience will recognize this recipe as a white sauce with cheese added. Any basic cookbook will offer other white-sauce variations; many of them are potential candidates for toppers.)

To use the least energy, bake potatoes in your microwave. The only exception would be if you are already baking something else in your conventional oven; then it makes sense to toss in some spuds. When we use the conventional oven, we string three or four potatoes on a skewer. This radiates heat inside them and cuts about ten minutes off the cooking time. We skip the foil and/or butter coating.

I cut each baked potato in quarters (or in eighths for a small child) before adding the chopped broccoli, cheese sauce, and bacon bits.

Even if we had to buy the broccoli, we could make a one-potato portion for under 20¢.

Another potato-topper combination we like is chili topped with shredded cheddar cheese. We make chili in large quantities and freeze the surplus in meal-size containers.

To learn about other possible topper combinations, I sent an undercover agent to check out a Mr. Potato fast-food joint in a local mall. Along with the combinations I've come up with, it sells: chives and sour cream; pizza-style; onion, bacon, chives, and sour cream; cheese and mushroom; meatball sauce; sweet-and-sour chicken; and spinach soufflé. It shouldn't take too much imagination to replicate these in your tightwad kitchen.

Far more breathtaking than the multitude of combinations we found were the prices: a "Broccoli 'n Cheese" goes for $3.39, and a "Chili Tex-Mex" is $3.54.

Need I say more?

SPACE: THE FRUGAL FRONTIER

Stocking up on good deals and saving things for future use—what I call "organized packrattery"—are essential to successful tightwaddery.

This is easy for us. With a 2,500-square-foot farmhouse attached to a 4,500-square-foot barn (this doesn't include the two attics, the carriage house, and the icehouse), we even store stuff for other people: boats, furniture, even a pinewood derby track for the Cub Scouts.

But I know what it's like not to have this luxury. I've lived more than half of my adult life in tiny, Boston-area apartments. Most of the other half was spent raising a big family in small, suburban ranch houses. It wasn't as convenient, but we always stockpiled and saved stuff in these places too.

Think of it this way: Would you rent out your closet for $75 a month? That could be what you'd save by having the space to bulk-buy groceries, or to keep a craft box for money-saving projects, or to stockpile great yard-sale purchases of kids' clothes. Conversely, if you think you don't have space to bulk-buy, you can figure it's costing you $75 a month to store bronzed baby shoes, fourth-grade toothpick constructions, and Engelbert Humperdinck records.

So here are some strategies for people for whom space is a precious resource:

1. Get rid of what you *don't* need. Clothes that no longer fit, books that you bought on a lark and haven't read in ten years, toys

your kids have outgrown, and impulse-buy kitchen gadgets (when did you last use that fondue pot?) can all be sold at a yard sale or through a consignment shop or donated to a thrift shop (many thrift shops will even come pick them up). If you make a mistake, it's not the end of the world. What you sell at a yard sale can probably be bought at another yard sale for the same price.

2. Buy things that have multiple uses. Example: A teakettle can only boil water. A saucepan can boil water and cook dinner. Instead of buying a bike and an exercise bike, get a trainer, a device that lets you convert your bike into an indoor exercise bike.

3. Buy furniture that has built-in storage space. The conventional coffee table with legs has several cubic feet of wasted space underneath it. A flat-topped trunk makes a suitable coffee table with storage space. Other examples include beds with built-in drawers underneath and cabinet-style end tables.

4. Buy smaller. A compact microwave will handle 95 percent of your microwaving needs. The money and space you save will more than offset having to use your oven for the other 5 percent. Technical advances mean you no longer need refrigerator-size speakers for good stereo sound. Many tiny systems get top ratings.

5. Buy foldable furniture like sofa beds and flip-down desks. Use folding chairs, card tables, and army cots for company. Similarly, buy collapsible items; instead of rigid suitcases, buy canvas travel bags.

6. Buy items specifically designed to store compactly, such as drinking glasses or chairs that stack. One of the mysteries of the modern world is that most plastic food-storage containers are not designed to fit into each other for compact storage.

7. When saving things for future reuse, keep only the small, useful parts. One reader, a former tiny-apartment dweller, wrote of how he baked bread in a toaster oven (I presume he didn't have a conventional oven.) After several years he learned the heating element was the only part of this toaster oven that didn't last. So, whenever he spotted another toaster-oven of the same make at a yard sale, he would buy it but save only the element.

I have saved two sets of couch-cushion covers for the zippers. If I had a space limitation, I would cut off the zippers and discard the remaining worn material.

8. Customize your furniture to fit. You can do this two ways: build furniture to fit, or modify an existing piece. When we lived in one of those miniature urban apartments, we shoehorned a nursery into a barely-bigger-than-a-twin-bed room by using both of these ideas. The room had a stairwell running under it, so there was this weird angle thing (see picture: Thank goodness I can draw) that chewed up a couple of feet of floor space. We bought a Salvation Army crib, cut off the two front legs, and bolted the headboard of the crib to the wall over the weird angle thing.

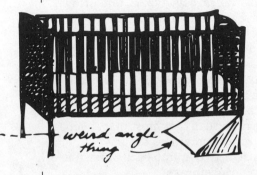

weird angle thing

Then we converted the closet to a baby-changing table and diaper storage area. We built a wide, lipped shelf with foam padding for changing, and kept diaper stuff and baby clothes on lower shelves. The room then had enough remaining space that we were also able to squeeze in a drafting table and a small filing cabinet.

9. Keep track to avoid duplication. Perhaps the major cause of household clutter is ignorance about what you have; you can't find that hinge you scavenged from your ruined screen door, so you buy another, while the original still rests at the bottom of a clutter pile. Instead, you might keep track with a list of what's in your freezer, detailed labels on boxes of kids' clothes, and carefully categorized workshop storage containers.

10. Think square. A square juice

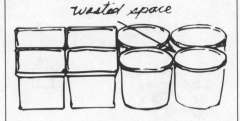

wasted space

jug and square freezer boxes fit more efficiently into refrigerator and freezer spaces than do their round counterparts. Odd items can be stored neatly in (square) boxes, which can be stacked.

11. Keep the right amount on hand. Tuna fish is on sale every other week, so we never buy more than six cans. Peanut butter goes on sale more rarely, so we purchase four cases at a time. Don't keep more plastic bread bags, egg cartons, or toilet-paper tubes than you could possibly reuse.

Sometimes an overstock sneaks up even on me. Upon investigating why my daughter's closet was so jammed, I realized she had fourteen size-4 dresses (most of my children's clothes have been given to us). I plan to donate half to our church thrift shop.

12. Share ownership. An infrequently used item can be owned by a group of families, and the family with the appropriate space can store it. For example, the one family in the group with workshop space keeps the table saw, which all other families are free to use. Meanwhile, the family with attic space keeps the electric train set up, while the family with pasture space keeps the horse.

13. Barter for space. One of my staff asked if we could temporarily store an organ for her. In exchange she gave us 20 pounds of hand-picked wild blueberries.

In a barter arrangement that resembles shared ownership, you can allow a friend to use something you own—a canoe, for example—in exchange for storing it.

14. Think vertical. Generally, the space above anything is potential storage space. Examples include the closet space above your shoes or the space in the garage above your car. If you live in an old house with high ceilings, a lightweight aluminum ladder kept in a handy spot can help you reach high storage spaces.

One architect, Malcolm Wells, sometimes designs homes with a shelf 1 foot below the ceiling. Because this design element is carried throughout the home, you soon forget it's there.

15. Be creative in thinking about other possible spaces: the spaces under, behind, or between. A double bed, 6 inches from the floor, has 16 cubic feet under it. Use the basement space between floor joists by nailing up strapping to store fishing poles, car racks, tents, and lumber. Most couch backs taper away from the wall, leaving 6 inches of unused floor space.

16. Hang it all! Bikes can hang from walls or ceilings. Pots and kitchen utensils can hang on pegboard. Hang your basket collection on the wall, making an attractive grouping. One woman told me she attached a crib side to her bed-

room wall and hangs wardrobe accessories on the slats.

17. Store things in untraditional places. Your bulk food could be kept in the nearby living-room closet. You could keep your oil filters and cans of motor oil in that coffee table/trunk.

For many people, saving space is saving money. Smaller places are generally cheaper to buy, rent, heat, cool, maintain, and pay taxes on. The extra effort required to find storage space in cramped quarters can be amply rewarded by those savings.

FLUSHED WITH SUCCESS

Dear Amy,

I've discovered my mother-in-law is trying to save on her water bill by not always flushing. I am wondering just how much water is used per flush, and what it costs. Hope you can help.

—Kathy from Kansas

Dear Kathy,

To figure out how much water is used per flush: Remove the tank cover. Mark the inside of the tank right at the "full" level.

Turn off the tank intake valve. Flush the toilet. Refill the empty tank with a gallon milk jug or measuring cup. The amount needed to reach the mark is the amount used per flush.

To figure the cost per flush: Most water bills are figured in cubic feet. There are 7.481 gallons in a cubic foot. We have a well, and we only pay for the tiny energy cost to pump water. So I had an employee from a nearby town

bring me his water bill for calculating purposes.

It said he had used 1,700 cubic feet during the billing period, and the cost was $24.78. So the cost per cubic foot is:

$24.78 ÷ 1,700 = $.0145764
So the cost per gallon is:

$.0145764 ÷ 7.481 =.0019484
Rounding up, a gallon of water costs him ²/₁₀ of a cent.

The average pre-1980 toilet uses about 5 gallons per flush. So, based on these figures, it costs 1¢ per flush. At 16 flushes per day (four each for a family of four) this is 16¢ daily, or $58 a year.

But water in Maine is relatively cheap. In Santa Barbara, California, which has one of the highest water rates in the nation, the cost is ½¢ per gallon, or 2.5¢ per flush. At that rate, 16 flushes per day would cost 40¢ daily, or $146 per year.

Another important cost to keep in mind is sewage fees. In many areas, these are based on water consumption rates, effectively doubling your cost per gallon.

Your own calculations may show that flushing is too expensive for you. Or you may be in a drought-stricken area and need to comply with water quotas. Or you may simply wish to save water out of environmental concerns. In any case, if you want to conserve:

1. Fill a plastic bottle halfway with pebbles, then fill it with water. Put the cap on, and place the bottle in the tank so that it is clear of the toilet mechanism. Experiment with different-size bottles so that you save the maximum amount of water and still get a good flush.

Some flush mechanisms allow you to lower the float ball by turning a screw.

2. Get a low-flush toilet. Sears sells one that uses 1½ gallons for about $100. Toilets are easy for a relatively handy person to install. If your water rates are high, this can pay for itself in a year. But be aware that the waste pipes in some older houses are pitched in such a way that at least a 3-gallon flush is required to avoid clogging. If you are unsure about your plumbing, consult a plumber who has plenty of experience with low-flush toilets before you install one.

3. Leave it. There is no refined way to phrase this, so let's just make up our own euphemisms: Some people allow "transparent" waste to collect between flushes, but draw the line, for esthetic, aromatic, and health reasons, at leaving "opaque" waste to accumulate. If you have young children or pets, I recommend flushing after each use, as they can be attracted to the toilet to play and drink, respectively.

BUT WHERE'S THE PRIZE?

Dear Amy,

Here's a Cracker-Jacks-ish snack that is quick, cheap, easy, and irresistible:

¾ cup packed brown sugar
¼ cup butter or margarine
3 tablespoons corn syrup
¼ teaspoon salt
¼ teaspoon baking soda
¼ teaspoon vanilla
8 cups popped popcorn
1 cup peanuts (optional)

Combine the brown sugar, butter, corn syrup, and salt over low heat until the butter is all melted. Cook without stirring for 3 minutes.

Add the baking soda and vanilla. Pour onto the popcorn and peanuts, and mix until evenly coated. Bake 15 minutes at 300 degrees. Break into pieces.

If you want a less sweet snack, use more popcorn. If you pop your popcorn in a saucepan, you can use the same oily pan to make the candy-coating mixture. The oil helps it slide right out.

—Lisa Smith
Cody, Wyoming

MAIL BAG

Dear Amy,

Did you know that you can use a small paper bag for a mailer? I was surprised to see one, and asked the post office if this was okay. They said yes. The maximum size allowable is 6⅛ inches by 11½ inches. The top can be folded down to meet length requirements, and stapled or taped.

—Laura Blyston
Crestline, California

CHECK OUT THE CHECKOUT

Dear Amy,

Now that the stores have electronic scanning and are trying to move people through the checkout as quickly as possible, I have found many errors. . . . For example, last week at Safeway I purchased bulk bridge mix marked at $2.99 a pound but was charged $3.09 at the register. When I questioned this, I received the item free because of the error.

At another store I was charged for three gallons of milk when I'd only gotten two. Also, coupons now have bar codes and are scanned. The scanners cannot always discriminate between a good coupon and an invalid one and will sometimes reject a good one, so baby-sit your grocery cashier.

—Pam Holcomb
Frederick, Maryland

(An article from the San Francisco Examiner, sent to me by reader Lesley Minearo of San Francisco, California, quotes a district attorney who estimates that there are millions of dollars in overcharges each year in Riverside County, California, alone. It occurs to me that there may also be millions of dollars in undercharges, too—in which case, one might feel ethically bound to report these errors as well. FZ)

TUX RELIEF

Dear Amy,

When both of my teenage sons (sophomore and junior) wanted to go to the homecoming dance, I talked them into going with me to several thrift stores looking (and hoping) for same appropriate clothing. By the end of our trek we had acquired two tuxedos in excellent condition and the exact sizes. We also found two cummerbunds. We borrowed shirts and broke down and bought two black bow ties. Then, a year later, when the senior prom came up, my son tried on his tuxedo, and it still fit perfectly. While all his friends were scurrying around trying to come up with the money to rent their formal duds, my son had only to shake off the dust and dress. Each ensemble cost $15. An added bonus was overhearing a conversation he recently had with a friend. "Where did you rent your tux?" My son proudly replied, "I didn't rent. I own."

—Judi Manolas
  Orlando, Florida

THE "WANTS" BULLETIN BOARD

You search thrift shops and scour yard sales, but you just can't find that elusive whatzit, so you break down and buy it new. When you tell a friend the sad tale, he slaps his forehead and says, "You

should have asked me! I've got a whole bushel of whatzits in my attic that I've been trying to get rid of since 1947!"

Here in Leeds, we have a close-knit group of friends at work and at church who freely exchange goods and services, but the scenario above happens to us, too. Weeks can pass before our paths cross—and even then, our needs may not come up in conversation.

So here at the *Gazette*'s palatial office complex, we came up with this idea: a "wants" bulletin board. This could be used wherever folks associate closely enough to become friends—at the dorm, church, or teachers' lounge.

To participate, people post notices stating their names and what they want.

For the most part, these should be free exchanges between friends who know that "what goes around, comes around." However, valuable items may need to be purchased, bartered, or loaned.

Even if they don't have the item on hand, making friends aware of your needs magnifies your bargain-hunting power. If you post a notice that you need size-7 girls' pants, the yard-sale junkie in your group will probably ask you, "If I see them, do you want me to pick them up for you? How much would you be willing to pay?" Naturally, this type of exchange requires trust, but if you set the amount you are willing to pay low enough, even if you wind up with electric-green punker pants, you'll probably be able to resell them at your yard sale for the same price (or make a Halloween costume).

All "wants" need not be material. You might list a need for storage space, a ride, baby-sitting, or

information on where to get something inexpensively.

The board can also include items that you would be willing to give away, such as surplus garden produce, baby stuff, or the avocado oven range that you are replacing.

This can also work for borrowing, such as if you need a lawn mower for a use or two while yours is in the shop.

I would stress that the "wants" board works best for small (fewer than 20 people) groups who share a generosity of spirit and a love for bargains. If it doesn't work in one of your circles of friends, try it in another.

IS FRUGALITY BAD FOR THE ECONOMY?

I'm sort of a politics/economics junkie. Every weeknight I forgo *Wheel of Fortune* to tune in to *The MacNeil/Lehrer NewsHour* on PBS. The show's format includes a panel of experts on a given topic—who sharply disagree. When the topic is the recession, typically you can see a professor of economics from Harvard Business School duke it out with some guy who won the Nobel Prize for economics.

Though I'm not an "expert," one question I have been asked to comment on is "If I'm frugal, isn't that bad for the economy?"

It's true that plenty of economists believe we need to get that American consumer confident and spending again. This thinking, that we can spend our way to economic prosperity, leads some to believe that those people who

don't spend money but save it instead, contribute to recession.

In fact, the reverse is true. Spending too much, and spending badly, got us into this mess. Frugality, in the long run, will get us out.

Here's why:

1. Former senator Paul Tsongas points out that business in America has suffered because of a lack of venture capital. Most businesses need capital to start up or to reinvest for greater productivity. This kind of borrowing is good debt, because in the long run it will create economic surplus.

Currently, there is a shortage of capital for two reasons. First, Americans save very little money, and second, what is available is sucked up by the federal government to pay for overspending. Americans typically save 4 percent of their total income, compared to Germans, who save 10 percent and the Japanese, who save 18 percent.

2. The average American has huge debts. To ask him to spend more to get the economy rolling is silly. It increases his economic vulnerability.

If that American declares bankruptcy, we all pay for it in higher costs from companies that had to eat the loss. If that person goes on public assistance, we all pay for it through higher taxes. And if chicken-hearted politicians are afraid to raise taxes, the government will have to borrow more money and . . . (see point #1).

3. The focus on spending our way to prosperity denies much deeper underlying reasons for the recession, such as the laws that make relocating manufacturing jobs to Mexico attractive for business. Consumer confidence will not bring back the thousands of manufacturing jobs we've lost in the last ten years. More people unemployed means the government pays out more unemployment benefits and—you guessed it—(see point #1).

To claim that we must borrow and spend our way to prosperity is shortsighted. We tried that to recover from the recession of 1982. The short-term economic gain was clear: More money was in circulation, which meant more jobs, and that meant more money, and that meant more jobs.

But this was a false "prosperity." The government "created jobs" through military buildup and expanding its own bureaucracy. Developers borrowed money to build office complexes when there was no market for them. Confident consumers bought CD players and snowmobiles on their credit cards. By trying to accelerate a recovery artificially, by going into debt on a government, business, and personal level, we eventually lost economic efficiency, because a larger and larger percentage of our money has had to be siphoned off to pay interest on our debt.

I'm not saying that debt is always bad. But debt must give you

value; it has to save you money in the long run.

And I'm not saying you should never spend a dime. Clearly, some spending is essential for the economy. We all enjoy a higher standard of living because we understand the benefits of trading goods and services. Imagine if we all grew our own cotton to weave our own material to sew our own clothes. It's more beneficial to trade our labor with those in our economy who have learned to make clothing more efficiently. Even if everyone were a tightwad, there would still be an exchange of goods and services, but this exchange would be sustainable over the long term.

If you're not impressed by economic theory as expressed by a housewife from Leeds, Maine, I refer you to two books that say the same thing about our need to save to rebuild the economy. They are *United We Stand* by Ross Perot and *A Call to Economic Arms* by Paul Tsongas, which is available for a suggested $5 donation from the Tsongas Committee, 20 Park Plaza, Room 230, Boston, MA 02116. By the way, this is not a political endorsement of either of these men.

So don't rationalize spending because it's "good for the economy." And don't feel guilty about being frugal because it's "bad for the economy."

A healthy economy is made up of economically healthy citizens. If you make choices that are financially sound for you, they will probably be financially sound for the economy in the long run.

CREDIT CARD THEORY

At Christmas, Americans tend to go nuts with bank cards such as Visa and MasterCard, but, frankly, Americans tend to go nuts with bank cards for the rest of the year as well. The average American is carrying a $2,500 balance on 2.5 bank cards, or about $1,000 per card, and paying an average interest rate of 18 percent. This means that the average American is throwing away $450 annually in bank-card interest. And these numbers don't even include store credit cards. Ack!

Because of these grim statistics, some tightwads avoid plastic like the plague. But cards *are* handy. They serve as identification, allow you to make telephone transactions, and can save you in an emergency.

So carry a card, but be sure to carry the right one for you.

You can find it by picking up (at the library, of course) the latest copy of *Money* magazine—the best bank-card deals are near the front of each issue.

But keep in mind that the best card for you depends upon your situation. If, like all good tightwads, you pay off your balance each month, you need a card with no annual fee and a grace period during which no interest is charged. Once those needs are met, *then* you need the lowest interest rate you can find, just to protect you in the unlikely event that you carry a balance someday.

On the other hand, if you are a new convert to tightwaddery, chances are you carry a balance from month to month. If you do, your aim should be to transfer your debt to the lowest-rate card you can find, and don't worry so much about the annual fee.

Why? Suppose your average balance is $5,000. If you can get an 8 percent interest rate rather than 12.5 percent, you'll save $225 per year. Most super-low-interest cards charge an annual fee of around $35, so the savings from the lower interest rate more than offset the higher fee. But keep in mind that once your balance drops under about $750, that lower-interest advantage disappears, and you'll be better off with a no-fee card.

Finally, let's explode a bit of tightwad credit card folklore. Some people like to buy everything with a credit card, reasoning that they profit because they can get free use of the money for up to 45 days. This looks like a better tip than it is: Remember, if you are getting 3 percent interest in your savings account, you must charge $77.33 to recoup the cost of the 29¢ stamp.

FILTER FACT

Dear Amy,

Instead of disposing of my disposable furnace and air-conditioning filters each month, I vacuum them and spray the clean filters with Endust. The Endust restores the dust-catching ability of the recycled filters. My air-conditioning repairman approves of this practice, and I recycle each filter two or three times before replacing it.

—Chuck Robinson
Bellaire, Texas

LOAF LESSON

Dear Amy,

When cutting homemade bread into slices, cut a whole loaf at one time. Then scrape all of the crumbs into a plastic bag that is kept in the freezer, and use when recipes call for bread crumbs.

—Julie Watner
Gramling,
South Carolina

DEALS ON WHEELS

Dear Amy,

My car-buying strategy is to buy the least expensive model from a top-quality car maker, to look for cars with extras like sport trim or better upholstery (it's important to me not to have a car that feels "cheap"), to buy cars two years old or less, to buy through the newspaper (not deal-ers), to buy from owners who have maintenance records on the car, and to buy from people who seem trustworthy and are selling for good reasons. When I've been interested in a car, I've given the other party a deposit and taken the car to a mechanic (at my expense) after writing up a short agreement, which we both sign. . . . I also check *Consumer Reports* and *The Yellow Book of Used Car Prices* at the library. . . .

Using the method, I have bought two trouble-free, attractive cars. . . . It is worth the time and work, and a careful buyer can virtually eliminate the extra risk.

—Susan M. Kuhn
Washington, D.C.

MEWS NEWS

Dear Amy,

I use newspaper cut into strips for cat litter. It smells better, is cleaner, and can be changed often. First, you mix the strips with real litter, then use less and less litter, then just newspaper. It's good for eyes and lungs, because there is no dust.

—Mrs. Paka Hussey
Odessa, Florida

NOT MILK DUDS

Dear Amy,

I go into the grocery store and look at the expiration dates on the milk. Usually, there is milk that has expired the day before, that day, or will expire the following day. I ask a store worker to mark the milk down since it's expired or about to expire, and they cheerfully do so. I get half-gallon cartons, which sell from $1.50 to $1.89 for 25¢ to 50¢. Since the milk stays fresh for five days after the expiration date and the half-gallon cartons can be stored in the freezer, we always have fresh milk.

—Karyn Price
   Rio Rancho, New Mexico

ONE PUMP OR TWO?

Dear Amy,

Most shampoo comes in a squeeze-type bottle or tube, leaving the portion control up to the user. With little ones and teenagers this can be expensive. Buy shampoo in bulk gallons and pour into pump-type dispensers for hand soap. Short hair: one pump. Long hair: two pumps.

—Jeannette Behr
   Twin Falls, Idaho

BUDGET QUENCHER

Dear Amy,

A cheap alternative to juice: I buy store-brand lemon juice for $1.49 and make my own lemonade more cheaply than I can buy juice in any form. It's delicious and far superior to the cheapest lemonade powder mix. A quart of lemon juice will yield 2 gallons of lemonade. Mix ½ cup of lemon juice and ½ cup of sugar to 1 quart of water.

—Rebecca Novakovich
   Cambridge, Massachusetts

THE FRUGAL FIXER-UPPER

The PBS TV series *This Old House* had a memorable episode a few years ago. Bob, the contractor, and Norm, the carpenter, had just finished renovation of the plus-200-year-old "Weatherby" house in Massachusetts. Here's the gist of their conversation:

Bob: We've finished her, Norm, and isn't she a beauty?

Norm: Yup. Though we did go a bit over budget.

Bob: Well . . . yes, the budget was $100,000, and we spent $200,000.

Norm: But isn't she a beauty!

As I watched, I cringed. *This Old House* inadvertently presents home renovation as discouragingly expensive. Many of their projects use costly, state-of-the-art materials and roar ahead quickly to meet the TV production schedule (which drives up costs).

But a fixer-upper doesn't have to mean financial insanity. Since my teenage years, I have consciously observed many renovations, noting what people did right and what they did wrong. Here's what I learned:

WHY GET A FIXER-UPPER?

By fixing up an old house, you can eventually own a home that is "technically" more than you can afford. Banks will rarely allow your mortgage payment to exceed 28 percent of your income—even if you prove you can handle more. But you can buy a fixer-upper with a small mortgage and put your surplus income toward renovation, eventually owning a more valuable home.

Usually, you can buy and fix up a house for less than it costs to build one or to buy one in good condition, particularly if you do much of the work. There are exceptions—like expensive top-to-bottom renovations of shacks. But if you do it right, you'll save money.

Fixer-uppers have other advantages over building new. You can more comfortably use recycled materials, and you don't have to be highly skilled to match existing old-house carpentry. Older homes usually have better construction and come with more land than newer homes.

WHO SHOULD BUY A FIXER-UPPER?

Because a fixer-upper is almost always an old house, you should appreciate old-house character: bumpy walls, sloping floors, and doors that don't quite fit. If you really want a new-looking house, don't buy an old house and try to make it look new. Not only will this be expensive, but you may destroy the architectural integrity of a historic building.

You'll need handyman skills, patience, persistence, and lots of time. In our case, Jim has the building skills, but I'm the one who loves the tedious work. If you or your spouse has a history of not finishing projects and you loathe this type of work, buy a home in good condition.

You should also have the imagination to see through grease-splattered walls, curling linoleum, and ancient crud and envision a cheerful kitchen.

HOW DO YOU SHOP?

Although most realtors are fine people, we found that many were hard of hearing. After specifically telling them we only wanted to look at older homes, we found ourselves being taken on frequent side trips to check out "a really interesting contemporary split level." We decided that shopping for fixer-uppers required a different strategy.

Unlike typical ranch houses, fixer-uppers vary greatly from property to property. Most drawbacks that are impossible or too expensive to change can be spotted by simply driving by, without time-consuming realtor-guided house tours. So, get copies of new listings that meet your criteria as soon as they come out and drive by the homes yourselves. Then arrange to have the realtor show you any that look interesting. We toured fewer than 10 percent of the homes we saw.

Because we looked at 176 houses in 15 months in a four-county area, we found we needed two important tools to save time and gasoline. We bought a book of area maps that showed street names. We also kept a notebook with the copies of listings taped to pages. Eventually we organized them by the town, in alphabetical order. When a realtor called we were able to tell him, in a matter of seconds, whether we had seen a particular house, and we avoided looking at the same house twice.

We developed a relationship with one realtor in each county, and they eventually understood we were saving them time too.

Obviously, how long you persist in your hunt has to do with variables in your situation. You'll spend less time shopping if this is a home you plan to own for a short period of time. We were shopping for a home to live in for the rest of our lives, and few homes within our price range met our criteria.

WHAT SHOULD YOU LOOK FOR?

Location is the most important aspect of any house purchase. You can sink unlimited funds into your dream home, but you will never be able to move the pig farm located across the road.

The fixer-upper should be valued below other homes in the neighborhood. If you spend $200,000 renovating and the neighboring houses are worth $75,000, you'll never recoup your investment if you decide to sell. The purchase price should be so low that it plus the total cost of renovation is much less than the cost of a comparable home in good condition.

During your tour with a realtor conduct your own building inspection to look for obvious problems that might rule out the purchase. If everything seems okay, hire a building inspector who is familiar with older homes. He can help you locate problems, advise you about some costs, and recommend contractors for any needed estimates. The most diligent inspectors and contractors will miss a few prob-

lems, so your budget should have room for surprises.

Avoid homes that require major changes, such as complete alterations of floor plans. Only consider major changes when the property is either extremely cheap or has other unique advantages. Otherwise, it's easier to keep looking.

The ideal fixer-upper has never been "remuddled." While it's a joy to remove cracked floor tiles and rusty sheet-metal sink cabinets, it's sickening to tear out newly installed orange-shag carpeting and plastic "Colonial-style" kitchen cabinets (that you just paid extra for).

HOW DO YOU FIX IT UP?

After you buy the house, develop a detailed plan; know, basically, what you want to do, from start to finish, *before* you lift a hammer. If you need to do major work, a floor plan is a must. Know what you'll need a contractor for and what you can do yourself. Also know the sequence in which things need to be done; don't put down the kitchen floor before you figure out the room's layout.

An advantage to a fixer-upper is that you can live there during the process. However, there may be some things you need to do before moving in to bring the home up to a livable standard. In our

case, we repaired a gaping hole in the kitchen ceiling and had a furnace installed in the unheated ell.

You may want to deal with lead-based paint before moving in, particularly if you have children. In Maine, painting over most surfaces is considered to be reasonable abatement. Some "chewable" surfaces, such as windowsills, can be covered with duct tape until there's time for more extensive treatment. With adequate research you can learn how to remove lead paint from small areas with little risk. If you are planning any large-scale removal of interior paint after moving in, such as sanding floors, take the kids to visit relatives.

Once you are in the house, tackle the big eyesores first. Things like a thorough cleaning, hauling trash to the dump, a quick coat of paint on ugly walls, and mowing down brush around the property will provide the most improvement for the least money and effort.

Do small sections at a time. Big messes are overwhelming—especially if you're living in them. Instead, you'll need the feeling of accomplishment that comes from completing each small job—as small as painting a single window at a time.

Don't start any projects that you don't have the time, energy, or money to finish. This way, you avoid ending up with a perpetually gutted, unlivable house. And if something unexpected comes along (like a brilliant idea for a newsletter or uh-oh twins), remaining projects can be postponed for a year or two.

Allow *lots* of time to make decisions. Consider the landscape ar-

chitect who planted grass in the new college's courtyard. He returned months later and designed walkways where the students had worn paths. Sometimes, you need to live in a place for a year or so before you know how to solve a problem.

In my pursuit of inexpensive solutions, I continually pore through magazines. I've noticed that the kitchens I like best are not the $30,000 renovations, but the ones based on simple solutions—refinished wood floors, original counters repainted, and simple, open shelves for storage. By doing this, I figure I can buy one or two strategic antiques for ambiance, and still save at least $27,000.

Always think of sources for recycled stuff, especially those that may already be in your fixer-upper. We found old, wide boards in our carriage house that we plan to use for countertops in our kitchen to match those in the pantry. If you need a door for a room, take it off a same-size doorway that doesn't need a door. Frequently, you can save money by waiting for salvage materials to become available.

Finally, don't do anything stupid. We saw an amazing number of botched renovations during our house hunt—like the mammoth brick fireplace that overwhelmed a tiny living room, a bedroom that could only be accessed by going through a bathroom, and a door that opened only partway because it banged against a counter.

Some people should be discouraged from tackling a fixer-upper. But the right person combined with the right house will result in great savings.

Used Shoes

. . . ARE THEY GOOD OR BAD?

When we were on the Donahue show, we skillfully fielded questions from skeptical audience members. But I sputtered when, after discussing what my children were wearing, a guy stood and asked, "Aren't used shoes bad for kids?"

"Uh . . . uh . . . I believe there's a difference of opinion on that," was my less skillful reply. I *had* always heard that the "experts" say used shoes are bad for kids. I confess: *My* opinion was the only one I knew of that was different.

This black-and-white opinion, that all used shoes are bad for kids, has always been a mystery to me. Although it is logical that an extremely worn, hard-soled leather shoe could cause problems, it didn't seem possible that all used tennis shoes, flip-flops, slippers, sandals, and twice-worn patent-leather church shoes would cause lifelong foot problems.

I recently learned of an article in one of the parenting magazines that said that some experts believe that hand-me-down shoes are *not* bad. Filled with joyful exuberance that I might indeed be right, I sent one of my staff to the library to obtain a copy of this article. She returned with two articles, which expressed opposite opinions.

The June 1990 issue of *Parents* magazine contained the familiar

expert advice. In it, Dr. Glenn Gastwirth, director of scientific affairs for the American Podiatric Medical Association, says that shoes mold to the individual foot, and shoes may become worn down in a way that is not outwardly visible. In addition, he says a natural bend develops in the shoe, and that bend might not be right for the next child. However, when I called him, he admitted that he knew of no studies showing that used shoes harm the feet.

He said the most important reason not to hand down shoes is that the only way to insure proper fit is with the help of a trained salesperson.

In other words, this doctor would not approve of a common, tightwaddy, new-shoe purchase method—trying on shoes yourself in a discount store. In his view, traditional, higher-priced shoe stores are the only option.

Just out of curiosity, we called a couple of shoe stores to inquire about the training procedure for clerks. The longest training course we found is two hours. A friend of mine, who was a shoe clerk for Sears, says her training lasted 60 seconds.

The second article appeared in *Parenting* magazine, in the June/July 1992 issue. This article, mainly about how to buy shoes for kids, devoted a couple of sentences to suggesting that some experts believe that hand-me-down shoes are acceptable.

Wanting a bit more information, we called Dr. Laurence Lembach, a professor at the Ohio College of Podiatric Medicine in Cleveland, who was one of the podiatrists interviewed in *Parenting*.

While stating that there is disagreement among professionals, Dr. Lembach said he believes that if a shoe is in good condition, and if it fits properly, it is okay to hand it down.

"Good condition," means that it is not badly worn along the outside edge of the heel or sole. He says a handed-down shoe may have "mild wear" on either side.

"Fits properly," means that there is about a thumb width between the end of the big toe and the end of the shoe (or a half inch for kids under two), and you cannot feel the bone or the little toe pushing against the side of the shoe.

He conceded that sneakers have much more give, and it's harder to get a good fit from a hard-sole leather shoe that laces tightly. In other words, choosing the type of used footwear, along with size and degree of wear, is also important.

Dr. Lembach practices what he preaches. He has six kids, and shoes are handed down within his family.

He noticed the same trend that I did: "Kids go through three or four size changes in the first two years. They outgrow shoes before they outwear them."

Both doctors agreed that proper fit is more important than whether a shoe is used (unless there is extreme wear). So, rigid adherence to the professionally fit new-shoe advice could be *more* likely to cause problems. Financially strapped parents may be unable to replace expensive shoes soon enough. In contrast, I can replace a pair of shoes in minutes, as soon as they are outgrown. Each of my kids has a box with a large selection of used shoes for them to grow into.

Doctors, who are very busy, are the most difficult experts to interview, and often return my calls several weeks later. As I wrapped up this article, more opinions straggled in. One podiatrist said that suggesting used shoes were fine was "awful advice," while Dr. Dennis Wenger, an orthopedic surgeon at Children's Hospital in San Diego, said that I was "on the right track." The only exception he made was for shoes previously worn by a teenager or adult with severe bunions. He said the idea that new shoes are essential for proper foot development is "a myth."

So there you go. Pick your expert opinion.

WRAPPING VERSUS UNWRAPPING: THE SLIPPERY TRUTH

One of the most ancient and respected bits of tightwad lore is that unwrapping soap several months before using it extends its life. The theory is that the soap dries out and therefore lasts longer. But is it true?

In the July 1992 issue of *Good Housekeeping,* Heloise addressed the question in her column (sent to me by reader Linda Bukvic of Williamsburg, Ohio). Heloise called the Soap and Detergent Association and was told that unwrapping soap does not prolong its life. In fact, the SDA stated that the wrapping protects the soap, and prematurely removing it could *speed up* the aging process.

I must admit that I have never unwrapped my soap to make it last longer, so I had no opinion one way or the other. But I suspected a conspiracy on the part of soap manufacturers to suppress this vital, soap-saving strategy—after all, they stand to sell more soap if it dissolves at an accelerated rate.

So I concluded that it was up to me, the dauntless researcher who ripped the lid off the cloth-versus-paper-napkin question, on page 20, to conduct the ultimate experiment to, once and for all, answer this critical question for tightwads everywhere. Yes, I would even fund the research myself and vowed to spend as much as $1 in pursuit of the truth.

I selected two bars of Coast soap that had been purchased in the same four-pack. I unwrapped one and put them both on my counter for several weeks. Then I unwrapped the second bar, put both bars in a glass loaf pan, covered them with water, and let them sit for two and a half days. I then precision-measured the remaining hard soap by shaping my thumb and index finger like a pair of calipers and squishing into the layer of goop. The measurement was the same for both bars. Finally, I scraped off the goop, and both bars appeared to be the same size.

I reported my findings to one of my staff, Carole, a longtime practitioner of unwrapping soap bars. She pointed to possible unscientific techniques in my experiment. Soap is not soaked in a dish, she observed, but rather used and left to dry between uses. She also theorized that different brands of soaps might react differently.

Carole conducted her own experiment with two brands of soap, Ivory and a facial soap with glycerine, both of which had been unwrapped for two months. She bought new soaps of the same brands. The unwrapped soaps did appear to be dryer, and weighed

½ ounce less than the wrapped soaps—even though all four bars were the 3-ounce size.

Using 120-degree water, she washed her hands for three minutes with each bar. She placed the bars on a rack to dry, turning them over when half dry. She repeated this process six times, for a total of 18 minutes of washing per bar. Both wrapped bars disintegrated after 18 minutes. The unwrapped bars disintegrated after 19½ minutes.

So, according to this experiment, unwrapping soap bars makes them last 7.69 percent longer. At 50¢ per bar, using 30 bars per year, our family of eight could save $1.15 annually.

But *wait*! Carole was prejudiced in favor of unwrapping soap, and she may have subconsciously washed 7.69 percent harder with the wrapped bars.

So watch for the unwrapping-the-soap-bar update: Our staff of *Tightwad Gazette* mechanical engineers is hard at work designing an experimental apparatus with robotic hands for precision soap dissolving, to be constructed of a trash-picked ceiling fan, scavenged bicycle parts, electronic gizmos, and four rubber gloves—wind-powered, of course.

FREEBIES

Actually, the only things that are truly "free" are those that would otherwise go to the dump—that's why the highest tightwad art, in my view, is legal trash picking.

Some of the offers below are government services—which taxpayers pay for eventually—so choose carefully. But as for the corporate freebies, if you feel at all guilty about accepting them, remember that some spendthrift (who's mocking your lifestyle) is paying inflated prices to finance these offers:

1. Do you wonder why your bank officer giggled when you asked for a loan? Maybe you need a free report on your credit status. Send your full name, addresses for the last five years, Social Security number, year of birth, and (if any) spouse's name to TRW Consumer Assistance, Box 2350, Chatsworth, CA 91313. Also include a copy of a letter or document that includes both your name and address, such as a bill. This prevents unauthorized release of your credit history.

2. Call *Consumer Reports* at (800) 234-1645 and request a trial subscription. You'll get a free issue and free copy of the latest buying guide. If you don't choose to subscribe, write "cancel" on the bill when it arrives, and the issue and book will remain yours to keep.

3. Free local attractions such as museums, gardens, and historical buildings are often listed in the calendar sections of newspapers. For free attractions nationwide, check out *Guide to Free Attractions, U.S.A.* It's available for $14.95 from Cottage Publications, 24396 Pleasant View Drive, Elkhart, IN 46517, (800) 303-7833, or get a copy from your library through interlibrary loan. For the same price, the same publisher sells *A Guide to Free Campgrounds*.

4. The federal government has dozens of free consumer booklets ranging from *The Student Guide: Financial Aid*, to *Understanding*

Social Security. To get the complete catalog, write S. James, Consumer Information Center-2D, P.O. Box 100, Pueblo, CO 81002.

5. Each month, the U.S. Postal Service sends an attractive poster promoting a new line of stamps to each post office around the country. We have a glossy, 2-foot-by-3-foot wild-animal-stamp poster hanging in five-year-old Neal's room that he loves. If you see one you like, ask your postmaster if you can have it when the office is through with it.

6. If you want to find loopholes in the tax law—or if you just can't get to sleep at night—bone up on tax law with free pamphlets from the government, including "Reporting of Real Estate Transactions to the IRS," and "Business Use of Your Home." Call (800) 829-3676.

7. If a flight is overbooked, you are usually offered a free round-trip ticket anywhere in the continental U.S. if you will give up your seat and take the next flight. You can increase the likelihood of getting bumped by casually striking up a conversation with a flight attendant over soda and peanuts and asking which times of the month or year the flight tends to be overbooked. In the future, fly at that time.

8. If you need to contact any large organization or company, start by calling toll-free directory assis-

tance at (800) 555-1212. I have found this extremely handy. It's a rare large organization that doesn't have a toll-free number.

9. Many newspaper classified-ad sections and "swap" publications list "free-for-the-taking" items. We recently picked up a nearly new range this way that only needed a $15 repair. Other freebies I've seen offered include free firewood, pets, and lumber (there's usually a slight "catch" for building materials—you have to tear down a building to get it).

10. The Service Corps of Retired Executives, more widely known as

SCORE, is the consulting arm of the Small Business Administration. It offers free advice from executives, most of whom are retired, to small-business owners and to people who want to start a business. I have used this organization and found it quite helpful. They advise over the phone and/or on-site. To find the office nearest you, call (800) 634-0245.

11. After you get your prescription, ask your doctor if she has any samples of the medicine she's prescribed. Doctors are swamped with samples from drug companies and are usually glad to unload them. Aside from the savings, this is marvelously handy if it is 11:00 P.M. and 20 miles to the drugstore.

12. Your congressperson's local office hands out free calendars, listing a significant event from American history for every date of the year. When visiting his or her office in Washington, D.C., ask for free passes to the House and Senate galleries, and for the V.I.P. tour of the White House, which has shorter lines and smaller tour groups than the regular tour.

13. Some fairs offer free admission if you do some volunteer work. Maine's Common Ground Country Fair offers free admittance, a free, attractive T-shirt, and a free meal in exchange for four hours of work. You can choose your hours and type of work—anything from parking cars to shoveling you-know-what. Similar arrangements can be worked out with community theaters. You can get free admission for ushering or selling tickets.

WE ATE LENTILS . . . AND LIVED

Lentils are a cheap, filling source of protein, and because they don't require soaking before cooking, they are the handy fast food of the legume family.

The only problem is that many people find them bland at best, mealy and unappetizing at worst. So, to review lentil recipes sent in by readers, I assembled a panel of unrepentant carnivores and diehard bean haters. I was seeking surefire recipes to excite the vegetarian virgins in your family.

While the vegetarian veterans around here enjoyed nearly all of the recipes received, this bean-hater panel narrow-mindedly rejected most of them. As it turns out, the only two recipes that received universal approval were not reader contributions but were developed by *The Tightwad Gazette*'s test kitchen. They both use a lentil-based meat substitute made of equal parts lentils and bulgur wheat (available from health-food stores). Simmer one part of this mixture with two parts water for 45 minutes.

LENTIL BURGERS FOR BEAN HATERS

2 cups cooked lentil-bulgur
    mixture
2 cups bread crumbs
1 cup chopped onion
½ cup chopped green pepper
4 tablespoons mixed Italian herbs
    (basil, oregano, thyme, etc.)
4 cloves garlic (or 4 teaspoons
    powdered garlic)
2 eggs (or 2 tablespoons soy flour
    and 2 tablespoons water)
½ cup milk

Mix the first six ingredients. Mix in eggs. Add milk and mix well. Chill ½ hour. Make into patties and fry 10 minutes per side, or bake on cookie sheet at 350 degrees, 10 minutes on each side.

BURRITOS

Combine 2 cups cooked lentil-bulgur mixture with ¼ cup taco-mix seasoning (purchased in bulk at a warehouse store, ¼ cup costs about 35¢).

Make tortillas as follows:

2 cups flour
½ teaspoon salt
¼ cup shortening
½ cup cold water

Combine flour and salt. Cut in shortening. Add water, mix until just combined. Divide into 10 balls and roll out flat. Fill with filling, roll up, and bake at 350 degrees for 20 minutes.

WHAT TO DO WITH . . .

A Crayon-Marked Blackboard. Use scouring powder to remove marks. We hung an extra child's blackboard in our pantry to write down shopping needs and things we want to remember to do.

An Egg Carton. Perfect for storing my 12 individually purchased jars of paste food-coloring. Usually purchased at a party-goods store, paste food-coloring can cost more than $1 per jar, but lasts longer and produces superior colors.

Jam Residue Left Inside Jar. Use for popsicle flavoring. Fill a popsicle mold with milk. Dump the milk into a jar that contains leftover jam. Tighten the lid on jar, and shake vigorously until the residue combines with the milk. Pour the milk back into the popsicle mold and freeze.

Ketchup Gunk in Empty Bottle. Pour ¼ cup hot water into the bottle and shake vigorously until the gunk combines with the water. Pour the water into your freezer container for leftover soup.

The Wrong-Color Liquid Foundation. Say you decide the shade you bought is too light. Buy a shade of the same brand that's too dark. Carefully combine small quantities of the two until you get the right shade.

Old Athletic Socks. Slit worn but clean socks lengthwise, and use  for dish rags. The thick material is ideal for this use. Or cut a thumb hole and use as a mitten liner. (Maryann Lalley, Bartonsville, Pennsylvania.)

No-Longer-Needed Crib Sheets. Graduate them to car use. Crib sheets fit neatly over the backseat to protect it from spilled toddler drinks and crayon marks. (Denisha Tremain, Mesquite, Texas.)

Stuck Envelopes. When new envelopes have sealed closed due to moisture, heat in the microwave for 20 seconds. This will open them all or partway. (Miriam Watto, Marietta, Pennsylvania.)

Old Mylar Balloons. Cut the seams off and use the two pieces to wrap small gifts. Place the gift in the center, pull up the mylar, and tie with a ribbon. Can be used many times. (Monica Kingston, Geneseo, New York.)

Old Room Deodorizers. Disassemble, soak the inner absorbent pad with pine cleaner, and reassemble. (Brenda Evans, Winston-Salem, North Carolina.)

Juice Lids. Glue a piece of magnetic tape (cheaper than magnets) to the back and a child's picture to the front. One teacher uses these on a metal board to keep track of classroom jobs or assignments. Parents could use this idea to rotate household chores among family members. (Ellen J. Urbina-Martin, Jamaica Plain, Massachusetts.)

Milk Jugs. Make a toss-and-catch game by cutting milk jugs as shown. Toss homemade beanbags. Invented by reader's six-year-old son. (Marilyn Bruggema, El Cajon, California.)

A Turkey Net . . . that your Thanksgiving turkey came in. Wash it, run an old shoelace through it several spaces down. Use to keep bath toys so they will drip dry. (Sue Reading, West Jordan, Utah.)

Musty Books. Put sheets of newspaper between some pages, and place the book along with crumpled newspaper in a suitcase or box. The newspaper will absorb the odor. (Denita Bradley, Knoxville, Tennessee.)

Six-Pack Rings. Acquire a large quantity from spendthrift friends. Tie them together with fishing line to make a hammock. Will last several seasons. (Jan Rusk, Roseville, California.)

Old Panty Hose. Use to make tiny pouches for fish bait, such as chicken liver. Helps keep bait on the hook. (Henry Howard, Smyrna, Tennessee.)

Old Kitchen Cabinets. Reuse them in the garage or workshop. (David and Cheryl Bernardi, Chicago, Illinois.)

Bacon Plastic. The plastic piece that comes in the bacon can be used to make stencils, such as for painting country designs on the walls.

GO WITH THE PRO

Dear Amy,

Please encourage readers to check the prices at their local janitorial-supply company (look in the Yellow Pages under janitorial supplies). Our local firm carries concentrated neutral cleaner, suitable for cleaning all surfaces including wood, for $7.70 a gallon. The label advises using 2 ounces of concentrate in a gallon of water. This works out to 12¢ a gallon of cleaning solution—a tightwad's delight!

—Rebecca Hodge
Raleigh, North Carolina

BIN BORROWING LATELY?

Dear Amy,

When visiting your local recycling center, spend a few minutes sorting through the magazine bins. You can find current or recent magazines, including some very interesting alternative publications. After reading these, I return them to the bins.

—John Raatz
Santa Monica, California

POSTAL PLEA

Dear Amy,

Here's an urgent warning to tightwads everywhere. As a new tightwad, my primary source of envelopes has become the return envelopes that come in advertisement/junk mail. There must be many tightwads who, like me, just throw a handwritten label over the printed address. However, postal workers have informed me it's important to put a label over those bar-code symbols on the bottom of the envelopes, too—because their computers will read the bar code and ignore my handwritten address label. I do know that some of my mail has seemingly been delayed or lost in the past year.

—Connie Boltz
Seattle, Washington

(By the time you slap two labels on an envelope, chances are you are spending more on labels than if you bought new envelopes in bulk from a warehouse store. A cheaper way to reuse junk-mail envelopes is to turn them inside out, as explained in the first book. In any case, don't mark over the code with marker. This prevents the post office from printing its own bar code in that space and slows down the mail. FZ)

THREE THRIFTY THOUGHTS

Dear Amy,

My sons don't like powdered milk, but they do enjoy it in a "purple cow." Fill a glass ⅔ with milk and ⅓ with grape juice.

If you have leftover salad, especially some to which dressing has already been applied, whir it in a blender with tomato juice, top with croutons and a few tiny cucumber bits, and serve as gazpacho.

After reading in your newsletter about the man who uses 1 square of toilet paper (yuck), I started using half of lots of things: shampoo, dish liquid, salt, and never noticed the difference.

—Marilyn Gibble
Lititz, Pennsylvania

CHANGE ON THE RANGE

Dear Amy,

   To extend the lives of burners on an electric range, rotate them just as you would tires on a car. It evens out the wear.

   —Nancy Deiter
   Platteville, Wisconsin

WIPE THE WIPER

Dear Amy,

   It is important to clean windshield wipers with vinegar and water in order to clean away the dirt and grime that accumulate. . . . I had thought my windshield wipers needed to be replaced, but after cleaning they were as good as new!

   —Margaret Landsborough
   Los Angeles, California

CREATIVE DEPRIVATION

At a yard sale I attended, a ten-year-old kid was barely visible behind a table piled with GI Joe paraphernalia. Along with about 30 Joe dolls, he was selling his Joe tanks, Joe bazookas, Joe rocket belts, and Joe you-name-it.

   What struck me was what contempt he seemed to have for the stuff—he was practically giving it away. It was clear that this huge collection, which must have cost several hundred dollars to buy, was now an immense bore to him. When I commented to his parents about the good deals at their son's table, they just rolled their eyes as if to say, "That's kids for you."

Increasingly, I see this trend toward excess in children's lives. A friend, who has one child, says his son is so bombarded with toys from friends and relatives that "I don't tell him to clean his room—I tell him to shovel it out."

   While we, as kids, might have been devastated to lose a favorite toy, kids today don't even bother to keep track of their stuff. When a friend found an $80 Game Boy, a hand-held video game, in his house, he was unable to learn whose it was. Six months later, the ten-year-old owner spotted her toy during a visit. She casually remarked, "Oh, I was wondering where I left that."

   And the excess problem is not just toys. The average kid spends more than four hours parked in front of a TV each day. If there's nothing good to watch on TV (or cable), they have an unlimited supply of video movies and games.

   As a result of all this stuff and stimulation, kids regard overload as a normal condition. Anything less—a walk in the woods, making cookies, or sitting in a classroom listening to a teacher—is boring.

   In contrast, using a concept I call "creative deprivation" is, in my view, a healthier way to raise children.

   The idea behind creative deprivation is that every event should have space around it, so that the event can stand out and be appreciated. A simple example is a frame around a picture, which provides a space to make it stand out from the busy wallpaper.

   Until this century, the space occurred naturally. Entertainment and material goods were hard to come by, so they were appreciated when they came along. A child cherished his few toys, and music was a special event, because it could only be heard when musicians were assembled.

The challenge of modern life is that we have to actively create the space. With mass production, toys are cheap enough to swamp even poorer families. With TV, videotapes, and video games, flashy entertainment can come into every home 24 hours a day.

That's why the best parents understand that their kids can have too much of a good thing. They place limitations on the stuff and stimulation. They are tough enough to slow down the flow of goodies.

Often, people think we refuse to avalanche our kids with toys because we're tightwads. But saving money is *not* the main reason. I just feel there's nothing sadder than a jaded eight-year-old.

Conversely, it's delightful to see a kid thrilled by a simple pleasure. During a rare trip to a mall a few years ago, we were shopping for a gift for one of our children, whose birthday falls in May—just before yard-sale season kicks in and just as I'm running out of the stuff from the previous season. To distract the kids while Jim went back to the store to pick up the gift and hide it in the car, we popped into an ice-cream shop and I ordered a junior cone for each child, which they consumed in complete silence, savoring every drip. I was very proud of my brood and their ability to enjoy these little treats.

Many parents, seeing their children appreciate junior cones, would buy them cones during each trip to the mall. Soon, seeing the kids' enthusiasm waning, they would assume they must wow them with banana splits. When those no longer produce the desired effect, they would move up to the jumbo deluxe sundae . . . and so on, until the kids became impossible to please.

But I see diminished appreciation as a barometer that shows when kids have had too much. Instead of moving up to the banana split, I decrease the frequency of junior cones.

While it's true I don't raise my kids this way to save money, saving is a natural by-product of creative deprivation. Not only do I save on the constant expense of the ever-increasing amount of stuff and stimulation, but when I *do* treat the kids, they get the same wow for far less money.

Creative deprivation does have a few rules. Limit the things kids don't need, but don't limit the things they do need—such as good nutrition and parenting attention. Second, provide them with alternatives. Our kids have their own "office" in my office where they do artwork, a tree house they can build on with scrap wood, a playhouse in an attic, and a selection of Legos and other toys that demand creativity. If you limit passive entertainment, kids eventually get beyond the boredom and begin to be creative.

Incidentally, this insight of mine, while brilliant, isn't new. About 2,500 years ago, the Chinese philosopher Lao-tzu wrote:

Guard the senses
And life is ever full . . .
Always be busy
And life is beyond hope.

Finally, creative deprivation works for adults too. If you seem to need increasingly expensive thrills and gadgets to keep from being bored, I suggest you step off the merry-go-round. Though this might seem *more* boring at first, eventually you'll come to enjoy a game of checkers with your nine-year-old, trying a new bread recipe—or, one of Jim's favorites, watching the freezer defrost.

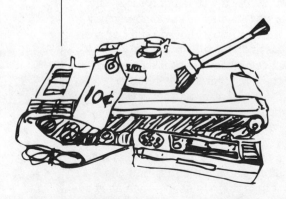

THE *X* SYSTEM

When you have several children and two or more are the same sex, it becomes difficult to keep their clothes straight at laundry-folding time.

One solution, which I read in an out-of-print thrift book, is to use a laundry marker to put *X*s in an inconspicuous place on children's clothes.

The oldest child is X, the next oldest is XX, and the next oldest is XXX, and so on. Every time an article of clothing is passed down, add another *X*.

Vicki Fisher of Clinton, Utah, uses a variation of this idea. She puts a tiny dot of acrylic paint on the inside of each article of clothing. Each time the article is passed down, she paints over the tiny dot with the color code for the next child.

Personally, I've developed a sixth sense, which allows me to detect even minute variations in white-sock size and sort accordingly. So to me, the attraction of the *X* system is that it would help my less gifted husband and kids to sort laundry.

LOW-COST COLOR

I had always suspected that paste-type food coloring, which is sold in party-goods stores, is cheaper to use than the liquid type sold in supermarkets. But I had never run a rigorous test to prove this. So when I was picked for classroom cookie duty recently, it seemed an excellent time to mix up a mountain of green frosting and settle the question.

Having used only paste food coloring for many years, I was surprised when I saw the high price of liquid coloring. A four-bottle box costs $2.29, or 58¢ for a bottle that contains 2 teaspoons, or 29¢ per teaspoon.

Paste colors last so long it had been a while since I'd priced those as well. The prices vary depending on the color. The average price is $1.79 a jar, which contains 6 teaspoons. Coincidentally, that also works out to 29¢ per teaspoon.

With this information, it was simple to compare them by making two large bowls of frosting and adding food coloring to each until we achieved the same shade of color.

To precision-measure the coloring, we used a chemist's $1/16$-teaspoon measure. It took $1/16$ teaspoon of paste to make a double batch of frosting turn medium green. In contrast, it took $7/16$ teaspoon of liquid to make a double batch turn the same green. So the paste coloring costs less than 1¢ per batch, versus more than 6¢ per batch for the liquid.

The cost advantage becomes clearer when you consider how much you save when you buy four jars of paste colors for $7.16. The equivalent amount of liquid color would cost over $50.

In addition to their economy, paste colors are much richer than liquids and have a greater range of hues, including brown and black. The liquid red will make pink, but won't produce a true-red frosting, and combining liquid red and blue won't make a nice lavender.

If you wonder whether you'd ever use up the paste colors, keep in mind that they last for years. My mother-in-law, who used the colors conservatively when she decorated, had bottles that were 20 years old and still good. I, on the other hand, am not of the pastel-flowers-on-white-frosting school of decorating. A basic tenet of my cake-decorating philosophy is that liberal use of wonderful, rich colors goes a long way toward concealing my pitiful lack of skill.

Paste colors can be used for other things besides frosting. I use them to jazz up bland-looking homemade popsicles and gelatin. they make wonderful modeling-dough colors too: passion pink, canary yellow, brilliant blue. I've even mixed up military colors to create camouflage modeling dough.

SIX WAYS TO REUSE OLD BLUE JEANS

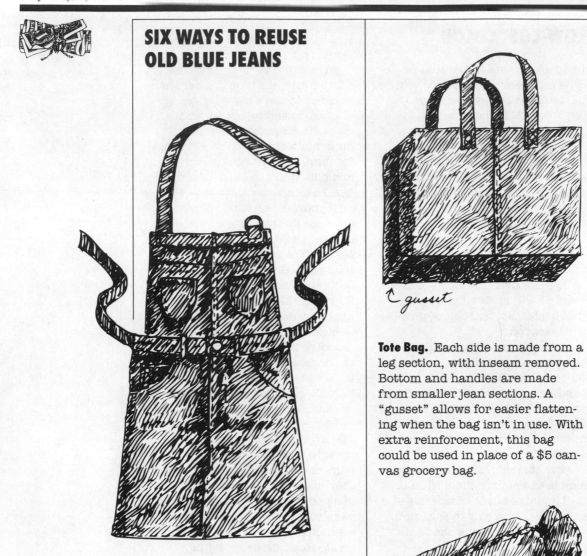

↳ *gusset*

Tote Bag. Each side is made from a leg section, with inseam removed. Bottom and handles are made from smaller jean sections. A "gusset" allows for easier flattening when the bag isn't in use. With extra reinforcement, this bag could be used in place of a $5 canvas grocery bag.

Workshop/Gardening Apron. Sew the front and back of jeans together as shown. Remove the inseam from the front section, and sew the legs together. Make neck and waist ties from surplus leg material. If you have one, sew on a D ring to adjust the neck tie.

Neck-Roll Pillow. Hem cut-off sections of leg, stuff, and fasten with rubber bands.

The apron, tote, and pillow ideas were sent in by Tammy Aramian of Haywood, California.

Wall Organizer. Collect a variety of old denim jeans, overalls, and jackets with interesting pockets. Cut a piece of plywood about 2 feet x 3 feet, or to the size you wish your organizer to be. Cover all four raw edges of the plywood with a denim strip. The denim should overlap the front and back about an inch, or with enough material to tack in place. Select the pockets you wish to use, thinking about variety and visual interest. You might use an overall bib pocket, a designer pocket, a pocket with a hammer loop, or a ruler pocket from a construction worker's jeans. Cut them out larger than you need, and tack them on the board using carpet tacks. Overlap the sections so that the wood doesn't show, and turn under the edges to be tacked that will show.

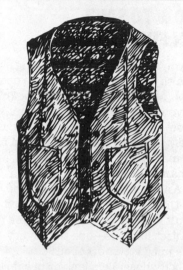

Jeans Vest for Teens. Buy a vest pattern, or improvise from a vest you own. Cut inseam of two jean legs and iron flat. Cut front sections of vest from these, positioning pattern over the double seam any way you like. Use other material teen approves of for back sections and lining. Remove jean patch pockets and sew on vest fronts. Sent in by Michele Steinbacher of Harrisburg, Pennsylvania.

Purse. Turn jeans inside out, sew across just above the crotch, and cut off legs. Make a strap from surplus denim. Lace a bandanna or piece of fabric through loops. Sent in by Peggy Ham of Salt Lake City, Utah.

HOW TO SAVE ON FUNERALS

If you're like me, you're young, healthy, and have no plans to deal with death in the near future. You have no more interest in learning about low-cost funerals than I did. But so many readers requested information on this topic that I began to do research.

And then I became fascinated by this subject. Yeah, *fascinated*. I don't know when I've run across a subject like this—one that everyone needs to know about but nobody does. This lack of preparation could cost your family thousands of dollars in needless and hidden funeral charges. The average funeral costs $5,000, and you can spend as much as $20,000.

Yet, as I studied, I realized that some readers would tend to skip to other articles. So this article is divided into three sections:

1. For Those Who Don't Think They Need This and/or for Those Who Are Squeamish About Death:

Someday you're going to be blindsided by an unexpected death. You won't have had any discussions about it with your family. Your first instinct will be to let a nearby funeral home handle everything for you, because you don't know that there's any other way. That's how expensive funerals happen.

So . . . the resource I want you to file away for future use is:

Continental Association of Funeral and Memorial Societies
33 University Square, Suite 333
Madison, WI 53715
(800) 458-5563

Memorial societies are member-supported organizations that work on behalf of consumers to keep funeral costs low. There are over 175 of them in North America. The CAFMS can be contacted 24 hours a day and can provide you with the name of the nonprofit memorial society that's closest to you. To receive a pamphlet that describes the benefits of memorial societies and a directory of memorial societies nationwide, send a SASE to the CAFMS address.

Remember, this is a nonprofit organization run primarily by volunteers, and it provides a much needed service. Always send SASE's when you request information through the mail, and donations are appreciated.

To join your local society, you pay a lifetime membership fee of about $25. There may be an additional small fee if membership papers are filed at the time of a death.

Among their other services, memorial societies have negotiated in advance with funeral directors and come up with low-cost, no-frills "package deals." For example, a "cooperating funeral director" here in Maine will deliver the body to a crematorium and provide a container and a place to hold the service for $550. A traditional funeral costs a little more. Remember, though, that if you want something different from what is contained in the package, the memorial society may not be able to accommodate you.

Memorial-society members generally don't believe in open-casket viewing and makeup. They also don't recommend embalming, which is unnecessary in most cases. They encourage the use of inexpensive caskets and simple, personalized services.

Memorial societies can also inform you about other options, such as:

• Handling arrangements without use of a mortuary, if it's legal in your state.

• Where to get inexpensive coffins—simple wooden ones might cost as little as $200.

• Laws regarding home burial plots.

• Using cement slabs instead of a more expensive vault.

Since the nonprofit memorial societies are operated by volunteers, in some cases you may get an answering machine with several numbers you can call in an emergency. If you have difficulty reaching the service in your area, call CAFMS again.

Although we have provided this information for you to use in an emergency, that is *not* the best time to use these organizations. When you join a society, you'll be sent a "prearrangement" form that helps you plan *before* the need arises.

This is not a contract, but merely a way to express your wishes, and a beginning point for family discussion. The society will also provide "Living Will" and "Durable Power of Attorney for Health Care" forms for members who are concerned about death with dignity.

Note: Not all businesses using the title "memorial society" are nonprofit organizations, but these may save you money if there is no nonprofit society in your area.

Finally, there are some potential downsides to these groups:

• While the overall concept of memorial societies is great, your local memorial society may not be one of the best. Have an extended talk with the volunteer who runs your society to get a feel for the quality of the group.

• There may not be a funeral home with a cooperating director near enough to suit your needs.

• In response to the good work done by memorial societies, many funeral homes have taken it upon themselves to offer "budget" funeral packages. If you find such a home, participation in a memorial society may be unnecessary.

2. For Those Who Want More Information:

If you're interested in some in-depth reading, go to the library and check out *Dealing Creatively with Death: A Manual of Death Education and Simple Burial,* by Ernest Morgan. This is considered to be the best book on the subject; at 170 pages, it tells you absolutely everything you could want to know about options in funeral and burial arrangements.

If you're not up for lengthy reading, a resource that might be helpful is "Funeral Information In-Home Seminar," by Dan Rohling, a former funeral director. This 60-page booklet is designed to be read in 1½ hours. It contains basic information on funerals and several worksheets including an obituary form, a vital information form, and a financial information form. It also includes a complaint form. If you have a problem with a funeral home, you can send Rohling the completed form and he will file it with the Federal Trade Commission for you.

I particularly liked the "Cemetery Pricing Survey," which lists all the questions you should ask—and most are questions I wouldn't have thought to ask. The questions are even phrased exactly as you should say them. All you have to do is read them aloud when you call for prices. Although some would think this is too basic, this simplicity would be very helpful if one were under stress. To purchase a copy, send $16 (includes shipping) to:

Funeral Information Service
3230 E. Flamingo Road, #287
Las Vegas, NV 89121

3. For Those Who Are Fascinated and Willing to Explore All Options.

If you're open to more "alternative" arrangements, you should read *Caring for Your Own Dead,* by Lisa Carlson. I am not the "alternative type" (I eat white sugar and give birth in hospitals), so I did not think I'd be receptive to this book. But I was extremely moved by three accounts she gave in which funeral arrangements had been made for less than $200. Within the context of these accounts, homemade coffins and hand-dug graves seemed loving and personal, rather than simply ways to cut some corners. The author makes a strong case that professionally arranged funerals tend to isolate you from the death, and that, in contrast, family participation is therapeutic. The book also lists regulations for different states and more specific information on other, more conventional, low-cost options. To order call Upper Access Press at (802) 482-2988. The softcover version costs $14.95.

Although I have never liked conventional funerals with their drawn-out, stressful ceremonies, I have further altered my thinking after having viewed this information. For the first time, I see the importance of writing down exactly what I would want. If my wishes weren't known, people might needlessly spend money on things I wouldn't like.

Also for the first time, the simplicity and practicality of cremation and scattering ashes seems very appealing. I like the idea of having an informal at-home memorial service at a later time, during which people may come in casual clothing and express their feelings to the family.

If all this stuff about cutting corners on funerals seems cheap and tacky to you, think about how the saved thousands could better be used. I feel it's better to spend money on the living—whether family or a charity—rather than for an expensive funeral.

HOW TO SAVE ON FUNERALS UPDATE

Another option that has been strongly recommended by several readers is donating your body to science.

Medical and dental schools in all states need bodies for anatomical studies. Many schools pay for transportation within the state. Most pay for cremation and will return the ashes on request. Reader Bob Balcomb of Findlay, Ohio, told me that by using this option, three funerals in his family have been "practically free."

It's always best to make advance preparations to donate your own body; many schools no longer accept body donations by relatives without such prior arrangements. Contact your nearby medical school, or get the address from the book *Caring for Your Own Dead* by Lisa Carlson, which lists medical schools in all states that accept body donations. The school will send you several forms to fill out and a Uniform Donor Card for you to sign and carry.

A final note: Carlson points out that many hospitals have a desperate need for organ transplants. Unlike donating bodies for study, organ donation can immediately save a life. Usually, corneas can be removed and the body can go on to medical-school study, but once a major organ has been taken from a body, medical schools usually don't want the rest of the body.

So, Carlson has specified on her Uniform Donor Card that her body be used for organ donation if possible; only if it's not needed for that should it be donated to a medical school. While organ donation may not be the absolutely cheapest alternative—because the family must still pay for final disposition of the body—it is probably the most compassionate.

PRETZEL VALENTINES

Every year I get pressed into sending "healthy" snacks to children's Valentine's Day parties at school. This year our stay-at-home dad will make heart-shaped pretzels, a variation on an animal-pretzel recipe sent in by David Westerberg of Middlebury, Vermont. Here's the recipe:

SOFT PRETZELS

1 package yeast
1½ cups warm water
1 tablespoon sugar
1 tablespoon salt
4 cups flour
1 egg

Combine yeast, water, sugar, and salt in a large bowl. Stir in flour. Knead on a table until the dough is smooth. Shape dough into heart or animal shapes, using water to "glue" two parts together. Place on a greased cookie sheet. Brush with beaten egg. Sprinkle with salt. Bake in a preheated oven at 425 degrees for 15 minutes.

TANGLE ANGLE

Dear Amy,

My small daughters took their Barbies into the bath, which made the doll hair tangle like a rat's nest. After trying to comb out the impossible hair, I decided to try hair conditioner on it. I let it sit for a while, rinsed it, and then was able to comb out the tangles. Although the doll hair doesn't look brand-new, I can now braid the hair or put bows in it.

—Matilda Carreras
　Billerica, Massachusetts

OUNCE OUCH

Dear Amy,

I made a discovery. I purchased a jar of generic honey that read "32 oz. net weight." I put the honey in a syrup bottle that read "24 fluid ounces." I discovered that 32 ounces net weight of honey fits in a bottle that holds 24 fluid ounces of syrup. This showed me that the price of the generic honey was average and I made no savings. Read the labels and know the difference in measurements.

—Lisa DeReese
　Alice, Texas

(Sixteen fluid ounces of water equals 16 ounces net weight. But 16 fluid ounces of oil, syrup, honey, or molasses equals 14, 20, 22, and 23 ounces net weight, respectively. When comparing same-size containers of these items, figure fluid ounces equals 114 percent, 80 percent, 73 percent, and 70 percent of the net-weight price, respectively. FZ)

CHEAP CHIC

Dear Amy,

I enrolled in a sewing class to learn to sew more complicated things and use fancy materials. The first thing I made was a party dress out of metallic fabric, very fancy, very chic. Last weekend we were invited to a benefit at the Chicago Lyric Opera. After quickly checking our coats (my ski parka and my husband's Colombo-style raincoat, both old) next to everyone else's furs, we went in to the fanciest party I've ever seen. I can't tell you how pleased I was when my friends commented on how nice my dress was (they didn't know I made it). Most of the dresses were probably worth over $200, while I spent $12 ($37 including the class).

—Katherine Richardson Kenward
　Homewood, Illinois

FZ PHONE HOME

Dear Amy,

The telephone company in our area offers three levels of phone service. The first: You pay $9.36 plus 9¢ for each outgoing call. The second, for $14.61, gives you 65 calls per month, then you pay 9¢ for each additional call. The third, for $19.18, gives you unlimited calls. Incoming calls are free for all three levels. I use the first service because I only make 30 to 35 calls a month. This month my cost was $12.42. I saved $6.76. It seems like a little, but it adds up to $80 to $84 a year.

—Elizabeth Bissett
　Huntingtown, Maryland

(We have a similar service in Maine. We switched to a more expensive service and saved money. Because we live 30 minutes from most places we shop, we make a lot of phone calls to compare prices. We save on phone bills, gasoline, and time. Factor in the money-saving aspects of using the telephone when figuring out which service works best for you. FZ)

BIRTHDAY BUCKS

Dear Amy,

Our two children had birthdays last month. They were pleasantly surprised that instead of the nice card their great-aunt usually sends each of them, they found $2 tucked inside a homemade card made from very old construction paper. Aunt Marg had selected cards at the local card shop, but when the lady added them up to $4.52, she sent the boys the money instead. The children were pleased with the $2 . . . and peeved when they calculated how much more money they would have received if other friends and family had been as clever as Great-Aunt Marg!

—Barbara Keltner
   Medicine Lodge, Kansas

EEK—A LEAK!

Dear Amy,

We had a water trap spring a leak under an old sink. It was such an old model that we could not find a replacement. Following the suggestion of a plumber, we bought a pack of chewing gum. One stick, well-chewed, filled the hole, and then some tape wound around it held the gum in place. It cost approximately 10¢ and saved a $100 plumber's bill.

—Ward Schori
   Evanston, Illinois

DELI DEALS

Dear Amy,

Many delis sell the end of a loaf of meat (some sell cheese, too) that cannot be reached by the electric slicer. After hand-slicing as much as possible, chop up the rest for German potato salad, scalloped potatoes, chef salad, or our favorite, potato soup!

—Karen Wilt
   Ann Arbor, Michigan

(This is a great tip, which I've used many times. More recently it seems as if the stores are catching on. The last time I asked for cheese ends, the price per pound was actually higher than the price per pound of 5-pound bricks of cheese at the warehouse store. So remember to keep checking prices. FZ)

CUT A RUG

Dear Amy,

When I took up the wall-to-wall carpeting in the bedroom, I found that the area under the bed was like new, so I cut it out for an area rug. Binding is available at carpet or fabric stores and can be glued on.

—Sharon Cribbs
   Jackson, South Carolina

THE FINE ART OF NEGOTIATION—OR HOW TO KEEP MORE OF YOUR CHEETOS

America is one of the few countries in the world in which shopping is a passive, "spectator" sport. In most other places, every purchase—whether of a piece of fruit or a home—is preceded by a long haggle. Jim, who has spent lots of time overseas, says some shopkeepers are actually offended if you don't haggle, because they enjoy the sport even more than they enjoy getting the full price.

In this country, somehow, the idea has developed that haggling is undignified, overly time-consuming, even unfair. None of this is true. The truth is that haggling is fun, need not take much time, and can benefit both the buyer and seller.

Jim and I are accomplished negotiators. This year, Jim got a new, $1,250 outboard motor at a boat show for $900 and a used Rototiller marked at $700 for $575, and I got a yard-sale "My Little Pony" marked at 25¢ for 10¢—I hope I wasn't too rough on the guy.

But for one of my readers, Daniel J. Mezick of North Haven, Connecticut, negotiating is his *life*. Mezick, a 35-year-old computer consultant, is addicted to negotiating. Virtually everything he owns is the result of haggling: He bought a complete aboveground swimming pool, with deck and filter, for $200; a top-quality $35 used coat for $5; and a Soloflex exercise machine for $90 that he sold six months later for $600.

Mezick has refined negotiating to a science. He has read books about it and even taken courses in negotiation. We called him and got these pointers:

1. **Everything is negotiable.** Most Americans haggle only over houses, cars, and yard-sale stuff (some don't even do this much). Mezick bargains for almost everything, including new retail goods such as shoes and motel rooms. The major exception is chain retail stores. The trick, he says, is to find the owner (generally, employees don't have the authority to haggle) and simply ask, "Would you take less?" The worst you'll hear is no, and you'll be surprised how often you'll hear yes. If you're negotiating with the owner of a small shop, you should do it discreetly, as he might be unwilling to let other customers know he is open to negotiation.

2. Negotiating is a human transaction as well as a financial one. Don't barge up and start haggling immediately. Chitchat, establish a relationship. This creates a bond between both parties; it also gives you a chance to assess the other person's character and motivation.

3. After this, gently guide the discussion to the item at hand. If you are the potential buyer, discuss it in a neutral way. Being too positive makes you seem overeager, but being too negative at this stage can lead the seller to dislike you and reject your offer.

4. Don't rush to discuss prices. As Mezick puts it, "The first one to name a price loses." This is because the person who names the price has given the other party the role of moving the price, and in negotiation, moving is everything.

5. Once you hear the proposal, never counter it immediately. "If you immediately counter a proposal, it makes the person think you didn't hear a word he said," says Mezick. By waiting and considering the proposal, you show respect for the other person and make him more receptive when you do respond.

(By the way, I used this technique with Mezick. When he sent me a letter offering to tell all about negotiating in exchange for a one-year subscription, I waited almost two years to call him back.)

6. When you *do* respond, give your reasons, *then* make your counteroffer. Most people do this the other way around, but the problem is that once the other party hears your counteroffer, he "shuts off" and does not want to hear your reasons. If you give your reasons first, the other party is *forced* to listen to them, because he is waiting to hear your counteroffer. Once he's heard your reasons, your counteroffer is usually more acceptable to him.

7. Suppose you go through this process and you still end up with a gap between what the buyer will pay and what the seller will take. Good negotiators bridge the gap with what Mezick calls "elegant currency." This is a noncash commodity that can "sweeten the deal" enough to satisfy both parties.

Example: The owner of a barber shop wants to buy your car. After haggling, you have a gap: He offers $2,000, you want $2,500. At this point, you might ask this barber to provide you with $500 in haircuts during his least busy days. This works much better for both parties than the usual "split the difference" route. You gain $500 in credit on something you really would have purchased out-of-pocket, and the barber's out-of-pocket expense is nil.

Mezick used this concept recently in a dispute with his auto-repair garage. He said he had been overcharged $300. He convinced the shop owner to drop $150 off the price and give him another $150 in repair credit.

While all of these concepts are important, the most important thing to remember about negotiating, says Mezick, is to *do it,* even if it makes you uncomfortable. Mezick describes his own personality as "extroverted, aggressive to the extreme," so haggling comes easily to him. If you are more the shy, introverted type, there is no easy answer, except, as Mezick says, "you have to be willing to climb out of your comfort zone."

Why should you do it? Mezick was very impressed with my concept of the "hourly wage" for various money-saving activities (for example, changing your car's oil and filter yourself saves $7 and takes 15 minutes, so it "pays" a tax-free $28 hourly wage. For more examples, see the first book). Negotiating, he says, can pay a higher hourly wage than any other activity.

Example: Recently, a junkyard Mezick visits frequently wanted to charge him $50 for a set of brake drums. He spread his arms wide and with a quizzical look said, "What? No preferred customer discount?" The owner immediately dropped $15 off the price. It took three seconds to say those five words; that works out to $18,000 an hour. Naturally, Mezick does not spend every minute negotiating, but he accumulates many hours worth of negotiation every year at a similar and sometimes better "hourly wage."

Because of the obvious value of negotiating, Mezick is making sure that his kids, ages eight, six, and four, all grow up skilled in the art.

He started them out early with this simple exercise: When each kid reached age three, he sat the child down and poured out a pile of Cheetos in front of the child, and another in front of himself.

"Would you like to play a game where you give me three Cheetos and I give you one?" he asks. The toddler agrees (toddlers agree to anything that sounds like a game) and soon discovers he's out of Cheetos. After what's happened sinks in, Mezick says, "Okay, let's play again, but this time *you* make the rules." The toddler considers and makes his own proposal, usu-

ally one that works to his own advantage. The parent makes a counterproposal, and the negotiation is on. The child is learning a crucial truth: You are better off if you don't let the other person make all the rules.

Interestingly, Mezick told me that the negotiation habit also eases family friction. His children constantly make deals with one another over disputes rather than running to their parents for mediation.

For those who think negotiating is unfair, here's my view: Everything in life is a negotiation. If you think that you never negotiate, you're wrong. Non-negotiators are, by their silence, saying, "You set all of the terms in this negotiation. I may accept it or reject it, but I refuse to seek a common ground that can meet both of our needs." While it's true that hustlers can fast-talk and cheat people, I find that honest negotiation is generally better for both parties than the silent, take-it-or-leave-it attitude that most people have.

My thanks to Daniel Mezick for his insights; but, as you might expect, I didn't get them for nothing. Mezick now has a one-year subscription to the *Tightwad Gazette* newsletter and a complete set of back issues—and I guarantee, we both feel we got good deals.

BUDGET BUG-BUSTING

Before you rush out to the home-and-garden store to arm yourself with your springtime bug-slaughtering arsenal, check out these clever, cheap, and safe bug-beating ideas from readers, and other sources:

REMEDIES FOR OUTDOORS

 This idea for vanquishing fruit-tree bugs comes from the Berne (Indiana) *Tri-Weekly*:

2-liter plastic bottle
string
1 banana peel
1 cup sugar
1 cup strong vinegar

Slice banana peel into strips and insert them into the plastic bottle. In a separate container, combine sugar and vinegar. Pour this mixture into the bottle, then fill it to within 2 inches of the neck with water. Tie the string around the neck of the bottle, then tie the other end around the lower branches of a tree.

Fruit and black flies, yellowjackets, and other insects find the fermenting banana, sugar, and vinegar more attractive than the fruit on the tree. Once they fly in, they get caught in the sticky mixture and drown. This reportedly works so well that it can make spraying fruit trees unnecessary.

Several other readers sent their favorite concoctions for defeating garden pests:

 Darcy Hutson of Tucson, Arizona, uses chopped garlic cloves and water in a spray bottle. She says to make the mixture extra-strong, boil tobacco and add the tobacco tea to mixture.

 Rey and Sandy Naranjo of Albuquerque, New Mexico, make a garden spray from 1 tablespoon dishwashing detergent and 1 cup vegetable oil. They mix 1 to 2 teaspoons of this mixture with 1 cup of water and spray it on their plants.

 Karen Hammond of Monroe, Georgia, waits for a day when the ground is dry and rain is at least a day away, then gently sprinkles a teaspoon of instant grits on each fire-ant hill in her yard. The worker ants carry the grits to the queen, who eats them. When she drinks water, the grits expand in her stomach and kill her. The remainder of the hill dies within a day.

REMEDIES FOR INDOORS

 Glenda DeSantis of El Reno, Oklahoma, sent this method for ridding your home of fleas:

Fill a pan with soapy water (a true tightwad, Glenda reuses the soapy water from the dinner dishes), and place under a nightlight in any room that you suspect contains fleas. Make sure it is the only light in the room. The fleas will jump at the light, fall in the pan of soapy water, and drown.

Michele Picozzi of Colorado Springs, Colorado, makes ant repellent by combining the following ingredients in a spray bottle:

10½ ounces water
3 ounces Tabasco sauce
2½ ounces Dr. Bronner's liquid peppermint soap (available at health-food stores)

Spray where ants enter the home.

Rhonda Barfield of St. Charles, Missouri, makes this "roach dough." It works because it creates gas when eaten. Roaches can't belch, so their digestive tracts explode.

½ cup sugar
¼ cup shortening or bacon drippings
½ cup chopped onion
½ cup flour
8 ounces baking soda

Combine sugar and shortening. Add onion, flour, and baking soda. Mix in just enough water to make a doughlike consistency. Put small balls in plastic sandwich bags and place in roach-infested areas. You should probably keep them out of areas where children and pets play.

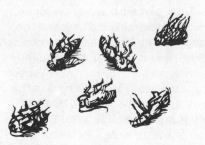

MIXES TAKE A BEATING

In my never-ending quest to shave more off my food bill, I read many books written by grocery-shopping experts. One surprising bit of information, which arose from three sources, was that some mixes and whack-'em-on-the-counter biscuits are cheaper than baking from scratch. But it wasn't until I read a more recent newspaper article suggesting that mixes were cheaper that I was finally inspired to get to the bottom of this apparent tightwad heresy.

To compare mixes to scratch baking, we bought the cheapest cake, biscuit, corn-muffin, and brownie mixes we could find at the supermarket, and for the purposes of calculation, we dropped their prices to the sale-price level. We also bought restaurant-supply cake mix (the chart price is based on a case that makes 24 cakes). And we tested whack-'em-on-the-counter biscuits as well.

We baked up each mix and its scratch counterpart, weighed them, and calculated the after-baked cost per ounce. The mix prices in the chart below include the cost of the ingredients you add at home (Example: 88¢ for the cake mix, plus 64¢ for eggs and oil equals $1.52).

As we baked and weighed, it quickly became obvious how the mixes-can-be-cheaper idea came about. If you compare only on the basis of *volume,* some mixes do indeed appear to be cheaper.

Scratch foods, however, tend to have more body and are heavier. Consequently, if you are interested in filling—rather than fooling—your family with baked

Baked Item	Weight Per Batch	Cost Per Batch	Cost Per Ounce	Taste Rating
Betty Crocker yellow cake mix	28 ounces	$1.52	.052	2
Restaurant yellow cake mix	38 ounces	$1.49	.039	3½
Scratch yellow cake	33 ounces	$1.05	.032	5
Jiffy biscuit mix (small box)	10½ ounces	.30	.028	1
Store-brand whack-'em biscuits	6½ ounces	.25	.038	2
Scratch biscuits	19 ounces	.30	.016	5
Jiffy baking mix (big box)	11 ounces	.10½	.009	2½
Jiffy corn-muffin mix	10 ounces	.38	.038	3
Scratch corn bread	24 ounces	.53	.022	5
Jiffy brownie mix	7 ounces	.40	.057	1
Homemade brownies	12 ounces	.35½	.030	5

goods, scratch is almost always cheaper.

Some would argue that mixes are quicker to make, but consider: To make a yellow cake from a mix, you combine four ingredients: mix, eggs, oil, and water. One from scratch takes eight ingredients: flour, eggs, shortening, milk, baking powder, sugar, salt, and vanilla. In my kitchen, it takes less than two minutes to add those extra items. (Presuming both cakes are equal, if it takes two minutes to save 47¢, that's like earning $14.10 per hour, tax-free.) In addition, by purchasing bulk baking goods, I save shopping time over buying individual cake mixes.

We also did a taste test. Six of our staff (including both those who grew up eating only scratch foods and those with a "mix" heritage) sampled everything. Our chart (above) contains a 1-to-5 taste rating. Because the scratch versions were the clear favorites, we gave those items a 5 and rated the mixes in comparison.

Scratch foods have at least two other advantages over mixes: They don't contain artificial ingredients, and they don't create nearly as much garbage as an endless succession of tiny mix boxes.

Our chart shows that Jiffy baking mix, when used to make biscuits, was the only mix we tested that was cheaper than scratch, although our staff did not like the taste as well. Its other disadvantage is that it has a white-flour base, and most of the scratch baking I do uses part oatmeal, cornmeal, or whole-wheat flour. I wouldn't be able to use these with a mix.

The only other way a mix could be cheaper than baking

from scratch is if you double a coupon or combine a coupon with a sale. For the mix price to be cheap enough, the after-baked cost per ounce has to be lower than the after-baked scratch cost per ounce. This is pretty complex, but if you really want to figure it out, wade through the following paragraph:

Multiply the cost per ounce of the after-baked scratch batch by the number of ounces in the after-baked mix batch. Then subtract the cost of ingredients that must be added to the mix batch. For example, to determine when a cake mix is cheap enough: Multiply 32¢ by 28 ounces, and you get 89¢.

Subtract 64¢ (cost of eggs and oil) from 89¢, and you get 25¢. So if the box of cake mix costs 25¢ or less, it's a good deal compared to scratch.

Just to be sure, after we ran the above tests, we also got some more expensive mixes and some chocolate cake mixes and tested them as well. Surprisingly, the more expensive mixes turned out to be slightly more economical than the cheaper mixes (because they made heavier batches), but still were not nearly as cheap as scratch. The chocolate cake mix versus scratch showed a similar spread to the yellow-cake results in the chart.

WHOOPIE PIES

Usually when I make snacks I opt for healthier alternatives, but every once in a while I make these junk-food substitutes. The recipe is a little time-consuming, so I make these with the kids to get in a little quality time in the process.

Cookie ingredients:
1½ cups sugar
¼ cup shortening
½ cup cocoa
1 egg
½ teaspoon cream of tartar
½ teaspoon baking soda

1 teaspoon salt
2 cups flour
¾ cup sour milk*
1 teaspoon vanilla

Filling ingredients:
½ cup milk
2½ teaspoons flour
½ cup shortening
½ cup sugar
pinch of salt
1 teaspoon vanilla

To make the cookie: Cream the sugar and the shortening. Add the cocoa and the egg; mix well. Sift the dry ingredients. Add alternately with the milk to the sugar/shortening mixture. Add the vanilla and mix well. Drop by teaspoons onto greased cookie sheets. Bake 12 minutes at 375 degrees.

To make the filling: Cook the milk and flour until thick. Chill until cool, then beat well with automatic beater. Add the remaining filling ingredients, and mix well.

Pair off cookies by size; add filling to make sandwiches. Because they tend to be gooey, preserve them by wrapping individually in plastic wrap.

*Make sour milk by adding 1 tablespoon vinegar or lemon juice to 1 cup milk, then let milk stand 10 minutes.

WONDERING ABOUT WAREHOUSE CLUBS

Dear Amy,

What is your opinion of warehouse clubs? I notice that some items are cheaper, but others seem more expensive. Is there really any savings when you pay the annual fee?

—Roseanne Olejarz
   Lombard, Illinois

You are right: Some items *are* cheaper, and some *are* more expensive than when purchased from other sources. Warehouse stores are cheap because they sell in bulk, have few employees, and have bare-bones "architecture" in their stores.

But other factors drive their prices *up.* Many don't take coupons, don't carry store brands or generics, and don't have loss-leader sales like traditional supermarkets.

So you must compare carefully. Unfortunately, warehouse stores make it difficult for you to compare. Unlike most supermarkets, they don't use unit pricing, and they carry products in unfamiliar (very large) sizes.

Another point is that warehouse stores carry bulk-purchase convenience foods and many other consumer goods that you don't need. I see people leaving them with cartfuls of dumb stuff—mirrored clocks, cases of juice packs, bushels of Lucky Charms cereal, and so on. People spend more than they should because "it's a good deal." At one point (years ago) we were bulk-buying fruit roll-ups until we came to our senses and realized that real fruit is cheaper.

Step one, then, is to make a price book. It is impossible to make an accurate comparison between stores unless you do this. I explain in detail how to make one in the first book, but basically, you use a loose-leaf notebook to record the lowest typical prices at various stores on goods you buy regularly.

To enter warehouse prices into your book, you'll have to do your own "unit pricing." It's simple and quick. Just take your calculator along, and divide the price by the units (pounds or ounces).

Don't sign up for a membership, which typically costs $25, until you do this. All of the warehouse stores in our area give you a one-day pass for free. If you buy anything, 5 percent is added to the purchase price.

Initially, we found that there were too few good deals for us to justify the membership fee. However, after we started our business, we found enough good deals on office supplies to make the fee worthwhile. If you aren't going to buy $500 worth of stuff per year, you would be better off getting the one-day pass with each visit and paying the 5 percent surcharge than paying a $25 annual fee.

After you've checked out the prices, chances are you'll find, as we did, that warehouse stores are a valuable part—and I emphasize the word *part*—of your overall shopping system. No single source has the cheapest price on everything. Know what items warehouse stores carry that have the cheapest price, and plan to stop in and get them once a month.

TAKE CHARGE OF CHARGES

One of the basic tenets of tight-waddery is to pay down your mortgage as quickly as possible—but how can you do it when you feel you don't have a cent to spare?

One answer is to chop out extra charges that you may be paying along with your mortgage payment, then use *that* money to pay down your principal. Much of this information comes from an interview we did with Marc Eisenson, who publishes a newsletter called *The Banker's Secret Bulletin*. (For a sample issue, send $1 to *The Banker's Secret*, Box 78, Elizaville, NY 12523).

Here are two examples of charges to examine:

1. Private mortgage insurance: Generally, if you make a down payment of less than 20 percent of the value of your house, you're required to buy private mortgage insurance. This insurance pays the lender if you default on your mortgage.

What the lender often *won't* tell you is that you don't have to keep the insurance forever. Usually, once you build up your equity beyond 20 percent of the value of your house, you can drop it. So ask your lender how much equity you need to be able to stop paying premiums. If property values have shifted in your area, you may also need to get an appraisal, which generally costs around $250 dollars.

The savings can be significant. According to the Mortgage Banker's Association, mortgage-insurance fees on a $67,500 loan average from $338 to $675 annually.

2. Property taxes and homeowner's insurance: No, you can't drop these, but you can pay them in a way that saves you money. If your down payment is less than 20 percent of the house's value, many lenders require you to put your property taxes and homeowner's insurance in escrow accounts, which you pay into monthly along with your mortgage payment. Some states require lenders to pay you interest on money in your escrow account, but the rate may not be as good as you'll get in another account. And some states don't require the lender to pay you a dime in interest.

So, contact your lender and ask whether you have enough equity to set up *your own* escrow account or can otherwise arrange to pay the property taxes and insurance yourself, and thus collect your own interest money. Again, the payoff makes the phone call worth it: Monthly payments of $250 at 4 percent interest would yield $65.73 annually.

Finally, Eisenson points out that the best time to explore these options is *before* you get the mortgage. When shopping for a mortgage (and if you can't plunk down at least 20 percent, which you really should try to do so that you can avoid all of these charges up front), be sure to ask the lenders when, exactly, you can drop the private mortgage insurance and pay property taxes and homeowner's insurance yourself.

TAKE THE PULSE

Dear Amy,

If the "pulse" (also known as rotary-dial) telephone service is cheaper each month than the "tone" (also known as touch-tone) signal, sign up for pulse and save $10 or more per year.

The usual concern with doing this is that you can't use automated answering machines—but you can! Use a "dual" phone with a "pulse/tone" switch when dialing long distance to any automated answering machine ("after the tone, press 1 for customer service, press 2 for account statements," etc.)

When you dial the long-distance call, use the pulse setting (you have to, if your signal is pulse), but when the machine answers, immediately switch to tone. It works perfectly!

—Steven P. Hill
Urbana, Illinois

(If you already have a dual phone, this is clearly a good idea. If you must buy one to do this, be sure to calculate whether the payback is worth the price of the new phone. FZ)

TRASH DANCE

Dear Amy,

As a high school teacher, I am routinely asked to chaperone the junior prom and the senior dinner dance. The students always do a fabulous job decorating the gym or cafeteria, but that night, or the next morning, all the decorations go into the trash. So, I always volunteer to help supervise the cleanup, and I scavenge as much as I can. I reuse the metallic paper, ribbons, streamers, bows, stars, bells, and plastic flowers for everything throughout the year. I decorate my classroom for the holidays, and I wrap and tie up boxes at home for Christmas. It makes me so happy!

—Anne Marie DeProspo
Hamilton, New York

USE THE RECYCLE CYCLE

Dear Amy,

Instead of washing your plastic bags in the sink, save them until you are doing your laundry. I turn them inside out and wash them with my white clothes. I use warm water, 1 teaspoon of bleach, and ½ cup of laundry soap. It seems to clean them better than washing them in the sink. It even cleans the greasy ones. I even wash the wrappers from store-bought goods so they are clean enough to be recycled. By washing our plastics we have reduced our garbage waste by half, which saves us $15 a month in garbage collection fees.

—Margaret Marsh
Hastings, Nebraska

PEEL A MEAL

Dear Amy,

Many of us either throw the stems of broccoli away or selflessly suffer through eating them. My coworker showed us that peeling the stems will make them amazingly tender. Now we like the stems better than the flowerettes!

—Carol Sabbar
　Kenosha, Wisconsin

A CLEARER MIRROR

Dear Amy,

To make any mirror fog-free, you need not purchase the expensive antifog products. Simply use liquid soap; spread it on glass with a cloth to cover completely, then polish dry with another cloth. This lasts for a long time.

—Patricia Stark
　St. Peter, Minnesota

SAVE THE SPOTTED TOWEL

Dear Amy,

I taught home economics for 27 years, and this recipe for homemade laundry pretreatment is one of the best tips I've seen:

½ cup vinegar
½ cup ammonia (sudsy or plain)
½ cup Wisk
½ cup water

Spray on grease or food spots, or dirty collars and cuffs. Wash garment as usual.

—Reader name withheld by
　request

PARLOR PAGES

Dear Amy,

The last time I got my hair cut, I asked my stylist what she did with the old magazines in the shop. She told me they were thrown out. I asked her if I could have them, and she said "Yes." Now, each month, she calls me, and I pick up 10 to 12 magazines for free! I clip coupons, find recipes, and read articles, all for no expense!

—Carol Foil
　Barnwell, South Carolina

CURDS GO A LONG WHEY

Dear Amy,

Does everyone out there know that when you find a terrific price on cottage cheese you can stock up without worrying about the expiration date? All you have to do is store it in its own container upside down in the fridge. This week we opened up our last container from my last cottage-cheese spree. The expiration date on the container was more than four and a half months ago. All I had to do was stir it some, since it had separated, but it tasted fresh. Once opened, continue to store it upside down.

—Dora Winzeler
　Waldron, Michigan

(To check this out, we called Kathy Gucfa, spokesperson for the United Dairy Industry Association. She said, "This is a fairly well-known household hint, and it does seem to extend shelf life, but there have been no studies or research to verify how long." We

called *several other medical and dairy-industry authorities, but none would go on record as saying keeping cottage cheese inverted for months was either safe or risky—they just didn't know. It's clear that inverting does extend the shelf life to some degree. FZ)*

SWF SEEKS SLIM, ATTRACTIVE FREEZER FOR COOL RELATIONSHIP

If you have a large family and a garden, you'd be crazy not to own a freezer. The largest available for home use costs under $500 and uses about $8 worth of electricity a month. It could easily pay for itself within a year. But does a freezer make sense if you are single, a working couple, or if you don't have a garden?

Yes, at least for certain lifestyles. To make my case, I only have to think back to my sorry past as an urban single and how not having a freezer made my life considerably more expensive.

I lived alone in the Boston area for over five years. Because keeping a car in the city is expensive, I always relied on public transportation and cabs. And I never lived anyplace that was convenient to a large supermarket.

If I used public transportation, I had to haul bags of groceries three blocks to the subway station, make a train change, catch a bus, and finally walk a couple of long blocks to my apartment. If I took a cab, it cost $5, plus a tip. If I walked, I might have to trudge up to 12 blocks with a pull-cart of groceries. I would be tired enough

so that when I arrived home, the flights of stairs seemed like the Washington Monument's—my sundry apartments included third-floor, fourth-floor, and fifth-floor walk-ups.

The apartments' refrigerators generally had only slightly-bigger-than-a-shoe-box freezers. So it was just as well that I was not inclined to lug home more—it would have rotted before I could eat it, anyway.

Because I had limited storage for frozen dinners, most meals I ate at home needed to be cooked from scratch after I came home from work—frequently after 7:00 P.M. I seldom felt like doing it.

Also, as an unattached single, I was far more susceptible to emotional valleys. If I had a bad day at work, there was no one waiting at home to cheer me up. So sometimes I was disinclined to go home to an empty apartment and fix a meal. Restaurant food was far more soothing. Like most spendthrifts, I felt I deserved this treat.

It was no wonder that I ate out so much, subsisted on convenience foods from high-priced neighborhood markets, and *never* bought food in bulk. In fact, I lived for two years in Boston before I made my first trip into a real supermarket.

I've recalled those years of late, mostly because of recent contact with New York singles in connection with my books. Food, they tell

Your Trendy Overpriced Gourmet Neighborhood Market

me, is one of their toughest financial challenges. When I've asked why they don't cook up and freeze large quantities of food, they tell me that they want more variety than they could store in a refrigerator-top freezer. Likewise, many working couples and seniors who live in the suburbs can relate to the problems I've described.

But I've also been thinking of those years because Elaine, our business manager, has shown me how freezers can benefit singles. Because circumstances vary greatly, the feasibility of freezer ownership must be considered from case to case, but it certainly works well for her.

Elaine is in her midthirties and has lived alone for a good part of her adult life—but she's *always* had a freezer, even when she lived in a trailer. At first I questioned the economics of this, until I learned how she uses her freezer.

Elaine cooks up large quantities of food, such as lasagna, chili, or tuna casserole, repackages it in meal-size portions, and puts them in her freezer. She skillfully rotates them so that every day she has something different to eat. If she takes the portion out to thaw before she leaves for work, she can pop it into the microwave when she gets home. So even when she's tired, she has tasty, varied, inexpensive, home-cooked food in minutes.

Sears sells a dishwasher-size freezer for $200, which uses about $2.25 worth of electricity per month. I could have fit this size freezer into three of my four apartments. If using Elaine's strategy had prevented me from succumbing to two restaurant meals per month, the freezer would have paid for itself in a year.

This ability to avoid restaurants is the biggest money-saver for singles or working couples. Other, smaller benefits, which may not have paid for a freezer by themselves, are a welcome bonus. A freezer can enable you to:

• Eat a healthier, more varied diet.

• Use cabs efficiently. If I had purchased larger quantities of sale items, the savings on food would have more than paid for the fare.

• Store bulk grains such as oatmeal, cornmeal, or rice. Freeze them for 24 hours to kill off bugs, then they can be stored at room temperature in airtight containers for months.

• Save time and energy, by shopping less often and preparing meals in quantity (the time and hot-water savings on dish-washing alone are significant).

• Take advantage of garden surplus offered by family and friends. For Elaine, a rural single, this is a significant advantage. But it could have helped me in my urban days, too; one of my landlords let the tenants have small gardens. I never bothered. If I'd had a freezer, such a hobby might have seemed worthwhile.

As a final note, I don't recommend buying an ancient, inexpensive, used freezer. Freezers built within the last five years are far more energy-efficient and take up less space than older models. If buying new, look for a sale, and be sure to compare the yellow "Energyguide" labels.

SLASH YOUR TRASH

Frugality naturally creates less trash, but even frugal people can learn to generate less than they do. It's important, because trash disposal *is* becoming expensive. As of January 1993, we are charged $1 per bag to dump trash in Leeds. Readers Greg and Linda Stewart of West Lafayette, Indiana, report they save $160 per year by actively reducing their trash.

Here are some tips for saving on trash fees:

1. Buy used items. Secondhand items rarely come with packaging.

2. Omit convenience foods, most of which have excess packaging.

3. Eliminate as many disposable items as possible, such as paper plates, disposable diapers, and plastic eating utensils. Use a mug, soap, and brush instead of canned shaving cream.

4. If given a choice, buy products in recyclable containers. Milk in a recyclable plastic jug costs the same as milk in a nonrecyclable wax-paper carton.

5. Buy concentrated products.

6. Buy bulk foods. A 25-pound sack of flour produces less packaging waste than five 5-pound bags. Some bulk-food stores let you bring your own container—although this may not be the cheapest way to buy the actual item.

7. Bring your own bags when you go shopping. Decline the "courtesy" bags store clerks automatically give you with each purchase of a single item.

8. Participate in your area's recycling program, and develop an easy system to encourage your family to follow through. One interesting method uses an old chest of drawers—one drawer per type of stuff.

9. Reuse everything as much as possible. An old athletic sock makes a great dishrag. Ultimately you throw away one sock-turned-rag instead of both a sock and dishrag.

10. Compost your grass clippings, leaves, and food waste. Even city folks can compost banana peels by taking waste to community gardens.

11. Buy with durability in mind. Especially avoid junk toys that break easily.

12. Reduce your incoming junk mail. The average American adult is on over more than 50 mailing lists. Send a written request to Mail Preference Service, c/o the Direct Marketing Association, P.O. Box 9008, Farmingdale, NY 11735. This will eliminate most national catalogs and solicitations from national charitable organizations for five years. To remove your name from other mailing lists, request the removal in a short note, put it in the organization's business reply envelope, and mail it back.

13. Cancel magazine subscriptions

(if you can't recycle magazines in your area), and borrow from the library. Or share subscriptions.

14. Instead of throwing things away, give them away or put them in your "free" box at your annual yard sale. I've even put a too-used-to-sell baby swing in my front yard with a sign that said FREE, and someone carted it away within the hour.

15. Make the extra effort to repair things before you throw them away.

16. If you live in a rural area, you may be able to get a permit for a burn barrel to burn nonrecyclable paper. With our newly acquired permit, we have dropped our monthly trash production to one bag.

17. Compact your trash by flattening it, cutting or breaking it into smaller pieces, or filling hard-to-flatten containers with other trash.

18. Try to locate a scrap-metal dealer in your area. Nondeposit (or road-flattened deposit) aluminum cans can be worth as much as a penny. Save them until you have enough to make the trip worthwhile.

19. Grow and preserve your own food. Canning jars, freezer containers, and jam-sealing wax can be reused from year to year.

20. Think hard about whether you really need Magic Mushrooms room deodorizers and other consumer items of recent invention.

CHALK IS CHEAP

As summer approaches, lock up the Nintendo and let your kids enjoy colorful graphics *outdoors* with this sidewalk/street chalk. The recipe was sent in by Sharon Hankins Crosswhite of Julian, California. She says it lasts longer than the expensive store-bought type.

We tried this and found it easy to do and very cost-effective. Ten cups of plaster of Paris at a hardware store cost $2.29, and six jars of liquid tempera, each containing 4 tablespoons of paint, cost $1.69 (we also experimented with powdered tempera and found it made even brighter colors). This makes 27 sticks for 15¢ each, and they are big: We used a manicotti noodle tray as a mold, and made sticks 5 inches long, 1½ inches wide, and ¾ inch thick. In other words, for $3.98, you've got a lifetime supply of sidewalk chalk.

1 cup plaster of Paris (do not pack)
Almost ½ cup cool water
Liquid tempera (your kid's
    teacher may "donate" the
    tempera in exchange for a few
    pieces of chalk)
Margarine tubs or other
    disposable mixing containers
Disposable molds

Pour plaster into a container. Using a disposable stick, stir in *most* of the water. Add 2 to 3 tablespoons of liquid tempera, mixing well, especially at the bottom. Add a little more water so the mixture thickens, stir well, and pour into the molds. Sharon uses the plastic tray from manicotti noodles; you can also use paper cups or toilet-paper tubes with foil bottoms. Remove the molds after the chalk is completely dry.

THE NAKED TOOTH

I am a big believer in using the least amount possible; whether it's of laundry detergent, salt, shampoo, even bath soap. When it comes to toothpaste, my intuition has always been that those ads showing a 1-inch glob were leading us astray, so I was gratified to receive the following letter from Lisa Murphy, a dental hygienist of nine years' experience from Medway, Massachusetts:

"Toothpaste does offer flavor, fluoride (which is necessary if you don't have it in your drinking water), and slight abrasives. It may also contain tartar inhibitor or baking soda (for gum problems).

"But it is not necessary to use toothpaste. Proper flossing and brushing are far more important. In fact, while our patients were learning the proper strokes, we would recommend not using toothpaste, so that they could see what they were doing.

"If you use the proper stroke and brush for a total of five minutes (yes, *five* minutes), getting *every* tooth, you should be able to remove most of the plaque.

"If you do use toothpaste, ask a dental professional for a recommendation of what would best suit your needs. When you use it, all that is needed is ¼ inch on your brush."

I had a chance to try this idea out on my last book tour—I forgot my toothpaste. With a toothpaste-less brush and glass of water, I performed dental hygiene while watching the news on TV. It worked great, and I also realized why most people—including me—have a hard time brushing for five minutes. It's hard to stand in front of the mirror for that amount of time watching yourself foam at the mouth. But I found I could watch TV brushing, swishing, and swallowing water for at least five minutes, if not longer. And my mouth did feel fresh and clean after brushing so thoroughly.

A TIGHTWAD TOY

This homemade toy is a variation of an idea one of my children saw on television. The original design called for a paper cup, which we didn't have. Instead my son improvised with a laundry scoop. He poked a tiny hole through the center of the "recycle" logo in the scoop-bottom. He knotted and threaded a 2-foot string through the hole. He made a ball from a wad of reused aluminum foil. He formed it so that the string end was secured inside the ball.

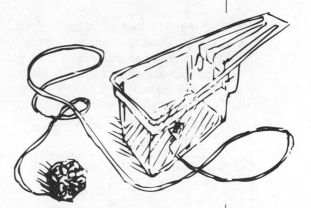

The younger children were entertained trying to land the ball in the scoop one time, whereas older ones competed to see how many consecutive times they could catch the ball in the scoop.

A BUDGET BURNER

"I'm looking for a tightwad way to make a camp stove," writes Sherri B. Saines of Marietta, Ohio.

Funny you should ask, Sherri. In our files we have a letter from Terri Ring of Lancaster, Pennsylvania, containing these instructions for making what she calls a "buddy burner":

1 empty, clean tuna can, label removed
1 empty, large coffee can
cardboard
paraffin

Cut the cardboard into a strip that is as wide as the tuna can is high. Roll it to fit tightly inside the tuna can.

Pour the melted paraffin over this. Cut a flap on the open end of the coffee can, and punch two holes on the opposite side of the can, near the closed end.

To cook, light the paraffin and place the coffee can over it. Place a pan on top to cook.

CHEAP SLEEPS

If I were going to travel a great distance with my family, I would, if possible:

1. Wait until summer.
2. Camp.
3. Stay with relatives who would love to host a family of eight (yes, I do have a few relatives who fit this description).

Obviously, travel is a low priority for me—going on a trip with six young children is more work than vacation.

But for those people who save their pennies so they can afford to travel and who don't like to camp, here are four alternative types of cheap travel lodging:

1. College dorms. Most dorms are empty during the summer, and several enterprising schools take advantage of that by offering overnight lodging.

For information, get *U.S. and Worldwide Travel Accommodations Guide for $12–$24 Per Day.* The 1993 edition is available from Campus Travel Service, P.O. Box 5486, Fullerton, CA 92635, (800) 525-6633. Cost is $14 postpaid.

Normally, I am unimpressed by the quality of many "save-money" publications, but this one is particularly well done. For each of the 700 colleges listed, the book gives the daily price for single and double accommodations; $12 to $24 is a typical single rate, with doubles usually less than twice that amount. But accommodations can run as low as $6 per night per person.

Along with prices, the book lists available dates (generally, Northern Hemisphere schools open their dorms to nonstudents in the summer months; Southern Hemisphere schools, such as those in Australia, open theirs during our winter), and what activities and attractions are nearby.

The quality of the accommodations varies greatly. Most rooms have two twin beds; the bathroom and showers are down the hall. But there are also some suites with private baths, or arrangements where two rooms share one bath. Most offer food service, and some have linen service.

The book suggests bringing sleeping bags for children; many colleges allow kids to sleep free in their parents' rooms. A small percentage of colleges don't allow children at all, so be sure to ask.

There is no central booking agency; make reservations by calling the schools directly. All necessary telephone numbers are listed in the book.

2. YMCA lodging. The same book also has a complete listing of YMCA accommodations: 43 lodging centers in 39 cities coast-to-coast, and 51 lodging centers in 26 overseas countries. Single accommodations average about $20, doubles around $35. Rooms for couples are widely available, and children are welcome, provided there is parental supervision.

You can call the YMCA's individually, but if you plan to stay in more than one and you know your itinerary in advance, you can book through the central New York office: The Y's Way, 224 E. 47th St., NY, NY 10017, (212) 308-2899. YMCA's also accommodate travelers on a drop-in basis when space is available.

3. Hostels. There are 6,000 hostels in 70 countries, including more than 200 in the United States. Many people think of these as "youth hostels" and imagine they are just for young people, but that is not the case. Many hostels have private rooms for families traveling together, and 10 percent of card-holding members of Hostelling International/American Youth Hostels are over 55. The price per person ranges from $5 to $22, with the most common price about $10. Children often receive a discount.

Each hostel is unique, but they share some common characteristics. All have dormitory-style sleeping quarters and bathroom facilities separated for males and females. They have fully equipped, self-service kitchens and dining rooms. Most have a night curfew. You are asked to clean up after yourself.

A spokesman at Hostelling International/American Youth Hostels told us that most hostels will admit nonmembers, but those without cards must pay a slightly higher fee, and during busy times of the year in major cities, cardholders receive preference. Membership is $10 for those under 18, $25 for adults, $15 for those 55 and over, and $35 for families. To join, contact the national office at 733 15th N.W., #840, Washington, D.C. 20005, (202) 783-6161. This office can send you information directly or direct you to one of the organization's thirty-nine local sales outlets.

When you sign up, you'll get a free copy of *Hostelling North America,* which lists 260 hostels in Canada and the United States. Purchased separately, the cost is $8 post-paid.

Another directory available from the national office is *Hostelling International: Guide to Budget Accommodations.* Volume 1 covers Europe and the Mediterranean; Volume 2 covers Africa, America, Asia, and Australia. These cost $13.95 each post-paid.

4. Vacation home exchange. An estimated 20,000 travelers will swap homes this year. Cars and even child-care arrangements can also be swapped. Several clearinghouses publish lists of homes offered to swap.

As you might expect, this is a more complex lodging arrangement than the three listed above. Logistics must be worked out carefully, and you'll have more success attracting swappers if you live in Hawaii than in Nebraska (I've got nothing against Nebraska, but that's how it works).

But people who do this generally love it.

Because home exchange is a big subject with its share of pitfalls (such as the other party backing out just as you're ready to make the swap), it's worthwhile to read a book on the subject before you begin. One good one is *Trading Places: The Wonderful World of Vacation Home Exchanging,* by Bill and Mary Barbour. Along with everything you want to know about the nuts and bolts of home vacation exchange, it has a complete directory of more than 40 home-exchange clearinghouses. It's available for $9.95 from Rutledge Hill Press, 211 7th Ave. North, Nashville, TN 37219-1823. Call (800) 234-4234 for shipping-and-handling charges, or get it from your local bookstore or library.

Here are a few of the larger home-exchange-listing organizations. They charge a fee for registering your home and sending out an exchange directory. For a fee, some will also put an exchange match together.

Vacation Exchange Club
P.O. Box 820, Haleiwa, HI 96712
(800) 638-3841

Lists 6,000 homes in 40 countries. Half are in North America, the rest are in Europe, Australia, and New Zealand.

Fee is $35.

Intervac/International Home
　Exchange
P.O. Box 590504
San Francisco, CA 94519
(415) 435-3497

Lists over 8,000 homes world-wide, 1,500 in the U.S. Membership is $45, but offers a free brochure.

Teacher Home Swap
P.O. Box 4130
Rocky Point, NY 11778

Exclusively for teachers. Has listings in 37 states, Canada, Virgin Islands, Germany, and Hungary.

GOOD TIMING

One of my he-man staffers has been bugging me for months to do an article about timing belts.

"Timing belt—is that a newfangled fashion accessory, kinda like a belt with a watch on the buckle?" I answered demurely, displaying my ignorance of both fashion and auto mechanics.

He scratched his tattoo, spat on the ground, and patiently explained that the timing belt connects the camshaft to the crankshaft. My eyes started to glaze over.

"Pull together some information and get back to me," I yawned, returning to my latest venture in dryer-lint mâché.

He returned with the book *Car Talk* by Ray and Tom Magliozzi with a bookmark in the appropriate chapter. He also suggested I interview Ray Fortin, owner of Autometrics repair shop in Brunswick, Maine, who has replaced hundreds of timing belts.

Turns out, the timing belt does indeed connect the camshaft, which opens and closes the valves, to the crankshaft. A durable timing chain (similar to a bike chain) used to do this, but today a more fragile rubber belt is often used because it's cheaper and easier to change.

In certain kinds of cars, if the timing belt breaks, it will severely damage the engine, because the pistons will smack into the valves, damaging the valves, the pistons, or both. Fortin says that generally, high-compression, 16-valve engines are most likely to incur damage if the belt breaks, but there are no hard-and-fast rules on this. Ask your mechanic whether your car is at risk for engine damage if its timing belt breaks.

Fortin says at least once a month he fixes an engine that was damaged by timing-belt failure. He told me that this is one of the most neglected areas of car maintenance.

Replacing a timing belt costs between $100 and $200, but if you have to open up your engine anyway to do other repairs, replacing the belt can cost as little as $30. Fixing a wrecked engine generally costs about $1,000.

While some types of cars' engines won't be damaged if the belt breaks, a broken timing belt *always* stops your car. If you've got one of these "invulnerable" cars, you might opt to take your chances, because these belts sometimes last more than 150,000 miles.

The timing belt is of particular

concern to my staffer because he had one snap in downtown Washington, D.C., during rush hour, and it cost a fortune in towing.

But the timing belt is just one of several parts that you might consider replacing *before* they fail because of the potential damage the failure could do to your car. Other such parts include brakes, belts, and hoses. Generally, these parts are easy to see, monitor, and replace.

Other parts to consider replacing before they fail are harder to get at. While the actual part cost may be low, labor costs for replacement are high. So if your engine has to be opened up for any work, use the opportunity to replace worn bearings, seals, and gaskets (make sure your mechanic charges by the hour, not by the standard part-replacement labor fee). Even if the part failure won't damage the engine, replacing it when it can be done cheaply often costs less than a tow.

The point is, you need to have a long, friendly, informative chat with a trustworthy mechanic who is specifically knowledgeable about your type of car. He can tell you when certain parts are likely to go (Fortin says, for example, that he's found that the timing belts on Subarus snap "like clockwork" at 70,000 miles) and whether it will be more expensive to wait until they do.

(By the way, I was just kidding about my staffer: He neither spat nor has a tattoo to scratch; he's a slender, well-mannered vegetarian.)

THE FEMME FRUGAL

"No, honey! Not supermaxi, round-edge, ultra-plus supers! I wanted ultra-absorbent, maxi-plus, super-thin regulars!"

Aside from fostering such marriage-testing experiences when hubby comes home from the supermarket, disposable tampons and napkins contribute to landfill problems and are overpriced (c'mon, how can a little cardboard tube, a wad of cotton, and a piece of string cost as much as a disposable diaper?). This has not gone unnoticed by my readers. I have a file labeled "feminine," full of letters from readers, that is impressively thick (partially because it contains a homemade sanitary napkin).

But I delayed writing about this subject until I found and tested a solution that seemed more workable for the average woman than cloth napkins, which must be soaked and washed.

The solution is the Keeper, a reusable rubber cup that replaces tampons. I learned of it through an article in *Garbage* magazine, through recommendations from readers, and from an employee who has used one for years.

The Keeper is accepted by the FDA and has a far lower toxic-shock risk than the 1-in-100,000 annual risk from tampon use.

Although the Keeper's initial cost is substantial—$37 postpaid—it is guaranteed for ten years, which works out to 31¢ a month. Compared to the cost of tampons, it would pay for itself in well under one year. (The company owner has used the same Keeper for 35 years.)

To try this out, I purchased five Keepers for staff and friends. All of us who tried it were very pleased. It works as well as a superabsorbent tampon, which means that if you use a napkin in conjunction with a superabsorbent tampon on days with heavy flow, you might use a napkin with this product as well. As you might imagine, removing a Keeper isn't as "neat" as removing a tampon, but this inconvenience is minor compared to the benefits.

So if this product is so great and has been available for decades, how come you've never heard of it before?

I asked the company owner. She told me that advertising is expensive and the company often does not recoup the cost of an ad. She added that she had tried to interest journalists in writing articles but with little success. She speculated that there were two problems: The "graphic" subject matter wasn't attractive to reporters, and women's magazines, which would seem to be the perfect place for a story, depend on advertising from companies that manufacture disposable feminine products and may be reluctant to publicize a product that might hurt those advertisers' business.

The Keeper comes in two sizes: A (after vaginal childbirth) and B (after C-section or before childbirth). Refunds are available if you aren't happy, although the company states that 92 percent of the women who try it are pleased with it. Order from The Keeper, P.O. Box 20023A, Cincinnati, OH 45220.

The Keeper seems to me to be the most appropriate option for most women, especially women who work outside the home. But if it doesn't appeal to you and you are willing to soak and wash them, consider nondisposable sanitary napkins. They are available through mail order for about $5 each. Write for information to Moon Pads, P.O. Box 166, Boulder Creek, CA 95006, or New Cycle, P.O. Box 3248, Santa Rosa, CA 95402. Figuring that you would need a couple days' supply, this option is a bit steep.

I do have three lengthy, detailed sets of instructions on how to make your own cloth napkins. For free copies, send us a SASE. Write to *The Tightwad Gazette,* RR1 Box 3570, Leeds, ME 04263.

If you decide to stay with disposables, keep in mind that pads are generally cheaper than tampons.

In addition to these alternatives, I have personally conducted a nine-year study on the pregnancy/breastfeeding method to avoid the purchase of these feminine products. After thorough and intense calculation, I have determined that one cannot fully recoup the cost of children through tampon savings.

THE INCREDIBLE SHRINKING GROCERIES

An article from Pennsylvania's *Daily Intelligencer* newspaper, sent to me by reader Debbie Rodrigo of Line Lexington, Pennsylvania, confirms something you may have suspected: that many grocery-store foods are "downsizing." Although the package size remains roughly the same and the price stays exactly the same, the net weight of the food inside has shrunk.

The story noted the following as just a few examples of recent downsizing:

• A box of Hershey's chocolate-milk mix that once held 16 ounces now contains 14.5 ounces.

• Gerber's strained baby food has gone from 4.5 ounces per jar to 4 ounces per jar.

• Identical-size cans of Maxwell House coffee weigh 16, 13, 12, and 11.5 ounces.

There's nothing illegal about downsizing as long as the correct net weight is listed on the package.

Your best defense, then, is to depend upon unit pricing. If the store where you shop does not offer it, keep track of net weights and do your own unit pricing with a calculator.

WORK OFF THE WORKOUT

Dear Amy,

My friend Linda has found a good way to get a "free" membership in a local health club. She works a four-hour-per-week shift in the child-care room; the club provides child care there as a free service to members. She takes her kids along to play. This club is always looking for moms to do this in exchange for a membership, and so is another health club in town.

—Jan C. Kass
Davis, California

OCEAN IN MOTION

Dear Amy,

Here is a cheap toy for a preschooler: Make a "tidal wave" soda bottle. Fill it half with cooking oil and half with water colored with food coloring.

—Sherry Mayer
Greensboro, North Carolina

(Children lose interest in new things after about two days, whether the things are store-bought or homemade. When your child loses interest in this, you can reuse the cooking oil. We made a tidal-wave bottle and learned you should not shake it vigorously: This makes the oil permanently cloudy. FZ)

FOIL HEAT LOSSES

Dear Amy,

Here's an energy-conservation idea for those with accordion-style radiators. Put foil-faced insulation board between the radiators and outside walls, with the foil side facing in toward the room. This reflects heat into the room that would otherwise radiate through the walls.

—Ellen Nagle Eggerton
  Silver Spring, Maryland

(Because the expense is minimal and the installation is not permanent, this is one of the rare energy-saving ideas that is useful to renters. FZ)

ATTACK THE RACK

Dear Amy,
    In our local paper, dry cleaners advertise that they will sell clothes for almost nothing. They will get rid of clothes left there for 60 days or longer. You just go into the dry cleaner, and there is a huge rack of clothes. Usually, they sell for what the dry-cleaning price was: $1 for a sweater, $2 for a coat, etc. I have bought a lot of clothes this way. It's worth checking into in other cities as well.

—Christi Kennedy
  Shirley Clasey
  Durham, North Carolina

SPECTACLE SAVINGS

Dear Amy,
    Save big bucks by buying used eyeglasses frames at thrift stores. You can then have new lenses made for your new prescription and save a bundle—especially if you, like me, like to have a backup pair of glasses or have children who destroy frames. Or be really

cheap and ask friends who are getting new glasses for their old frames. Since new frames cost from $30 to $100-plus, the savings can be substantial.

—Beverly Carlson
  Carmichael, California

STALKING A GREAT KITE

Dear Amy,
    The dead stalks of last year's goldenrod, ragweed, and various other species of medium and tall weeds make good frame members for a kite. For covering, we use ultrathin polyethylene film from dry-cleaning bags. This is the kind that can suffocate babies and small children, so use plenty of common-sense precautions to keep all pieces under control. To stick it on a kite, cut to the kite shape plus 1 inch all around. Fold the inch over the string, then hold it down with clear tape. The result is an ultra-lightweight kite.

—James R. Jenness, Jr.
  State College, Pennsylvania

RUB-A-DUB TUB

Dear Amy,
    When we moved into our house over 25 years ago, the surface of our bathtub was slightly rough and became stained after a while. I tried various cleansers, including the strongest ones, but nothing seemed to work.
    Then I saw the craziest idea in the newspaper—and it worked!
    Wet the surface, sprinkle it with cream of tartar, and rub this with the cut surface of a lemon. Then,

with some elbow grease, the tub will be as white as new within 20–30 minutes. I use two lemons and about ¼ can of cream of tartar on my tub, and it does not have to be done very often.

Today, I checked the prices for refinishing a tub. The range was between $225 and $250. One can buy a lot of lemons for that amount. The surface of the tub is still a little rough, but then, one is less likely to slip on a rough surface than a smooth one.

—Sally Weitlauf
  Dayton, Ohio

CARPET TACTIC

Dear Amy,

Call carpet stores for carpet samples. When colors or styles change, carpet samples are usually thrown out. Samples can be used in cars, bathrooms, doorways, or cut to fit benches or chairs. Toss in washer to clean.

—Ann Williams
  Rochester, New York

BAND AID

Dear Amy,

Never buy a band instrument from the companies that come to the school. We made that mistake with our first child, and one flute ended up costing us $816.00! This was with their handy-dandy payment plan that at the time did not seem like much, ha ha. With our second child, we have been shopping yard sales and already found several to choose from. Prices vary from $35 to $100 for a clar-

inet. Even if they need new pads and a cleaning, this is still quite a savings.

—Chawn Stiers
  Cumberland, Ohio

FENDER MENDER

Dear Amy,

Even a minor car accident can require major amounts of cash for repairs. After our fender bender, we took our car to the vocational school. They saved us money by pounding out the fender and repainting. A body shop would have replaced the entire fender due to the high labor cost. At the vocational school, there was no labor charge. We paid only for the paint and parts.

—Dawn Hancock
  Auburn, Indiana

SELECTIVE SQUEAMISHNESS

In the early years of my zealous frugality, I eagerly and naïvely offered money-saving ideas to the unappreciative. Usually, my suggestions would be rejected with such responses as: "I couldn't be bothered," or "My family wouldn't eat that."

I recall when I first identified a common reason for rejecting ways to save money. It's an attitude I call "selective squeamishness."

Seven years ago we lived in a suburb near Norfolk, Virginia. As I chatted with my neighbor, who was raking leaves in her yard, I spotted a patch of scarlet among the brown leaves in her trash barrel. Propelled by my scavenger instincts, I zoomed in and saw a large, shiny, Delicious apple with two fresh bites missing.

Thinking she hadn't noticed this waste, I pointed out the apple to her. She casually responded that her four-year-old didn't want to finish it. So I helpfully offered my solution to this common dilemma. "You know what I do with an apple one of my kids doesn't finish? I save it in the refrigerator. Later, I cut it up, sprinkle on some apple-crisp topping, put it in the microwave, and presto-chango, he has his own apple crisp. He thinks it's a treat!"

I expected my neighbor would marvel at my resourcefulness. Instead, she recoiled in horror. "Ugh! I couldn't put her germy apple back in the refrigerator!"

My rejection radar went off. I dropped the subject and silently wondered if the fear of germs ever prevented my neighbor from exchanging kisses with her small children.

Since then, I've observed the same sort of situation time and time again. Americans are curiously inconsistent when it comes to squeamishness. We often reject "odd" or "germy" practices that are frugal, while happily indulging in equally "gross" activities that are expensive and wasteful.

As for "odd" ideas: When I was on *Donahue,* I demonstrated how

the burned bottom of a cookie could be very easily scraped off with a grater. The audience emitted a collective "Eeeeew!" Yet I'd wager that this same group of skeptics routinely salivates over charred filet mignon.

On the same show, I explained how you could make a popsicle from jam-jar remains by adding milk, shaking, and pouring into a mold. The audience's groan made it clear they rejected my all-natural solution, apparently preferring to feed their children expensive popsicles made from unpronounceable ingredients.

People have expressed squeamishness over my practice of making soup from leftovers, yet if the same soup had been assembled from virgin ingredients, they would regard it as good home cooking.

As for "germy" suggestions: I've been taken to task for my "unsanitary" practice of trash picking. Although I draw the line at rummaging deep in trash barrels or taking things that are hard to clean, I feel quite comfortable carting away something from a pile that appears to be the result of a recent garage cleaning. Yet most people aren't squeamish about buying exactly the same stuff at a garage sale. I have been mystified by parents who throw away cookies their baby tosses on the floor. Yet the same parents let their baby crawl on the floor and pick up toys to chew.

The American public has been duped by advertisers to believe that a few invisible cooties in the toilet bowl are evil, threatening, and untouchable. But automatic, blue-tinged toilet-bowl cleaners—which may contain muriatic acid, paradichlorobenzene, and other caustic stuff and should be treated as hazardous waste, according to the Environmental Hazards Management Institute—are supposedly our salvation.

One of the most curious areas of germ squeamishness is second-hand clothes. Some people would never wear a yard-sale shirt, even after laundering it in germ-killing 120-degree water, yet blithely try on department-store clothing that dozens of people might have tried on before them.

I've encountered a few people who are squeamish about buying used sheets. Yet I'll bet these people don't take their own sheets when they stay in a hotel or at the home of relatives. Likewise, they don't give a second thought to using a cloth napkin in a restaurant.

Even people who feel comfortable with used clothes may take exception to wearing used undergarments. Although I have never purchased used underwear, I've swapped a bra or two in my time. Can you imagine the groans if I had advocated such a thing on a national talk show? Yet, think back to other talk shows that featured guests who had multiple sex partners. Although some audience members might have objected on a moral basis or because of AIDS, have you ever heard audiences groan over how "gross" such a thing is? It's fascinating that people who are squeamish about swapping bras are not squeamish about swapping spouses.

The fact is that germs are an unavoidable part of our lives. When we talk on a public phone, we are exposed to the germs of the person who previously used it. If we eat in a restaurant, we rarely wash up despite our recent contact with door handles, counters, booths, and chairs. When we purchase fresh produce, which may have been handled by many previous shoppers and clerks, we never feel compelled to sterilize it in 120-degree water. The simple act of breathing in a public place exposes us to germs of strangers.

Although some effort to minimize germ exposure is important, we also need to remember that we have immune systems designed to handle the majority of germs we encounter.

The things we regard as odd or germy are often unique to our culture. Many frugal practices I advocate are common in most parts of the world today and were common a generation ago in this country. In modern society our sense of squeamishness has become heightened because we are insulated from the most basic human activities—cooking, cleaning, and dealing with waste. Now convenience foods, disposable products, and mechanical devices keep us "from getting our hands dirty." But the price of squeamishness is high, both in financial and environmental terms.

So . . . next time an idea about saving money seems gross to you, consider whether you are merely being selective, and whether you accept a similar activity as okay. In other words, think before you squeam.

MIXED EMULSIONS

In every basement, just to the left of the tattered lawn chairs awaiting rewebbing, sits a stack of paint cans, left over from dozens of household projects. A new project arises, you scan the cans and discover that you don't have quite enough for this particular task. So you buy another can, use three quarters of it, and add it to the pile. Eventually, sick of the mess, you decide to take the whole lot to the dump, even though a lot of it is, technically, toxic waste.

There's a solution to this common dilemma. Mix it and use it!

In Snohomish County in Washington, solid-waste officials have been accepting old cans of paint from residents for the last three years. They mix the paint, seal it, and give it away—over 12,000 gallons so far. For an insight on how this can be done at home, we discussed the program with David Shea, project specialist for the Snohomish County Solid Waste Authority, and with Philip Morely, who ran a similar, larger project for the nearby city of Seattle.

The #1 rule of paint mixing is play it safe. Lead paint for residential use was banned in 1973, so if you have any paint that even *might* be older than that, don't mix it. Also, paints that say prominently on the label that they kill fungus and mildew may have high levels of pesticides and/or mercury and should be avoided, especially for interior use.

When it comes to mixing, combine latex with latex, and oil-based with oil-based—never latex with oil-based. But don't worry about mixing flat, semigloss, and high-gloss together. As Shea puts it, "We've found that paint is paint, and it generally comes out durable and looking good." If you mix interior and exterior grades and use it outdoors, you can lose some durability, but if you use the mixed paint for undercoats and "pure" paint for the final coat, you'll probably have good results.

In any case, paint mixing works. Shea says after distributing thousands of gallons, "We've never had a complaint."

Using mixed paint will require you to be a bit less picky about color—you won't be able to get precisely the shade you may want. But keep in mind that probably everyone you know has old paint and will be glad to donate it. Perhaps teaming up with friends and neighbors will give you the proper colors to at least approximate what you want.

In the past I've used this technique. I have several partially filled cans of odd-colored paint that I trash-picked. I found that by combining latex paints I could make small amounts of good colors. I use them to rejuvenate the beat-up yard-sale furniture that we have in our children's rooms. I refuse to buy my kids good furniture until we're beyond the little-kid, furniture-abuse years.

Reader Joan Lovering of Scarborough, Ontario sent in another ancient-paint-revival technique:

"My tightwad son-in-law found that his four large cans of latex paint had settled to near-cement-like sludge after sitting in the basement for years. Inspired, he took a chance on using his wife's food blender, hoping for the best. To his delight, it worked wonderfully well. He salvaged all four cans of paint, thus saving at least $60. And the blender cleaned itself nicely with warm water and detergent."

Before publishing this idea we didn't run it by the Food and Drug Administration, so I can't give it my official endorsement. But clearly it will pose a serious health risk if this guy's wife ever finds out.

THE SLED SOLUTION

In March of '93 we had just weathered the "blizzard of the century." All of our sleds had long ago vanished under previous snowfalls, and we had been scooting Brad and Laura, the 20-month-old twins, around in cardboard boxes and a large plastic cooler. It never occurred to us to *buy* more sleds, knowing that ours would reappear with the spring thaw. But with this new, huge, wonderful snowfall, we felt we needed something that worked a bit better than the substitutes. Suddenly, Jim remembered the obsolete-but-not-antique wooden skis we trash-picked in the last book. He disappeared into his workshop. After two hours of the usual roaring, whacking, buzzing, and cursing, he emerged from a sawdust cloud bearing this contraption—a sort of double-stroller ski-sled, built entirely from salvaged materials. With this we were able to run the twins around our snowy driveway and push them down the small slope in front of our barn, much to their wide-eyed delight. Other ski-sled creations could be made in a similar way. Our original idea was to use the skis for a sled to haul firewood. I can also imagine four skis used to make a toboggan. If you build one, put a guard over the pointy tips, or use it on an uncrowded slope where collisions are unlikely.

You don't have toddler twins, you don't have old skis in your attic, you don't lose your sleds . . . why am I telling you about our double-stroller ski-sled?

Because this is yet another example of how being resourceful and creative with materials you have on hand, instead of spending money, can ultimately be much more fun.

SHARE—AND SHARE ALIKE

Many readers have sent me literature about SHARE (Self-Help and Resource Exchange). This nationwide, neighborhood-based, self-help food-distribution program is sponsored by a network of churches, community centers, unions, and other groups.

It works like this: You sign up one month in advance with a host organization and do two hours of community service. You then qual-

ify to buy a package of groceries worth $30 to $35 retail for $14 in cash or food stamps. You have to pick up the food at a specified place and time. The SHARE program buys the food from wholesalers or directly from growers. This is not a government program or charity, and you do not have to meet income requirements to participate. One brochure I received provided a list of the contents of a typical food package. The monthly packages vary, but each contains 15 items including 6 to 10 pounds of meat, 4 to 7 pounds of fresh vegetables, and 2 to 4 pounds of fruits. I estimated the value of the list based on typical sale prices in my area.

5 pounds chicken-leg qtrs.	$1.50
1 pound ground beef	.99
1 pound fishsticks	1.49
1 pound pork sausage	.69
1 bunch celery	.99
3 cucumbers	.99
1 head lettuce	.69
2 pounds onions	.80
4½ pounds potatoes	1.12
1 pound tomatoes	.75
5 pounds apples	2.59
2 pounds oranges	1.00
1 cantaloupe	1.49
1 pound pinto beans	.50
1 pound spaghetti	.33
1 package frozen vegetables	.99
1 can fruit	.79
1 package "Touch of Butter"	.44
Total	$18.14

Our shopping style, as I've explained in "Let's Go Shopping with Jim," on page 228, allows us to get these prices regularly with no extra travel or effort. So SHARE would save us only $4.14 for two hours of community work.

Still, I think this is a good program for many people, for a few reasons:

People who lack desire or have no transportation options, won't shop like we do. And our shopping style does require you to have enough money to buy in bulk. If you are really broke, this program can be a big help.

SHARE buys only nutritious food. It ensures that people with poor food-buying habits are getting some healthy food.

People who face hard financial times often isolate themselves. The community-service requirement forces people into the community, where they make friends and contacts and gain the self-esteem that comes from helping others.

To find the SHARE program nearest you, or to start one, contact:

SHARE U.S.A.
3350 E St.
San Diego, CA 92102
(619) 525-2200

SENSIBLE SUBSTITUTES

Many of the "nouveau frugal" are enchanted with making their own convenience foods—no matter how inconvenient the process may be. Take the time I tried a homemade Grape-Nuts recipe, which required making a dough, rolling it thin, baking it forever, and then running the concretelike chunks through a food processor. Not only did this require a lot of electricity and time, but I nearly burned out the motor on my food processor. I decided I would prefer to eat hot cereal.

In books I've seen about making your own convenience foods, many recipes have you jumping through hoops to replicate the recent invention of a manufacturer. Instead of eating tightwad versions of spendthrift foods, it's easier to switch your diet to simpler foods.

But here are some sensible homemade convenience-food recipes. The only possible exception is the homemade stove-top stuffing mix, which is the most time-consuming and yields the least savings. Personally, I'd rather boil some rice, but if your family loves stuffing, give it a try.

I've provided a cost comparison of each homemade product to its store-bought counterpart. These numbers are based on our own painstaking calculations—figured down to the cost of ⅛ teaspoon of salt (¹⁄₁₀ ¢).

By combining coupons and sales, you may be able to beat these prices. (If you use coupons to buy convenience foods, you should calculate the cost of preparing food from scratch and develop "rules of thumb for coupon use.")

But remember: Aside from cost savings, preparing foods from scratch has other benefits:
• Less packaging.
• No artificial ingredients.
• Staples require less space and shopping time than convenience foods.
• Homemade almost always tastes better.
• Homemade can be modified to taste or to meet dietary restrictions—such as reducing salt.

SEASONED SALT

8 tablespoons salt
3 tablespoons pepper
2 tablespoons paprika
½ tablespoon onion powder
½ tablespoon garlic powder

Mix all ingredients in a bowl, and store in an airtight container (an empty, store-bought spice shaker works well).

Durkee's seasoned salt: 98¢ for 3.5 ounces, or 28¢ per ounce.
Homemade: 14¢ per ounce.

TACO-SEASONING MIX

6 teaspoons chili powder
4½ teaspoons cumin
5 teaspoons paprika
3 teaspoons onion powder
2½ teaspoons garlic powder
⅛ to ¼ teaspoon cayenne pepper

Mix all the ingredients, and store in an airtight container. The home-made mix is twice as strong as the store-bought one, so add only half as much.

Old El Paso taco-seasoning mix: $4.95 for 1 pound, or 31¢ per ounce.
Homemade: 13¢ per ounce.
Contributed by Mary Jane Mandl of Lee's Summit, Montana.

STUFFING

6 cups cubed bread
1 tablespoon parsley flakes
3 tablespoons chicken-bouillon powder
¼ cup dried minced onion
½ cup dried minced celery (or fresh celery may be sautéed and added just before cooking)
1 teaspoon thyme
1 teaspoon pepper
½ teaspoon sage
⅛ teaspoon salt

Preheat oven to 350 degrees. Spread the cubes on a cookie sheet and bake for 8 to 10 minutes, turning to brown evenly. Cool. In a plastic bag or bowl, toss the cubes with the rest of the ingredients until well coated. Store in a tightly closed container in the pantry for up to 4 months, or in the freezer for up to a year. To use: Combine 2 cups stuffing mix with ½ cup water and 2 tablespoons melted butter. Stir to combine thoroughly. Warm on the stove top or in a microwave. Stir again just before serving.

Stove Top stuffing mix: $3.45 for 6-cup package, or 57¢ per cup.

Homemade: 46¢ per cup.

Contributed by Margaret Gatz of Hiawatha, Kansas.

TOMATO SOUP

1 6-ounce can tomato paste
24 ounces milk (refill tomato
    paste can four times)
1 teaspoon salt or to taste
1 teaspoon celery seed

Put tomato paste in a small saucepan. Add the milk using the can, rinsing thoroughly. Add the salt and the celery seed. Cook on medium heat, stirring occasionally.

Campbell's tomato soup: 69¢ for a 10-ounce can, plus 11¢ for 10 ounces of milk equals 80¢ for 20 ounces, or 32¢ per cup.

Homemade: 21¢ per cup.

Contributed by "an appreciative reader in Boston."

ONION-SOUP MIX

¾ cup instant minced onion
4 teaspoons onion powder
⅛ cup beef-flavored bouillon
    powder
¼ teaspoon celery seed, crushed
¼ teaspoon sugar

Mix all the ingredients, and store in an airtight container. To use, add 2 tablespoons mix to 1 cup boiling water. Cover and simmer for 15 minutes. This makes a

stronger soup than the store-bought mix, so you can use less.

Lipton onion-soup mix: 99¢ for 2 ounces, or 50¢ per ounce.

Homemade: 33¢ per ounce.

CHOCOLATE SYRUP

½ cup cocoa
1 cup water
2 cups sugar
⅛ teaspoon salt
¼ teaspoon vanilla

Mix the cocoa and the water in a saucepan. Heat and stir to dissolve the cocoa. Add the sugar, and stir to dissolve. Boil 3 minutes. Add the salt and the vanilla. Pour into a sterilized pint jar, and store covered in refrigerator. Keeps for several months.

Hershey chocolate syrup: $1.69 for 24 ounces, or 7¢ per ounce.

Homemade: 3¢ per ounce.

Contributed by Doris Schaefer of Corunna, Indiana.

CREAM-SOUP MIX

2 cups dry milk
1¼ cups cornstarch, or 2½ cups
    flour
¼ cup chicken-bouillon powder
2 tablespoons dried onion flakes
½ teaspoon pepper
1 teaspoon thyme (optional)
1 teaspoon basil (optional)

Mix all the ingredients, and store in airtight container. If the mix is made with cornstarch, add ⅓ cup mix to 1¼ cups water; if made with flour, add ½ cup mix to 1¼ cups water. This makes a concentrated casserole consistency. For soup consistency, double the water.

Store-brand soup: 64¢ for a 10-ounce can.

Homemade: Recipe makes ten 12-ounce batches at 18¢ per batch.

Contributed by Kathy Brown of Lakewood, Colorado.

SEASONED-RICE MIX

3 cups uncooked rice
¼ cup dried parsley flakes
6 tablespoons instant chicken or
   beef bouillon powder
2 teaspoons onion powder
½ teaspoon garlic powder
¼ teaspoon dried thyme

Mix all the ingredients, and store in an airtight container. To use, put 1 cup mix, 2 tablespoons margarine, and 2 cups water in a saucepan. Bring to a boil, cover, reduce heat, and simmer for 15 minutes or until the rice is tender. To more closely approximate Rice-A-Roni, substitute a cup of broken pieces of uncooked spaghetti for a cup of rice.

Rice-A-Roni: 89¢ per 1-cup box.
Homemade: 44¢ per cup of mix.

CALCULATING THE NET VALUE OF THE SECOND INCOME UPDATE

In the first book, I explored the idea that for many couples a second, smaller income may not be worth it when one considers the extra expenses that are incurred.

The second income could be a good idea, if: both incomes are low—say under $15,000; both spouses love their jobs; and/or the lower income provides medical benefits that are needed for a pre-existing condition.

But I received a letter that illustrates the possible economic benefit from going from two incomes to one. Linda Prentiss of Lake Ronkonkoma, New York, writes, "After leaving my art-teaching job last spring, I was worried that we couldn't make it on my husband's salary. Thanks to your newsletter, we are doing fine!"

She says she was making $13,000 gross, with no benefits. She realized the following savings by quitting and using the time she freed up to live more frugally:

Transportation:	$265
Clothing:	$200
Breakfast and lunch at work:	$720
Extra convenience food:	$2,080
Fast food:	$1,560
Day care (not tax-deductible in her case):	$5,000
Teacher supplies:	$200
Taxes and Social Security:	$3,380
Late fines, bank fees, and finance charges:	$720
Occasional housekeeper:	$100
Total:	$14,225

Prentiss says these are conservative estimates; her family has $2,300 more in savings than it had six months ago. As a further benefit, their lower income may help them qualify for more financial aid for their daughter's college education.

Certainly Prentiss could have avoided some of her work-related expenses. But most people in that situation do rely on meals out and convenience foods, so her example applies widely.

UNDER ONE ROOF

One of the most powerful frugal concepts is sharing. Whether it's tools, cars, or cookware, when more than one person or family uses it, money is saved.

Consequently, sharing makes a lot of sense when it comes to the biggest expense most of us face: housing.

That's the basic idea behind the more than 400 shared-housing programs in 43 states across the nation. With this country full of huge houses left over from the six-kids-per-family days and more and more people living alone (7 percent of the population lived alone in 1980, 12 percent in 1990), shared housing could be the wave of the future.

According to Margaret Harmon, codirector of the National Shared Housing Resource Center, there are two kinds of shared housing:

Match-ups. In these, homeowners share their homes with homeseekers who pay rent and/or provide service. For example, an elderly widow might share her home with a college student, who pays minimal rent, does some home or yard maintenance, and provides some companionship. Or single mothers may live together in a home one of them owns and share child-care duties.

Group-shared Residences. These involve a number of people living cooperatively in a single, large dwelling, usually rented. In the case of elderly or disabled residents, the home may be owned by a church or other sponsoring organization, and cooking, laundry, and housekeeping may be pro-

vided. Last year in Massachusetts, 230 people moved out of nursing homes and into shared housing.

Harmon says many young people work out their own shared-housing arrangements through newspaper classified ads, bulletin boards, and word of mouth. But older or disabled people, who may be more wary of potential problems and who may lack the time or energy to screen house mates themselves, often use shared-housing programs. These programs are sponsored by churches, housing authorities, social-service agencies, and other nonprofit groups. They carefully screen potential house mates to make sure they will be compatible.

To find the shared-housing program nearest you or to learn about how to start one in your community, call or write:

National Shared Housing Resource
  Center
431 Pine St.
Burlington, VT 05401
(802) 862-2727

A final note: According to a study done at Columbia University and St. Luke's-Roosevelt Hospital in New York, people who live alone are twice as likely to have second heart attacks and die from them as people living with family or friends. Another study at Duke University Medical Center found that unmarried heart-attack patients with no close friends were much more likely to die within five years than those with close attachments to family and friends.

In short, concludes the *Journal of the American Medical Association,* isolation and loneliness can actually be life-threatening. It seems clear, then, that sharing housing and forming friendships and attachments could actually save lives.

THANK YOU, TANK GOO

Dear Amy,

I've learned that aquarium sealant works better on wet joints than anything else I've tried. I use Dow-Corning, 100-percent silicone rubber aquarium sealant, $2.79 at a pet shop. I learned by fixing a leak in my car trunk. . . . My repair has held up for six years. Later, after two different dive shops had failed to seal my diver's faceplate to the rubber part, I fixed it the same way.

—Leonce W. Many
    New Orleans, Louisiana

GOOD-BYE, OLD FLAME

Dear Amy,

We've turned off the pilot light on our gas stove and use a flintless lighter. We've done this for at least ten years, and my husband estimates that we save $7 a month.

—Beatrice E. Lewis
    West Newton, Massachusetts

SAVE A BUNCH

Dear Amy,

If you keep bananas in a closed plastic bag, they will keep at least two weeks on your counter. I experimented with this. I bought two bunches of bananas at the green, barely yellow stage. I put one in a closed plastic bag and one in an open plastic bag. By the end of one week, the open-bag bananas were

brown-spotted and almost at the banana-bread stage. At the end of two weeks, the closed-bag bananas were just starting to get small brown spots, and the stems still showed some green. Once the bag is opened and left open, the bananas ripen at a faster rate.

—Margie Jamison
    Lynchburg, Virginia

MOM'S WATCHFUL EYE

Dear Amy,

When we received our copy of a bill from the hospital after our third child's birth, we discovered that the hospital had charged the insurance company twice for the birthing room (which added over $1,200 to the bill). Our insurance company has a hospital-audit program. If the patient finds an error that saves the company money, the patient receives 50 percent of the savings up to $500. After we followed the procedure required, the insurance authority issued us a check for $500. Not a bad return for a few moments of work.

—James and Ann Gallegos
Thoreau, New Mexico

COTTON TALE

Dear Amy,

This costume only cost me 50¢. I went to a garage sale, and they had a large, stuffed bunny for that price. I removed the stuffing . . . outdoors because of the mess . . . and cut out the face, hands, and feet. The costume was then ready for Halloween.

—Dianne Willis
Sterling Heights, Michigan

FOAM FOR FREE

Dear Amy,

My wife and I live in the Northern California foothills, where the temperature drops below freezing in the winter. I had some PVC water pipes to insulate. . . . I went to the local retail carpet business and asked if I could have some discarded foam pads from their Dumpster. They were happy to get rid of them. I cut the pads into strips about 2 inches or 3 inches wide. I secured one end of the strip to the start of the pipe with duct tape and wound the strip around the pipe, being careful not to overlap. When I reached the end of the pipe, I secured the foam with more duct tape and the pipe was insulated.

—David Stroble and Diane Hall
Nevada City, California

CAMP TIGHTOWADDIE

Dear Amy,

If you are unable (or unwilling) to spend money to send your children to camp, have some neighborhood mothers join you to make a neighborhood day camp. Two mothers form a team to take care of one afternoon's activities according to talent and interest: crafts on Monday, sports and contests on Tuesday, nature skills on Wednesday, cooking on Thursday, skits and songs on Friday. Friday evening can be a families-included barbecue (bring your own meat and a pot-luck dish), and the children display crafts and perform skits. If you are really brave, you could also include a Friday sleepover.

Moms meet a couple of months before to plan dates, activities, and pool resources.

—Colette Hymas
South Jordan, Utah

KITTY LETTER

Dear Amy,

After practically killing my cat, and running up a $300 vet bill, by using too many flea products, I bought a $6 flea comb. I combed my cat four times daily and got out an average of about 20 fleas a day for two weeks. Within a month of this, every trace of a flea was gone. Now I comb her one time a day, just to be sure. Nary a flea have I found.

—H. P. Peasley
Seattle, Washington

PERIODICAL PICK-UPS

Dear Amy,

I get free magazines from my local library. They keep magazines for one year only, and then put them out in the foyer for anyone who wants them. I go one step further and reserve particular magazines. They call when they've got them sorted and I go pick them up. I got a full year's worth of "Organic Gardening," "Mother Earth News," "Money," "Coinage," and "Bicycling," (for the husband) all for free.

—Janine M. Ott
Jacksonville, Arkansas

(We called our local libraries and inquired about their policies.

Smaller libraries have little storage space and dispose of magazines far more frequently . . . they can't keep them a full year. We were advised to ask anytime we went in to see if any were available. The larger libraries keep magazines for 5 to 15 years. They suggested we call back in December to learn which publications would be available, and when. FZ)

BIDS FOR BIKES

Dear Amy,

In our small town, the police station holds a yearly auction of unclaimed bikes. These range from trikes to top-of-the-line racers. This year, we were able to get a midsize boy's 5-speed mountain bike for $25 (retail value, Sears catalog, is $149–$159). We also picked up a men's 12-speed in perfect condition for another $25 (approximate value $199 at Sears).

—Rhonda James
Fergus, Ontario, Canada

WEAR AND WASH

Dear Amy,

I make my washcloths from terrycloth garments bought at garage sales. I cut or rip the garments apart, cut in the right-size squares, round the corners a bit, and zigzag around the edges. After washing, the edges will need to be trimmed. If you end up with enough for two halves, sew them together. The seam through the center doesn't matter.

—Myrtle Usher
Ottosen, Iowa

CALCULATING PAYBACK TIME

Decaying leaves, sticks, and debris obscured the rusty remains of the trailer. Hardy vegetation had arrogantly sprung from the humus layer on the trailer floor. The pock-marked trailer sides, of beer-can strength, flapped loosely.

In a former life it had been a pop-up-tent camper-trailer, then it was gutted and used for hauling wood, and finally, it was abandoned to the elements. Although free for the taking, it wasn't clear we were getting the better end of the deal.

the investment purchase

But diligent scouring of the classifieds during the previous months failed to turn up a bargain utility trailer. So when we located this derelict, Jim's vision overrode his pride and he set forth to make something of the wreckage.

In the next days, Jim stripped away everything that didn't look like a respectable trailer, leaving only a sturdy skeleton of axle and frame. He spent $335 on mail-ordered wheels, sale-purchased, pressure-treated lumber, hardware, wiring, and lights. Up from the humble beginning miraculously arose a handsome utility trailer that became the envy of his coworkers.

We had an imminent need for a heavy-duty trailer to move our family's belongings over the 40 bumpy miles between our Navy house and our new pre-1900 farmhouse with attached barn.

By moving on weekends, the process took ten days. Renting a utility trailer of equal size would have cost $15 per day or a total of $150. During its initial use, nearly half of the cost of the trailer had been paid back.

In the last five years, the remaining cost of the trailer has been paid back in savings on delivery charges and the ability to haul free-for-the-taking items. We have bartered the use of the trailer, and it has saved us hundreds of hours of work.

A $335 utility trailer would not have sufficient payback for everyone. With each investment purchase, do the math to figure out whether it's worthwhile for you.

Calculating payback is a simple but often overlooked process and is a fundamental practice of successful tightwaddery. You divide the cost of the item by the savings per use to determine how many times you would have to use something to pay back the cost.

Example: A pair of hair-salon-quality scissors cost $14. A child's haircut costs $7. Two home haircuts will pay for the scissors.

You should also figure out how long the payback time is.

Example: If it takes two home haircuts to pay back the cost of the scissors, and your child needs a cut every six weeks, multiply two haircuts by six weeks. The payback time is 12 weeks.

People often mistakenly assume that any investment that pays for itself is a good one. When figuring payback time, consider these points:

1. Factor in the life expectancy of the item you plan to buy.

Example: If the more expensive sneakers will last 30 percent longer than the cheap ones and cost 30 percent more, you are not gaining ground—and you would be better off using your money to invest in something else.

2. Similarly, consider how long you will need the item. If you are buying a tool you will only use briefly, try to buy it used so you can recover the cost when you re-sell it. Or you may find it's better to rent.

Example: Rent or buy used rather than new pump jacks to help you paint your house.

3. Generally, put your money in items that have the quickest payback time first.

Example: You estimate in your case the payback time on insulated windows is 20 years. You also can find many smaller investment purchases that pay back in 10 years that add up to the cost of the windows. The smaller purchases will pay for themselves two times in 20 years—and so you would save twice as much.

4. If a new product comes on the market that might save you money in the future, wait to buy it: The price may drop dramatically.

Example: You decide to buy a computer because your grade-school kids will need one when they get to high school. In the meantime you plan to use it to write letters to save money on your phone bill. But a computer that cost $2,500 seven years ago can be purchased used today for $250. Unless the item will give you immediate, significant payback, wait for the price to drop, for a great deal to come along, or for the technology to improve.

5. Consider the 90/10 rule. Sometimes for 10 percent of the money you can buy a tool that will do 90 percent of the job.

Example: You can buy a small, used, portable sewing machine for $50 that will do 90 percent of the sewing you need. Or you can buy a new, $500, whiz-bang sewing machine with all the attachments that will do 100 percent of the sewing. So you are paying $450 to get that 10 percent more.

Let's say you buy the smaller machine, and every two years you encounter a sewing job it cannot handle. If hiring a professional seamstress costs $45 per sewing job, the more expensive machine would take 20 years to pay for itself.

6. With great reluctance, I suggest you factor in time savings. People frequently and erroneously cite time savings as an excuse to buy expensive "toys." You can buy time-saving purchases to create more leisure time, but time-savers become money-savers only when you genuinely, absolutely have no spare time—and when you use the free time you gain to save money by doing something else.

Example: When we first moved to Leeds, Jim wanted to buy a riding lawn mower with snow- and garden-plowing capabilities. I resisted until I mowed our front yard for the first time. With our push mower, that one small section required two hours—ample time for me to ponder how many hours I would have to spend every day to maintain the entire lawn. Mowing this way would have made it impossible for us to have a garden or do some renovations or other money-saving activities.

In cases like this, calculate the payback by transference.

We bought a used garden tractor for $1,600. The tractor frees up ten hours per week. If I use those hours to do home renovation instead of hiring an $8-per-hour contractor, then I can transfer those savings toward the cost of the tractor. It will pay for itself when I have completed 200 hours of renovations.

We feel economic triumph when we hitch our paid-for-itself tractor to haul leaves, brush, and garden debris around our 7-acre spread. The ultimate thrill for our little tightwads comes when, after the chores, we load them in the trailer and ride off, giggling and squealing, into the sunset.

TOYS FOR TIGHTWAD TOTS

As an experienced parent, I have noticed that for my kids the transition from "It's-the-greatest-toy-in-the-universe-thank-you-thank-you-Mommy," to "big deal," is about two days.

It's this rapid disenchantment that makes many parents swamp their kids with toys. One recent survey revealed that the average five-year-old has "cycled through" about 250 toys.

As an alternative, I was in-

trigued by the concept of a "toy library." There are more than 200 around the country. One opened two months ago in nearby Lewiston, Maine.

Its director, Anne Belden, says her nonprofit, volunteer-run facility is actually a combination of indoor play space and toy library. A family pays a $20 annual membership fee, and the kids, ranging from infants to eight-year-olds, can play in the library, which is located in donated space in a church. Belden says indoor play spaces are particularly needed in cold climates like ours, where snowed-in parents and kids can go a little nutty.

Kids can check out toys for two weeks. The Lewiston toy library has 300 toys, mostly donated.

To find out whether there is a toy library (with or without a play space) near you, contact: The U.S.A. Toy Library Association, 2530 Crawford Ave., Suite 111, Evanston, IL 60201, (708) 864-3330. The association publishes a national directory of member libraries. If you want to start one, Belden suggests visiting the nearest operating toy library for suggestions.

PRESSED-FLOWER PICTURES

Before I lose the male audience with this "woman's" article, let me say that I first became intrigued by pressed-flower pictures when a *guy* on my staff made one for Mother's Day about a year ago. His mother loved it. I realized this was a great tightwad endeavor for several reasons:

• Wildflowers are free and plentiful in rural and suburban areas. Cultivated flowers may also be pressed.

• Flower presses can be easily made from free materials.

• No special tools, materials, or talent is required.

• Pictures can be designed to fit in secondhand frames (I've got a box full of long, thin, rectangular frames for which this would be perfect).

• A variety of backgrounds can be used, including papers, matboards, and cloth, depending on what you have available.

• Pressed-flower pictures make great all-occasion gifts, and you can get a jump on Christmas by starting in the summer.

To learn more, I consulted four library books as well as spoke with a woman in my community, Joanne D'Unger, who has been pressing flowers since she studied botany in college ten years ago.

The familiar method of pressing flowers in heavy books is somewhat inconvenient. To prevent stained pages, you have to press flowers between facial tissues in-side the book for 24 hours, remove the tissues, and press the flowers in the books with weights stacked on top for several weeks, meaning that you have a semipermanent pile of stuff taking up space. Then, Murphy's Law of Flower Pressing dictates, "If you've used your 'A' encyclopedia, your child will have to write a school paper on Albania." And after the flowers dry, you'll want to transfer them out of the books to some sort of file for safe keeping.

In contrast, Joanne's flower press consists

of two wooden sections made of glued-and-nailed-together slats (left over from a building project) in a style similar to the metal-rack type she used in college. You could also use discards like scrap plywood, oven racks, or our no-longer-needed homemade baby gate, which, if cut in half, would closely resemble Joanne's press.

To apply pressure, Joanne uses

cinch straps (that she trash-picked), but you could also use weights or bolts with wing nuts. If you use bolts, drill the holes through the center of the sides, as opposed to the corners, for even distribution of pressure.

Flowers have to be pressed between pieces of absorbent paper. Two authors suggest newspaper without colored ink. Joanne uses a plain, nonsmooth paper (which she scavenged from the trash at work) and has used the same sheets for many years. She places the paper sheets, with flowers, between layers of corrugated cardboard (which she cut from packing boxes); this helps to circulate air.

Joanne sandwiches many flower/paper/cardboard layers between the outside wooden sections, cinches the press tight, and stores it in a dry place for several weeks. This type of press is compact, portable, and makes a permanent place to store flowers.

When you're selecting wildflowers to press, avoid endangered species. Flowers along roadsides are usually fine, but don't pick them in parks. Some types of flowers may spot or turn brown, and learning which type works best requires experimentation. Small flowers, ferns, and grasses are easiest for beginners. Already-dead butterflies may be pressed and are suitable for making pictures as well.

Pick flowers in the middle of the day when they're the driest, and more than a day after the most recent rain.

When laying out flowers to press, curve the stems and press flowers to present both side and top views. Depending on humidity and type of flower, drying time can vary from two to six weeks. During the drying period, one book suggests, inspect the flowers to find and smooth any folded petals or remove any that have mildewed.

While you're hitting the yard sales in the summer, pick up inexpensive frames. If you're a beginner and planning to make gifts, you'll want smaller frames for two reasons: They require smaller, less complicated arrangements; and most people's homes can accommodate a sweet little picture, but giving any large piece of artwork is risky and may not be appreciated.

When you're ready to assemble a picture, choose a frame and background material. Trace the glass on the background, and cut the background to the right size. Next, lay out your pressed flowers on your background, using tweezers or a dry watercolor brush to position them, until you find a pleasing design. During this stage you'll want to avoid any coughing, slamming of doors, or whirlwinds created by careening three-year-old twins.

After you've settled on a design, carefully pick up each item, use a toothpick to apply a tiny dab of Elmer's glue to the back of the flower, and replace it in the arrangement. Once everything is glued, the finished picture can be framed. Be sure to use glass to protect the picture, and seal the back with tape to prevent problems from humidity.

To learn more about advanced techniques (such as for pressing bulkier flowers), design styles, and other applications for pressed flowers, consult one of those many books at your library.

TVP: A BAD NAME FOR GOOD FOOD

Who thought up this name, anyway? "TVP" sounds like an emissions control device, or maybe the knob next to "vertical hold" on your television. It doesn't even remotely sound like food—no wonder it's been around for 20 years and never really caught on. In fact, I had never heard of it until a friend, whose two daughters suddenly "went vegetarian" on her, introduced me to it. After some experimentation, I've concluded it is a reasonable product for people to explore.

TVP stands for "texturized vegetable protein." It is the same stuff that those convenience-food manufacturers sneak into your food to make it seem like it has more meat than it really does; it's often listed in the ingredients as "textured soy flour."

TVP is a staple food in many vegetarian households. But unlike tofu, brewer's yeast, mung bean sprouts, and other vegetarian mainstays with unique flavors and textures, TVP was designed as a substitute for meat, so mainstream families should find it easy to swallow.

All TVP is made by one company: the Archer Daniels Midland Company in Decatur, Illinois. Although it's made in America's heartland, ironically, TVP is much more widely used in Europe.

TVP comes in dry form in three sizes: flakes, granules, and chunks (kitty-food size). Before cooking it in any form, you reconstitute it by adding warm water.

Although TVP has little flavor of its own, it has a texture that is very difficult to distinguish from that of ground turkey or hamburger (You can trust me on this: I'm not the kind of person who oversells vegetarian dishes. I'd be the first to tell you that spaghetti with lentils just doesn't cut it). So TVP works very well in spicy foods, like spaghetti sauce and chili. When we made blander

Which of the following is a low-cost meat substitute?

TV

ATV

CFC

PVC

VP

RV

TP

TVP

ET

foods, like TVP gravy on biscuits, we decided we would add Worcestershire sauce in the future.

If you find you don't like it in meatless meals, try mixing it with hamburger. Instead of buying 85 percent lean ground beef at top dollar, you could buy bargain-priced 75 percent lean and mix it half-and-half with TVP; this mix would have a slightly lower fat content than the expensive hamburger.

Aside from any health benefits, the obvious advantage of TVP is its price. When we happen upon an amazing sale on ground beef, we can buy 75 percent lean for $1.19 per pound. We almost always fry and drain the meat before we use it in a casserole or spaghetti sauce. This means we're really buying 12 ounces for $1.19, which works out to $1.58 per pound of usable meat.

TVP, when purchased by the 25-pound bag from our local natural-food store, costs $21.50, or 86¢ per pound. But a pound of dry chunks, when rehydrated, weighs about 3¾ pounds. This means the price for the usable product is about 23¢ per pound, or 14 percent of the cost of usable hamburger.

What about nutrition? TVP is a good source of fiber and protein. Rehydrated TVP has about 60 percent of the protein of hamburger,

and it has almost no fat. Here's how the vitamins and minerals in 400 grams of rehydrated TVP stack up with those in 400 grams of hamburger, in milligrams.

As you can see in the chart (below left), TVP has more of some nutrients and less of others.

But isn't this some kind of weird "chemical food"? No. TVP is a by product of the process of making soybean oil. Although chemicals are used in this process, TVP has been repeatedly tested and has been found to have no trace of those chemicals. But if you're skeptical, you can buy organic TVP, which costs $1.05 per pound (of dry chunks) at my natural-food store.

How can you find TVP? Many natural-food stores carry the flake or granule types, but TVP chunks may have to be specially ordered for you. I recommend that you go to the extra effort of ordering the chunks, as these most closely approximate meat. If you cannot find a local source, TVP chunks can be ordered through *The Mail Order Catalog* by calling (800) 695-2241. The price, including delivery, is $37.25 per 25 pounds. This means the dry price is $1.49 per pound, which works out to about 40¢ per pound for rehydrated. If this quantity seems like a risky experiment, I suggest you pool resources with other families and split the quantity.

This same company sells *The TVP Cookbook* for $6.95, plus shipping and handling. But most cooks of any experience will be able to adapt recipes by simply substituting rehydrated TVP for ground meat, and perhaps adding more spices and onions to blander recipes.

	TVP	Hamburger
Calcium	340	28
Phosphorus	700	878
Iron	8	15
Potassium	2,200	1,795
Thiamine	.60	.61
Niacin	3	14
Riboflavin	.33	.7

A BOOK REVIEW

If you are in the market for a new appliance—or just want to learn how to make the ones you've got work better—I highly recommend *Consumer Guide to Home Energy Savings,* by Alex Wilson and John Morrill.

Unlike a lot of wimpy energy-efficiency publications ("Be sure to caulk those windows!"), this one goes into great detail on how to get the maximum energy savings from lightbulbs, furnaces, washing machines, water heaters—any appliance that uses energy.

Particularly helpful are the up-to-date, model-by-model listings of annual energy costs for various appliances. But I was also interested in the charts that help you maximize energy efficiency when you *use* your existing appliances—for example, the one below, which shows the most and least expensive appliances you can choose when cooking a casserole. The costs are based on 8¢ per kilowatt-hour for electricity and 60¢ per therm for natural gas:

	Temperature	Time	Cost
Electric oven	350	1 hr.	16¢
Toaster oven	425	50 min.	8¢
Gas oven	350	1 hr.	7¢
Frying pan	420	1 hr.	7¢
Crockpot	200	7 hrs.	6¢
Microwave oven	High	15 min.	3¢

To order, send $6.95 (California residents add 8.25 percent sales tax) plus $2.00 shipping to:

American Council for an Energy-
  Efficient Economy
2140 Shattuck Ave., Suite 202
Berkeley, CA 94704

CONTACTS BY MAIL

I have managed to stumble to the advanced age of 39 without needing corrective lenses. Readers who are not so fortunate have told me that contact lenses can make a big dent in a frugal budget, but some said they had heard that good deals are available from mail-order sources. So I plunged into research and discovered that the subject is both complex and controversial.

Cheryle Baker Dusinberre of Boiling Springs, Pennsylvania, sent me a newspaper clipping that indicated that the American Optometric Association didn't fully support mail-order replacement lenses. So I talked with Dr. Burt Dubow, chairman of the contact-lens section of the A.O.A., who cited these concerns:

• Consumers who buy mail-order contacts might skip regular checkups.

• A discount supplier might accidentally fill an outdated prescription.

• Any custom-made lenses, like torics, gas-permeables, or bifocals, should not be mail-ordered because they should be checked by your optometrist for any imperfections.

But Dr. Dubow said that if consumers have checkups, make sure their prescriptions are still good, and purchase daily-wear or extended-wear lenses (which aren't custom-made), mail-order lenses pose no problem.

In addition, Dr. Dubow confirmed what I had heard from other sources. Many optometrists are now offering replacement lenses at discount. If your optometrist isn't, try negotiating, using prices from mail-order suppliers to make your case. If your optometrist still won't budge, shop around with other optometrists.

Also check your warehouse club. Sharon Nelson of Auburn, California, said a pair of lenses that costs $150 through her optometrist costs $60.35 at Lens Express—but she found that the pair costs $36 at the optical shop at her warehouse store, Price Club. (Ironically, the mail-order suppliers have the same criticism of warehouse clubs that some optometrists have about mail-order suppliers: They are more likely to make mistakes and don't provide personal service.)

If you can't get lenses at discount prices locally and opt for purchasing them through the mail, consider these points:

Two discounters I surveyed, Lens Express and LenSmart, charge a three-year membership fee of $25, but their discount prices were still higher than those of other discounters who charge no membership fee. Although LenSmart offers no other benefits for this fee, Lens Express does; if you refer a friend who joins, you save $15 on your next purchase. Lens Express also may help you save on eye exams through an associated doctor. But the contact-lens industry is changing so rapidly, it may not be wise to lock into one discounter that long.

Shipping and handling fees vary considerably—from zero to $8.95—and may vary based on where you live in the country.

Most discounters quote prices for *pairs* of lenses, but we found a few that quote them for *individual* lenses. In the case of one catalog I inspected, this was only evident in the teeny-weeny print at the bottom of the page.

Lens Express guarantees the lowest price, which means it will "match any price at the time of order." In other words, the company's usual price may not be the

Mail-Order Company	Phone Number	Daily Wear	Extended Wear	Shipping
Lens Express ($25/3-year fee)	(800) 666-LENS	$45.90	$105.40	$8.95
LenSmart ($25/3-year fee)	(800) 231-LENS	$40.00	$84.00	$5.95
Contact Lens Replacement Center	(800) 779-2654	$49.00	$89.00	$4.50
Contact Lens Connection	(800) 695-LENS	$38.00	$98.00	none
Dial A Contact Lens	(800) 233-LENS	$19.50*	$89.00	$3 or $8
Contact Lens Supply	(800) 833-7525	$48.00	$93.00	$4.00
Prism Optical	(800) 637-4104	$45.00	$90.00	$5.00
Soft Lens Express	(800) 872-1880	$60.00	$148.00	$5.00

*Price is for a special offer of two pairs.

lowest, it's up to you to find a lower price, which Lens Express will match. A company representative told me the company would also adjust its price to compensate for its higher shipping charges and the membership fee. However, each time you place an order, you'll have to renegotiate.

By calling around each time you order replacements, you might locate a "special," as indicated by the asterisk (*) in the chart on page 136. At the time I researched this article, this company offered this price for a pair of lenses, but only if you bought two pairs.

This chart compares the prices of two specific types of brand-name lenses, from companies recommended by readers. All the prices are based on one pair of lenses. As you can see, no company offers the lowest prices on every type of lens, and there are over 100 types. You have to shop around yourself to find the best deal.

Finally, the bottom price isn't always the final consideration. Some companies may offer poor service and/or may not be well established. I omitted any company with a perpetually busy phone or that didn't return my call after I left a message on its answering machine. But I couldn't research the reliability of any of these companies.

Ultimately, you have to work out the best package of options for yourself. Some optometrists charge less for exams and mark up replacement lenses. According to Elizabeth Rhymer of Naples, Florida, these optometrists might not even release your prescription so you can buy lenses elsewhere. Other optometrists charge more

for exams but sell discounted lenses or let you fill the prescription through a discounter. So in addition to factoring in membership fees and shipping, you may also need to factor in the cost of exams.

FLOWERS ARE FOREVER

Dear Amy,

Perennial flowers are a much better buy for the garden than annuals. You buy them once and they're there forever. While perennials are more expensive than annuals, there are ways to minimize the expense. Many can be started from seed. Others can be started from cuttings you take from the mother plant in the spring and fall. Still others can be divided in a couple of years. For advice, I specifically recommend *The Victory Garden Flower Book* by Bob Thompson and *The Perennial Garden* by Marilyn and Jeff Ball.

—Diana Bauer
  Cincinnati, Ohio

DITCH PITCH TO SWITCH

Dear Amy,

I received a check in the mail for $75 to switch my long-distance carrier. I phoned my current carrier and asked them what pertinent questions I could ask the competition when I called to see if they had any similar plans to my current carrier. The service representative I spoke to was very honest and told me the competition probably had something similar, and although he could not send me a check for cash with the promise to switch like the competition, he would credit my account for $75 if I mailed my check to their office. I could have switched, but then I would have had to pay new service fees. Instead, I spent 29¢ to mail in the competition's check and will get $75 credited to my account.

—Vera Ziegler
　Bremerton, Washington

SCHOOL BUDGET CUTS

Dear Amy,

I admire those who can cut their own hair, but I can't. And I certainly don't trust my husband or two-year-old. My way to save money is going to a cosmetology school. Their prices on services are greatly reduced; I save $7 on a haircut. Having my hair just cut, and not dried/styled, has saved about $7 more.

—Dawn Hancock
　Auburn, Indiana

SAUCE SAVER

Dear Amy,

I had found a bargain on a huge and slightly dented can of tomato sauce at a grocery warehouse. I really didn't know how I was going to freeze the sauce in usable portions with little waste after I opened the can. My mom told me to freeze the sauce in ice-cube trays and then put them in a freezer bag. It worked great. A homemade pizza takes us exactly five cubes. There is absolutely zero wasted.

—Melanie Wisdom
　New Caney, Texas

WHAT BASEBALL TEAM WON THE 1939 WORLD SERIES?

SPEED DIAL

Dear Amy,

Often, radio stations have trivia contests where the first person to call with the correct answer is the winner. Many times, the questions aren't that difficult; the hard part is being the first caller. The secret: Dial the last number before they've finished asking the question. I've won two meals in the last month this way.

—Paul Stynsberg
　Roseau, Minnesota

CHOO-CHOO CHEAPIES

Dear Amy,

In preparing a fourth birthday party for my rail-fan son, I remembered those little paper engineer hats they always gave to him on station visits. Thanks to the courtesy of the Amtrak representative, our guests had *free* theme-appropriate hats.

—Jill Zacharie
　Alexandria, Virginia

BAGS IN A BOX

Dear Amy,

I used to feel that empty plastic grocery bags had invaded my pantries and closets. Now, I store plastic bags in an empty tissue box. It dispenses them one at a time and saves a lot of space.

—Name withheld by request
Peekskill, New York

GIANT FLOWER PRESSES?

Dear Amy,

Wood pallets (no deposit) are often available from stores, lumberyards, feed stores, etc. Ask the store manager if he/she has any no-deposit pallets for free. They can be used for:

1. Most obvious, storing things off the ground.
2. Firewood. Most pallets are hardwood and make great fires. We cut the 1 x 4 from between the rails and then cut the rails to the proper size for the wood stove.
3. Fences. Nail them together with a 2 x 4 along the top and use an occasional fence post to help hold the row up.
4. Tables and work counters . . . use your imagination.
5. Garbage and trash bins, to keep the neighborhood dogs out.

We have found pallets to be a great resource, especially for temporary-type projects when money is in short supply.

—Bob and Rusty Taylor
Poulsbo, Washington

USE IT OR LOSE IT

I've observed a problem common to nearly all the gardeners I've encountered throughout my life: How do you use up all that you've canned and frozen—but make what you have last until the next year's harvest?

Home-canned goods last a couple of years, so ending up with extra isn't terrible—every once in a while you have a bad tomato year, and last year's surplus spaghetti sauce can be handy. But frozen vegetables should be used up within the year; they begin to lose their vitamins and develop a freezer taste if they're too old.

Throughout the year most gardeners, being unsure whether they have enough to last to the next season, buy supermarket fruits and vegetables. Then, as the new season rolls around, they find they have too much left over. So they have to throw away last year's surplus (or the year-before-that's surplus) to make room for this year's. As a result, money, effort, and energy are wasted.

Of the gardeners who keep any records at all, most use a notebook system. They write in how much they freeze or can, and then throughout the year they make a mark every

Beans	49 qts	HHT HHT HH II
Cauliflower	10 qts	HHT IIII
Peas	27 qts	HHT HHT HH HHT I
Rhubarb	31 qts	HHT HH I
Spinach	46 qts	HHT HH II
Strawberries	39 qts	HHT HH HHT

time they use something. This system, while good, doesn't insure the maximum use of garden produce. At some point, usually during the late spring, it becomes evident that their family has to eat beet greens three nights a week but only has two jars of spaghetti sauce to last four months. So, they lose the nutritional advantage—and pleasure—that comes with variety.

Being of a more precise, frugal mind-set, this seems to have been a greater vexation to me than to others. If I didn't use my garden produce evenly throughout the year, my food bill would fluctuate greatly, and it would take me 12 months to know for sure whether it was going up or down.

So I decided I wanted a better system to schedule produce consumption. It would take into account that vegetables are harvested during different months, from June to October, so vegetables would be scheduled to last accordingly. I also wanted a system that would schedule canned and frozen-food

consumption together—as opposed to a notebook by my freezer in the laundry room and another near the canned goods in the cellar.

So I decided to make up a calendar of sorts. First, I went through my freezer and canning shelves and recorded how many jars or packages I had of each fruit or vegetable.

Then I made up a time-line calendar, as shown below, on the backside of attached sheets of used computer paper. I listed the items vertically, in alphabetical order. I made horizontal spaces for the upcoming months. Noting the projected date of harvest, I divided the number of items by the number of remaining months. If I have 20 packages of spinach to consume in four months, I put five X's in each month's space. If I have 13 packages of shredded zucchini to consume in five months, I alternately allot two and three X's: $3 + 2 + 3 + 2 + 3 = 13$.

Months of light consumption could be scheduled for the summer, since some fresh garden vegetables are available during those months. People who have small gardens might want to schedule their heaviest consumption during the winter months when supermarket produce gets most expensive.

This schedule is now taped up in our pantry with a pencil nearby. We look at it before planning our daily menu. When we use something, we circle the appropriate X. It took

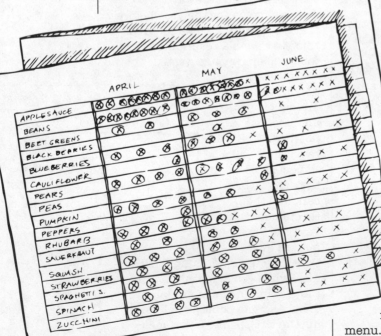

me about an hour and a half to inventory and make this schedule, and it requires no more than ten seconds a day to use.

I started my schedule in April, because that's when I devised this system. Next fall, after all of our garden is harvested, I will make a 12-month schedule.

This garden schedule illustrates a larger point. If you lack control over any area of your life—be it time, money, or other resources—design a system to manage it. Order will save you stress as well as money.

SAVE THOSE SEEDS

A dilemma that faces gardeners each year is whether to buy new seeds or take a chance on seeds left over from last year. Many gardeners, believing that seeds become much less viable each year, toss out all of the leftovers and buy a new batch "just to be sure."

But this isn't necessary, according to reader Pam West of Batavia, Illinois. She says that when she worked for one of the largest seed companies in the nation, one of her duties was to relabel the seed packages from the year before with the current germination information after the seeds were tested in the lab.

West wrote, "I was amazed to find out that in most cases, the germination percentage actually went up from the previous year, sometimes as much as 10 to 15 percent. So use those seeds from last year, and save your new seeds for next year."

According to *The Year Round Vegetable Gardener* by Anne Halpin, only onion seeds need to

be purchased fresh each year. Here are the average storage limits for other varieties of seeds.

One to two years: corn, lettuce, parsley, and parsnips.

Three to five years: asparagus, beans, cabbage, carrots, celery, chicory, endive, okra, peas, peppers, radishes, and spinach.

Five or more years: beets, cucumbers, and tomatoes.

In *Square Foot Gardening* (a book that, incidentally, has been

recommended by at least a dozen of my readers), author Mel Bartholomew recommends storing seeds in airtight containers in a refrigerator. But even if you lack the room to store them in your fridge, there is a great chance they will be good next year if you store them in a cool, dry place.

If you don't want to risk devoting a large space in your garden to risky seeds, do your own germination test a few weeks before planting time. Sandwich ten seeds in a paper towel, and keep it moist. If at least seven sprout, your seeds are approximately as viable as new ones.

BUDGET PHILOSOPHY

Dear Amy,

I want to find out how to budget correctly. I've tried several methods but end up confused. Since my husband's and my income comes in sporadically, I have a hard time figuring out when I should start to figure; from the first of the month, or when all the income has come in, or when I pay monthly bills?

—Susan Sandoval
Elm Creek, Nebraska

Our personal budgeting system is so simple it doesn't seem like a budget, and I have often claimed that we don't have one.

Before I broached this subject, I consulted a couple of personal-finance books. Their systems seemed complicated and/or tedious. Sylvia Porter has four forms you need to fill out monthly. Likewise, readers have written to me about systems involving filling jars or envelopes with monthly expense money or even setting up an in-house checking system, which again seemed needlessly complicated. Conversely, many well-known personal-finance experts claim that budgets are like diets: Don't bother, because they don't work.

I'm in the middle. I do believe that every family needs a basic plan, but that plan should be extremely simple and flexible.

Early in our marriage, Jim and I spent an evening working out our plan. First, we pulled out our old bills and figured our average monthly fixed expenses: rent, insurance, utilities, and so on. Any bills that occurred annually were divided by 12, so that we knew how much to allocate for each month. Next, we estimated our nonfixed expenses: food, household expenses, clothing, gifts, transportation costs. By this point, we had accounted for every expense we could anticipate.

Then we subtracted our fixed and nonfixed expenses from Jim's take-home pay. If your income fluctuates wildly, base your monthly income on last year's after-tax income and divide by 12, and allow a huge amount for savings in case your income is less this year.

From this process, we determined we had a theoretical $500 per month surplus, or about 20 percent of Jim's take-home pay. Had this surplus worked out to less than 10 percent of our income, we would have done some refiguring.

By keeping a personal expense diary—a small notebook in which we recorded each expense as it occurred—we were able to make sure we stayed, on the average, within our budget.

It's easiest to keep records monthly, so start your records from the first of the month. Try to pay bills the same month in which they arrive, so that you know in which month to record the expense.

Budget gurus suggest putting 10 percent of your income into

savings each month, religiously, as if you were paying a bill. But this hard-and-fast rule "allows" you to spend the other 90 percent and doesn't challenge you to save more. It may also prevent you from paying off a high-interest debt or from buying an appliance that will save you money. They also insist on adherence to this rule whether your income is $10,000 or $100,000 per year.

Instead, I regard the budget as a beginning point only. Rather than seeing it as what you're allowed to spend, try to lower each area of the budget until you reach the point where it no longer feels comfortable, and then spend slightly more.

For example, we budgeted $200 a month for food, but over a period of years I whittled this to an average of $145 (back when we had three children). We only spent half of what we allowed for birthdays and rarely spent any of the money allocated for entertainment. By doing this in each budget category, we were able to increase our surplus to put into savings.

Additionally, sometimes you should overspend when it will save money in the long run. We average $180 a month for food (including school lunches and gardening supplies), but some months we spend $250 and other months we spend $100. The overspending occurs when we bulk-buy sale items or when we spend a lot for canning supplies during the summer months. If we have too many high months in a row, I figure out how much we should "underspend" this month to bring our average in line, and we eat from the items we have stocked up.

The physical management of our money was equally simple. We kept $1,000 in our checking account. Because we sought to spend as little as possible, our checking account naturally grew. When it grew to $1,500 we would transfer $500 into savings. We kept $2,500 in a savings account. When that grew to $3,500, we transferred $1,000 into an investment or paid off a debt. Some experts suggest keeping as much as six months' income in savings and liquid investments.

A question I've been asked is "How do you handle emergencies?" Plan your budget to include any expenses you can anticipate. If you drive an old car, figure on $1,000 per year for repairs. If you drive a new car under warranty, don't plan for any repairs. But if an unexpected fender bender occurs, pay for the repair, or the insurance deductible, with savings. Only dip into savings for emergencies or for buying something you can prove will pay for itself very quickly.

By deliberately living beneath our means we have *always,* I repeat, *always,* had enough money in savings for unexpected expenses. And because we always worked to save more than we had budgeted, even with emergencies, we saved an average of 21 percent of our income for seven years.

But everyone is different. Some people seem to need to put money into savings as if they were paying a monthly bill, or have it automatically withdrawn from their paychecks. For those with low incomes or little discipline, a more complicated and tedious system may be essential.

DARE TO DUMPSTER DIVE

As you become an accomplished tightwad, you find fewer and fewer new ideas that can significantly cut your expenses, so when you find one, you get excited. *The Art and Science of Dumpster Diving* by John Hoffman increased my awareness of a frugal frontier I had yet to explore.

Before I go any further, let me emphasize that I understand this subject crosses the line even for many hard-core tightwads; however, I am willing to risk the criticism. Dumpster diving can yield huge savings that may make a significant difference for some families.

In his book, Hoffman makes three basic points:

1. Americans are incredibly wasteful and throw away all sorts of good stuff.

2. Americans are snobby and afraid of germs.

3. Because of the first two points, the brave soul who is willing to poke his head into these forbidding urban caverns will be well rewarded.

Hoffman, who is now 29, writes with authority. He's a third-generation Dumpster diver (his grandmother took it up late in life) with over 20 years of diving experience. Much of what he owns, wears, and (yes, even) eats comes from Dumpsters. He now has a college education and a good job but continues to Dumpster-dive because he finds it a profitable, enjoyable, environmentally responsible pastime. The information in this article is based on both the book and a telephone interview we did with Hoffman.

Just as in Dumpster diving, where one must pick through the trash to find the treasures, it takes some effort to focus on the good stuff in the book. I had to ignore Hoffman's disrespectful attitudes toward authority figures, his profanity, and his slippery ethics (he has snipped locks on Dumpsters). And his tips on snooping for information and dealing with police are sure to offend all but the most ardent libertarian. At times, it seemed hard to find a single page without some offensive element.

Durable Nondescript Clothes

Flashlight

Gloves

Duffel Bag

Dive Stick

Thick-Soled Shoes

But the saving grace of the book is that the guy is actually a skilled, entertaining writer, and I did learn a great deal. For example:

• If you dive consistently and well, you'll never have to buy any of this stuff again: manila envelopes, clothing, clothes hangers, boxes, houseplants, Christmas decorations, videotapes and audiotapes, furniture, candles, most toiletry items, books, magazines, newspapers, low-cost jewelry, and much more.

• The idea that Dumpsters are rat-infested is false, according to Hoffman. In 20 years of diving, he has seen exactly one rat. Even so, he keeps his eyes open for white powder sprinkled on a Dumpster's contents; it may be rat poison.

• The idea that Dumpsters are full of AIDS-contaminated syringes from drug abusers is also false, according to Hoffman. He has not seen a single syringe in the tens of thousands of Dumpsters he's inspected. (Nevertheless, be careful.)

• For food, Hoffman favors bakery and grocery-store Dumpsters, because the food is packaged or has been minimally handled. In an average week, about 50 percent of the food he eats comes from Dumpsters. Along with canned and packaged food, he salvages lightly bruised fruit and cheese with a tiny mold spot. Clearly, Hoffman is less squeamish than most people would be, but his hints about finding and using Dumpster food (he even includes two pages of recipes, such as "Bad-Banana Whipped Cream Substitute") could, at least, be valuable to people in dire economic circumstances. Any food that is questionable could be salvaged to feed to farm animals.

• Hoffman's other favorite Dumpsters are at motels (endless free soap), discount stores, wholesale florists (you'll be able to carry on multiple romances), candy stores, bookstores, toy stores, and garden stores (he planted his parents' orchard with discarded fruit trees).

• Madonna, the rock star, was once a Dumpster diver.

• The best time for diving is the early evening, because apartment dwellers put out trash after supper, and businesses put out trash at the end of the business day.

• Dress in nondescript, durable clothing. Wear gloves and thick-soled shoes. If using a car, bring a long stick with a bent nail on the end for poking and prodding. When on foot, Hoffman uses an antenna from a discarded CB radio for a prodding stick. His grandmother uses her cane. Bring a flashlight for night dives and a shoulder bag for finds.

• For sheer fun and variety, residential Dumpsters, such as those serving large apartment complexes, can't be beat. Hoffman also recommends hitting the Dumpsters of college dorms. As he puts it—and this is a sample of his prose style—"Lots of college kids are wasteful little pukoids." The day the dorms must be vacated is best, but fall, spring, and Christmas breaks are also hot.

• Diving success comes in "streaks." When you hit a good Dumpster, go through it thoroughly.

• When you Dumpster dive, you become invisible. People walk past you as though you don't exist. But if you are approached, Hoffman suggests using the universally accepted excuse: Say you're "looking for boxes." You may actually need to scavenge boxes for the loot you hope to find.

Throughout the book, I appreciated Hoffman's concern for safety. He carefully explains specific techniques to avoid injury from common Dumpster hazards such as broken glass, deranged cats, aerosol can "mines," and Dumpster-lid-slam decapitation. He suggests avoiding actually climbing into Dumpsters.

And I enjoyed his hints on converting trash to cash through yard sales and other outlets. (Basic hint: Never reveal that the item came from a Dumpster. Hoffman supplies several vague, evasive answers you can use regarding the origin of your stuff.)

The book does have a few gaps. Hoffman spends little time discussing the legality of Dumpster diving, except to note that laws vary from city to city and that he's never been arrested.

To find out about laws in our area, I made a few calls to local police stations. The officers knew of no laws in Maine that prohibit Dumpster diving. The only legal problem they could imagine was if the Dumpster was located on private property and the owner complained; then, technically, you'd be trespassing. But even then, the police would merely give you a

warning. The police in one town said they knew of several local people who Dumpster-dived regularly; it never occurred to these officers to stop them.

Furthermore, since shop owners pay for disposal, by removing things from Dumpsters you're saving them money. Hoffman routinely leaves a site cleaner than when he found it to avoid any ill feelings.

My personal experience with Dumpster diving had been previously limited to retrieving cardboard boxes. So I decided I needed to make a field trip (all in the name of research, mind you) to verify Hoffman's claims. My business manager, Elaine, and I paired up one evening (we called ourselves The Dumpster Divas) and drove a long distance to a city that shall remain nameless.

Most of the Dumpsters we found were located in the fronts of stores, and lacking Hoffman's bravado, we passed them up. The ones that were secluded contained mainly cardboard.

But just as we were becoming completely discouraged, we hit the mother lode. We found inexpensive toys still in their packaging, a case of dog biscuits, a case of "moist burgers" for dogs, a shrink-wrapped case of bottled juice in which one bottle had been broken, tuna-fish cans minus their labels, and several jars of Classico spaghetti sauce.

There was far more in that Dumpster, and most of it just as good, but as we were sifting and retrieving, a pickup pulled up. We were about to make a quick getaway when we realized that it was another Dumpster diver. We struck up a conversation, compared our loot, and he shared a valuable bit of information: "Never, ever, reveal your sources." Dumpsters divers are quiet about their hobby, not out of shame, but because it would be akin to telling everyone where the good fishing hole is.

As a result of my experience, I would add this to Hoffman's tips:

• If you wait until dusk, you'll feel braver about checking out less-secluded Dumpsters.

• Bring boxes.

• The buddy system is a good idea for women divers.

• Once we saw the actual food in impermeable packaging, we were more receptive to it than we thought we would be. However, we left behind the food in cardboard packaging.

I doubt, despite our success, that I will make Dumpster-diving a regular part of my life, simply because it is such a long drive from our country home to the nearest Dumpster. Hoffman suggests—and I agree—that diving works best when it's incorporated into an urban or suburban lifestyle. He checks his six favorite Dumpsters each day as part of his commute home from work.

If you are willing to sift through Hoffman's offensive language and opinions to glean the finer points of Dumpster diving, you can get his book by sending $12.95 plus $4.00 shipping and handling to:

Loompanics Unlimited
P.O. Box 1197
Port Townsend, WA 98368

With each book order, Loompanics sends a copy of its catalog of offbeat, dishonest, weird, and sometimes useful books.

DARE TO DUMPSTER DIVE UPDATE

My "Dare to Dumpster Dive" article attracted a spirited and generally positive response from readers. A listing of readers' great finds alone would fill a page. Even so, enough concerns were raised that I decided to lift the lid on this subject and rummage around a second time.

If you feel Dumpster diving goes too far, consider this scenario: You take your trash bags to your apartment building's Dumpster. As you make your deposit, you spot a $20 bill within easy reach. Do you take it?

This question illustrates an important point. Dumpster diving encompasses a range of activities. At the most cautious end, you can quickly check the contents of your apartment building's Dumpster whenever you dump your trash, and if you see some item that's right at hand, clean and useful, you snatch it. At the most daring end, you can rummage through dozens of Dumpsters nightly, taking whatever treasures, including food, they hold. And there are infinite gradations between those two.

Dumpster diving isn't a viable option for me because I live in a rural area. If it were, I would not approach it as aggressively as some, but I respect the hard-core divers. By helping to conserve natural resources, as well as tax dollars to pay for landfills, I figure they're doing the rest of us a service.

At the same time, I feel we should respect the views of others who feel diving isn't socially acceptable. Some divers are becoming bolder about rummaging in Dumpsters in daylight or in visible areas. Although I don't feel diving is shameful, we should consider the discomfort other people may feel. Dumpster dive discreetly.

Several readers expressed concern about the legality of Dumpster diving. My original article pointed out that the police departments of several towns in Maine told me that there was no law against it. I've called several more law-enforcement officials since then. These sources confirmed that Dumpster diving is generally considered to be legal, with the following exceptions:

• If the container is on *clearly marked* private land, behind a fence, or locked up. However, most Dumpsters in "semipublic" areas such as parking lots are fair game.

• If the discarded items are outside the Dumpster, they should not be taken.

Dear Amy, Your Dumpster article changed my life...

• If you make a mess. Leave a Dumpster site cleaner than you found it.

One of the public officials with whom we spoke is Michael Adams, deputy district attorney for California's Santa Clara County. Because, by some estimates, there are hundreds of Dumpster divers mining the rich veins of discards behind the Silicon Valley high-tech firms, Adams has made a careful study of the legality of Dumpster diving.

"People have thrown this stuff away," he said. "The idea that people are stealing is not a prosecutable case." He said that by putting items in a Dumpster, the companies have "abandoned ownership."

Adams doubts that any municipality anywhere in the country could craft a law that specifically banned Dumpster diving under all circumstances. Nevertheless, four readers reported they knew of such towns.

A couple of readers brought up sanitation issues. Yet in some modern landfills, there are people who stand at a conveyor belt picking the recyclables from trash all day. If there really were a serious health risk, it wouldn't be allowed. If, as we did, you wear gloves and wash your finds immediately upon returning home, I feel you face less of a health risk than you would riding a crowded subway car during flu season.

Some readers questioned my confidence in foods with impermeable packaging. To learn more about the safety of packaged food, we called the National Food Processors Association in Washington, D.C., Spokesman Roger Coleman confirmed that although such things as broken glass, mold, and contaminants can collect under the rim of a jar, they can't get through a vacuum seal. He added that a dented or rusty can is safe as long as the can doesn't leak or bulge. As for the possibility that recalled food could end up in a Dumpster, Coleman said that supermarkets are extremely careful to return recalled items to the manufacturer.

Then why do businesses throw away good stuff? Frequently, it's because the labor costs to fix, reuse, or even give it away are too high. One former supermarket employee told me it was illegal for stores to sell canned goods with missing labels. His store tried to give these unlabeled cans to food banks, but none wanted them. It can also be illegal to sell goods with dampened labels (as happens when one jar in a case breaks). To prevent pilferage, many businesses prohibit employees from taking home good but unsaleable items.

There were also suggestions that the act of Dumpster diving itself is unsafe. Safety issues were among the reasons I promoted *The Art and Science of Dumpster Diving;* the book takes pains to discuss how to avoid hazards. I would rate Dumpster diving as less dangerous than using a circular saw. The key is simply to learn safety rules and apply them.

Finally, I'd emphasize that if I published only information that *no one* could find objectionable, this would be a very boring—and short—book. Our foray into Dumpster diving was a reflection of the fact that a wide range of people read my book and newsletter, and I need to provide information to readers who are willing to stretch the boundaries of the frugal life.

GREAT QUOTES

"Much ingenuity with a little money is vastly more profitable and amusing than much money without ingenuity."

—Arnold Bennett

"Those who have little, if they are good at managing, must be counted among the rich."

—Socrates 470–399 B.C.

"Beware of little expenses; a small leak will sink a great ship."

—Benjamin Franklin

WHIP UP A WALKWAY

Dear Amy,

In Seattle, the price for a single, round aggregate stepping stone ranged from $4.59 to $5.99. Since I needed five, I felt this was highway robbery. So I took a large bucket that is slightly wider at the top (5-gallon paint or joint-compound buckets work well). Buy one bag of concrete for $1.69 (total cost of the project). Mix the concrete right in the bucket to a 2-inch level. Let set for a couple of hours, but while still wet, press in aggregate stone if desired, or imprint a design (I used my children's footprints). Mist frequently with a water sprayer to keep the concrete from cracking. After two to three days, turn the stone out gently onto soft ground, so as not to break it.

—Marilee Thompson Duer
  Mercer Island, Washington

BASKET CASE

Dear Amy,

When we moved from Massachusetts to Pennsylvania, we needed to bring our cats with us. Large plastic cat carriers in pet stores cost $40 to $60. They're nice, but seemed like a lot of money, especially if you need two.

I made a carrier of similar size by buying two large plastic laundry baskets. I flipped one basket over the other and used two bolts to fasten them together in the back. Then I tied them together securely in the front. The baskets could be separated and used for laundry after you reach your destination.

—James DeHulu
Edgewood, Pennsylvania

SEE SPOT GO

Dear Amy,

There is an easy way to remove stains off of white or lightly colored parts of a garment, where stains are always prominent. I've had great success renovating hand-me-downs and yard-sale finds for my toddler. It works great on garments that have bright patterns that would fade if I soaked or bleached the whole thing. Pour a little liquid bleach into the bottle's cap. With a Q-tip or paintbrush, dab a bit of the bleach on the soiled area. Within a minute, most stains are gone. Wash as usual. Use more bleach and leave on longer for stubborn stains.

—Rachelle Purcell
Peru, Indiana

(Based on my own tests and advice from experienced launderers, I would add that 1) be sure to rinse the bleach out immediately after the stain disappears, or holes can develop after a few washings, and 2) straight bleach can remove color from some fabrics. So reserve this tip for otherwise hopeless stains. FZ)

DISPOSAL AND PROPOSAL

Dear Amy,

What attracted my now-husband to me, and me to him, was that we always made use of what we had, or what was readily available. His first encounter with me and my junk picking was my ceiling fan, which he and I installed in my bedroom. When he asked where I bought it, I honestly told him that I found it down in the alley on garbage day. He then proposed.

—Jamie Bunch Elliott
Brinnon, Washington

I DREAM OF JEAN-KNEE

Dear Amy,

When I want a little more use out of old work jeans, instead of having to rip open and sew up seams, I just get my glue gun out and glue the patch on. My husband is a welder, and his overalls are expensive.

—Penny Oberlander
  Eagle Point, Oregon

HOLE-ISTIC REMEDY

Dear Amy,
   I think I have discovered the ultimate in shower curtain solutions! I had one that lasted 17 years, and I finally got rid of it because it was so totally out of style. I don't repair; I prevent damage. When a shower curtain is new, I sew a strip of appropriate-colored heavy cotton duck cloth over the top 1½ inches of the curtain (folding the cloth over both sides of the curtain) and make buttonholes at the hanger holes. I have never had a hole tear. I am the mother of seven children, so this has been tested.

—Lynn Davis
  Escondido, California

NO-MEAT FEAT

Dear Amy,
   Here is a recipe you might enjoy. Even my husband, a die-hard meat eater, asks for more:

LENTIL-RICE CASSEROLE

3 cups chicken broth, or use water
    and 1 tablespoon vegetable
    seasoning
¾ cup lentils, uncooked
½ cup brown rice, uncooked
¾ cup chopped fresh onion
½ teaspoon sweet basil
¼ teaspoon oregano
¼ teaspoon thyme
¼ teaspoon garlic powder

Blend all together in a casserole dish. Bake, covered, for 1½ hours at 300 degrees. During the last 20 minutes, you may top with ½ cup grated cheddar cheese, if desired.

—Christina Parli
  Springfield, Ohio

(We tried this recipe, and Jim rated it a "9" on the 1-to-10 lentil scale. Because of the lengthy cooking time, plan to bake other items at the same time or use your solar cooker or crockpot. FZ)

BEATS A DEAD MOUSE

Dear Amy,
   My brother and I have the perfect cheap—oops, I mean thrifty—cat toy. Place any object that will rattle (paper clip, pen top, etc.) into an empty 35-millimeter film canister. My cat Martha loves hers, although several have mysteriously disappeared beneath the entertainment center.

—Michelle Stanton
  Medina, New York

CHEAT SHEETS

Dear Amy,
   When it's time to change the sheets on the beds, if I changed them the week before, I just turn them around so the unused end is now at the top of the bed. It works well on the beds of children who aren't tall enough to touch the bottom portion of the sheets.

—Shelbey Dutter
  Kalispell, Montana

THE CHILI CHART

It's always interesting to examine how widely the costs can vary when you purchase or prepare a particular dish in different ways— in this case, chili. Whenever I do one of these charts, I'm reminded of how there can be such a huge difference in the food bills of two families who eat almost identical meals.

Using the same basic recipe, we costed out several versions. We calculated it using the most expensive ingredients we could find at the supermarket, including canned kidney beans. We also used the cheapest store-bought ingredients, and substituted 2½ cups of cooked dry kidney beans for the 40 ounces of canned beans. We substituted rehydrated TVP (see page 133) for the hamburger. We calculated another version made with TVP and homegrown ingredients (peppers, onions, tomatoes, and dried beans).

Here's the recipe we used:

HOMEMADE CHILI

1 tablespoon oil
1 cup chopped onions
1 cup chopped green pepper
1 pound hamburger
1 40-ounce can kidney beans
1 28-ounce can tomatoes
1 6-ounce can tomato paste
1 tablespoon chili powder

Heat oil in a large skillet. Brown onions and peppers. Add hamburger and brown well. Add beans, tomatoes, tomato paste, and chili powder. Add ¾ cup water and simmer, covered, for one hour.

Some observations:

• If you spend an hour making 12 cups of homemade, dry-bean, hamburger chili and packaging it in meal-size freezer containers, versus buying microwaveable chili, even if you factor in energy usage, you will earn $10 per hour, tax-free, for your time.

• Hormel's microwave chili in individual-serving containers is so expensive that it's cheaper to buy chili from Wendy's.

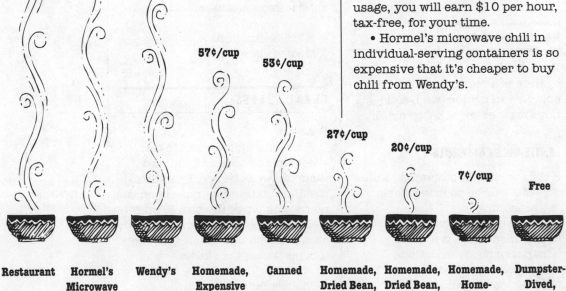

Restaurant	Hormel's Microwave	Wendy's	Homemade, Expensive	Canned	Homemade, Dried Bean, Hamburger	Homemade, Dried Bean, TVP	Homemade, Home-grown, TVP	Dumpster-Dived, Canned
$1.66/cup	$1.07/cup	99¢/cup	57¢/cup	53¢/cup	27¢/cup	20¢/cup	7¢/cup	Free

• Making homemade chili from the most expensive store-bought ingredients is more expensive than buying canned chili.

• It's worth your time to cook up dried beans. A store-brand, 40-ounce can of cooked kidney beans costs $1.15. The same amount of beans cooked up from dry costs 25¢, based on 42¢-per-pound beans at a wholesale club. It takes about 5 minutes of hands-on time and 30 minutes of cooking to prepare beans in a pressure cooker.

• Having a garden is not essential to making huge savings on your food bill. Compared to microwave chili, you save 87¢ per cup by making scratch chili with the cheapest store-bought ingredients. You save only 13¢ more per cup by using homegrown ingredients.

• If you use a coupon to buy store-bought chili, the final cost should be less than 3¢ per ounce, as compared to hamburger chili made with dried beans, and less than 1¢ per ounce as compared to hamburger chili with homegrown ingredients.

"ARE BREAD MACHINES A GOOD VALUE?"

This question was posed by reader Heidee Lindsey of Fremont, California, and it's a good one to explore. My mail tells me that many beginning tightwads are buying or considering the purchase of these gadgets, propelled by a vague notion that "it will pay for itself."

People think this because they know homemade bread is cheaper, but they think the traditional, hand-kneaded bread is too time-consuming to be worthwhile. Because it takes five minutes to make bread using a bread machine, people presume it's a money-saving device.

To research this question, my crack investigative staff mooched machines from acquaintances, girlfriends, and brothers-in-law (you didn't think we'd *buy* one, did you?) and put them through a grueling series of trials. Bread machines cost between $99 and $199. *Consumer Reports* recommends the Sanyo Home Bakery, which costs $140, so we used that cost as the basis for payback calculations.

Before we go any further, let's talk about the positive aspects of bread machines:

• You make one loaf at a time, so you can have freshly baked bread every day.

• Bread machines make bread that tastes better than store-bought—although our staff unanimously agreed that this bread is not as good as traditional homemade bread.

• Bread machines require no exertion, which is important if you have physical limitations.

• You don't have to be home while your bread is baking; you can put in the ingredients, set the timer, and the machine will mix, knead, and bake, and shut off automatically.

In short, if you demand fresh, homemade bread every day, and cannot or won't make it yourself, a machine could be a worthwhile luxury.

But if you're buying a bread machine to save time or money, think again. Our calculations show it's doubtful a bread machine will accomplish either of these goals.

THE MACHINE VERSUS TRADITIONAL HOME-BAKING METHODS

Let's look first at time savings. It takes five minutes to load ingredients into a bread machine and push the appropriate buttons to make a single loaf.

In contrast, when using the hand-knead method, you can bake four loaves at a time. Although you must be around for a few hours as the bread rises and bakes, the actual amount of hands-on time required, based on our careful timing of three cooks of average ability, is 25 minutes for four loaves, or 6 minutes, fifteen seconds per loaf.

However, a bread bucket, which features a hand-cranked dough hook, will save some time. We

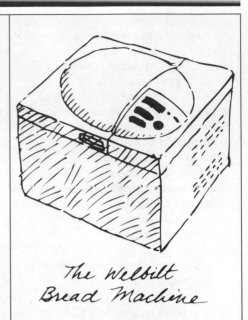

The Welbilt Bread Machine

timed three breadmakers using a bucket. Each was able to make four loaves with 20 minutes hands-on time—or the same 5 minutes per loaf required by bread machines.

Although it does take some muscle, one bread-bucket user I know is in her fifties, another is under 5 feet tall, and they have no trouble. (Think of it as a tightwad exercise machine: If you have a hard time doing this, you *need* the exercise.) Because these buckets last for decades, you should be able to dig up a used one. Of the five bucket users I know, four procured theirs secondhand. The average yard-sale price is about $3. New buckets cost from $20 to $45.

Aside from time saving,

the bucket method is neater than hand kneading.

You can make bread in a food processor, one loaf at a time, and this would take five minutes per loaf. Or you can buy frozen dough, which requires one minute per loaf of hands-on time.

So, if you have a freezer to store extra loaves and have reasonable physical capabilities, a bread machine doesn't save time.

Does it save money? The same ingredients are used however you make bread, so the only possible savings would be in energy usage.

Including preheating, an oven will run for an hour to bake four loaves of bread. At 8¢ per kilowatt-hour, it costs 16¢ to run an oven at 350 degrees for one hour, or 4¢ per loaf.

Finding out how much energy bread machines use proved to be extremely difficult. The machines come with wattage information, but they run intermittently during the cycle. We called all of the manufacturers, and none would tell us the cost of running their machines. We called Underwriter's Laboratories, which among other things, tests products for energy usage. The UL representative was not allowed to give us this information and suggested we call the manufacturers. Finally, one of my staffers ran the machine, carefully noting every time the machine went on and off during the cycle, and computed the energy usage as about 3¢ per cycle. This figure is the same as I have read in other sources.

So using a bread machine may save you 1¢ per loaf over other methods of home baking. If you have a gas oven, it won't save anything.

THE MACHINE VERSUS THE STORE

Let's suppose you'll make bread only if you have a bread machine. Compared to store-bought bread, will a machine pay for itself?

Most store-bought bread weighs 19 to 22 ounces. Frozen dough makes 14-ounce loaves. Bread machines vary in the size loaf they make. Most bread recipes make two 1½-pound loaves. Because of this variation, we calculated the figures based on an "ideal" loaf of 1½ pounds and added in energy cost where applicable. The homemade and bread-machine prices are based on

The Yard Sale Bread Bucket

sale-priced ingredients. We used bulk yeast from a health-food store, which costs $2.00 per pound. If you use those little packets of yeast, figure another 15¢ per loaf. All the prices are for a whole-wheat loaf, which contains two thirds white flour and one third whole-wheat flour.

Supermarket	$1.49
Wholesale club	$1.46
Frozen dough	$ .68
Thrift store	$ .57
Homemade	$ .27
Bread machine	$ .26

Bakery thrift shops are common throughout the country. Without making a special trip, or perhaps by cooperating with friends, most people can buy day-old bread and keep it in their freezer.

So if a bread-machine loaf saves you 31¢ over a thrift-shop loaf, you would have to bake 451 loaves to pay back the cost of the machine. At four loaves a week, the machine would pay for itself in a little more than two years.

We wondered how long bread machines last, since they're fairly new devices, they have a lot of moving parts, and there's competition to bring the price down. Of the four companies we called, three wouldn't say how long their machines would last. Welbilt said its machine would last from four and a half to nine years, based on making four or five loaves a week. So although a bread machine might last long enough to pay for itself, it isn't a once-in-a-lifetime purchase.

Getting repairs and replacement parts for bread machines may be tricky; I know of two dead machines. In one case, the needed replacement part is no longer available. A second machine lies dormant because the owner decided the cost of getting his repaired was too high.

A further disadvantage of the bread machine is that it eats up a square foot of precious counter space. In contrast, a bread bucket stores easily in a cupboard.

IN CONCLUSION

As long as you have no physical limitations, a bread machine isn't a true time- or money-saver. Those people who want homemade bread should use traditional methods. With a little planning, traditional bread-making can fit into a busy life as easily as the bread-machine method.

Finally, making bread by any method is not essential to the tightwad lifestyle. Our bakery thrift shop is conveniently located near our printer, and we buy 15 loaves at a time. If we made bread, we would spend five minutes to save 30¢, which is like earning $3.60 per hour. In addition, our family consumes homemade bread at a significantly faster rate than storebought—11 loaves versus 7 loaves a week—so it's hard to keep up. We make bread when we can, but when life gets hectic, it's among the money-saving activities we skip.

By the way, for those really lazy folks out there, you can now buy gourmet bread-machine mixes. A mix that makes one 1½-pound loaf costs between $3.50 and $4.95.

WOODEN REINCARNATIONS

Wood is great stuff. Compared to concrete, metal, and glass, it is easy to reuse. Somehow, it's deeply fulfilling to disassemble some hideous and/or no-longer-needed wooden item and create just the thing you need.

Sources are everywhere. Frequently people discard or give

away something because they no longer need it in its original form. We scavenge wooden things because they are a resource—like the 42-inch-square frame for a dog bed, which we made into a seedling table.

Hammers alone aren't enough for most disassembly operations. But if you get a flatbar . . .

and a cat's paw . . .

you can take apart nearly anything. Wood is like wrapping paper: It gets smaller with each incarnation.

The examples on this page are taken from real life.

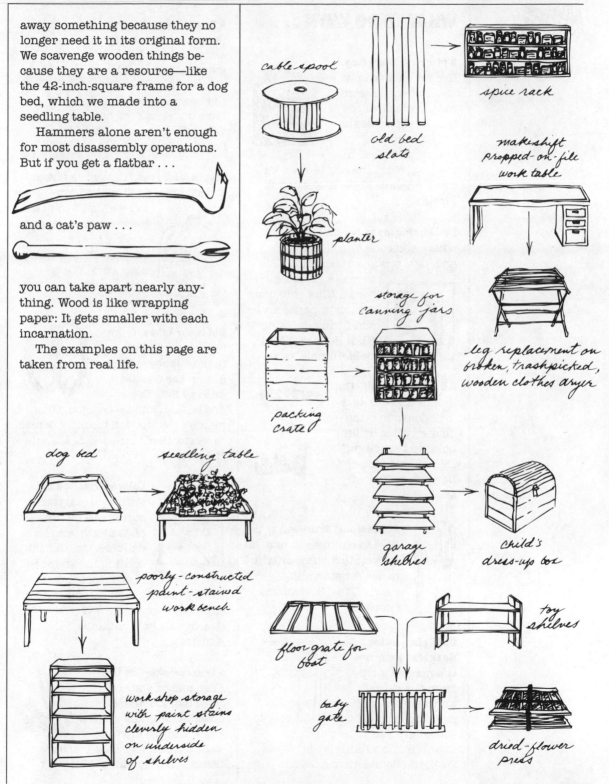

cable spool

old bed slats

spice rack

makeshift propped-on-file work table

planter

storage for canning jars

packing crate

leg replacement on broken, trashpicked, wooden clothes dryer

dog bed

seedling table

garage shelves

child's dress-up box

poorly-constructed paint-stained work bench

workshop storage with paint stains cleverly hidden on underside of shelves

floor grate for boat

toy shelves

baby gate

dried-flower press

WHAT TO DO WITH . . .

A Plastic Grocery Bag.
Use for a salad spin-
ner. Put a dish towel
in the bottom of the
bag. Shake loose the
water from the
greens and place in
the bag. Whirl the bag ten revolu-
tions. (George Silvera, Springhill,
Florida.)

Bad Photographs . . . the ones
where someone had closed eyes
and/or a strange expression. Use
to make all-occasion
cards. Glue onto con-
struction paper and
add funny captions.
(Gail Bedard, Wood
Dale, Illinois.)

A Dead Volleyball. Cut
in half and use as a
drill guard to catch
plaster when drilling
holes in the ceiling.
(Maxel and Stacey
Newberry, Ithaca,
Michigan.)

Old Compact Brushes.
Give to children to use
for paintbrushes, or trim
to use for stenciling.
(Carol Case, Statesboro,
Georgia.)

**Old Refrigerator
Gaskets.** Remove
the magnet strip
from the gasket,
and save for craft
projects. Snip off
the length you
need. (Sharon Dahlmeyer,
Durham, Connecticut.)

A Dead Umbrella. Use
to make a poncho for
a small child. Re-
move all the metal
pieces. Cut a hole for
the head. If you don't
have a waterproof hat, add a
hood. (Karen Schneider-Chen,
Seattle, Washington.)

Plastic Milk Jugs. Cut circles from
the side panels to make hamburger disks to place
between patties when
storing in the
freezer. Plastic lids
also work. (Ginger
Player, Williston, Ver-
mont.)

Old Inner Tubes from
bike tires. Use to
make rubber stamps.
Slit up the middle
and lay flat. Draw
and cut out simple designs. Glue
pieces onto wooden blocks. (Denise
Augusto, Shelburne Falls, Massachusetts.)

Colored Plastic Bags,
such as department-
store bags or the
bags newspapers are
delivered in. Cut into
continuous strips to
make ribbons to
wrap presents. You can pull the
edges to create a ruffled effect.
(Norma Kelly, Huntsville,
Alabama.)

A Frozen-Juice-Can Lid.
Keep one in your bi-
cycle tool kit. Use to
place under your
kickstand when you
want to park in a sandy area.
(Fran Misterly, Citra, Florida.)

IF YOU DREAD IT, SHRED IT

Around August each year, your garden begins to crank out more zucchinis than you can eat, and friends stop answering the door when they see you staggering up the walkway with a double arm-load. Eventually, as you fall further behind in production, the zucchinis grow to baseball-bat proportions, with tough skins and huge seeds. The dilemma is worsened because your garden is producing so much *other* fresh produce that you can barely keep up with the hoeing and canning.

baseball bat

monster zucchini

I handle this problem by waiting until I have a pile of these overgrown zucchinis. I get out my food processor and start slicing, shredding, and filling Ziploc bags. These bags go into the freezer to be saved for baking during the more tranquil winter months.

When shredded zucchini thaws, it is very watery. If the recipe calls for milk, I frequently combine this juice with dry milk powder and use it for the milk in the recipe.

Shredded zucchini (as well as shredded yellow summer squash) gives a wide variety of baked goods more moisture, fiber, and nutrition. I use it in muffins (zucchini-pineapple or zucchini-raisin), brownies, pancakes, and quick breads. Shredded zucchini is interchangeable with common baking ingredients like pumpkin purée, applesauce, mashed bananas, or shredded carrots. Because zucchini has little flavor, I usually add spices like cinnamon, nutmeg, and dried orange peel, or combine it with a more flavorful fruit or vegetable. A recent experiment, a zucchini-blackberry crisp, was extremely successful.

WALLPAPER SOLUTION

Personally, I like white walls. They are classic, go with everything, and paint stores don't have to custom-mix the color.

But some people love the look of wallpaper. For them, here's an idea from reader Sara Brown of Longview, Washington. She makes incredibly cheap wallpaper that isn't wallpaper at all.

For a floral effect, paint a wall a base color in latex paint. Then take about 1 cup of that base color and add a small amount of another color—for example, add a little white to a blue base color to make a light blue. Add water to thin down the light blue. Then wet the feathers of a cheap feather duster, shake it out, and dip it in the tinted color. Practice on some cardboard first, then touch the wall in a random pattern (not rows) to make a floral pattern.

You can mix in other colors. As long as you begin by mixing with the base colors, they will go together. Other objects can be used as "daubers" to create different effects: crumpled newspapers, sponges, bristle brushes, and broom ends. For kids' rooms, use handprints, or cut sponges into shapes and "rubber-stamp" the walls.

Sara's technique has clear financial advantages. Wallpapering a 12-foot-by-15-foot room costs about $18 for the sizing (stuff that's painted on to make the walls receptive to the paper) and $107 (at discount prices) for the required six double rolls of wallpaper, for a total of $125. In contrast, primer and top-quality paint to do the same-size room, including enough extra paint for this wallpaper-look technique, at a cost of less than $35.

A further advantage is that Sara's technique can be done solo by anyone who can wield a paintbrush. A quality wallpapering job is extremely fussy. A friend told me he and his wife nearly got divorced after they attempted to paper a bathroom and argued about the acceptable tolerances for error. If one factors in the savings in avoiding divorce proceedings, this technique could be worth thousands of dollars.

A DEAL TO DYE FOR

Dear Amy,

Here's a "tightwad" way of getting the most out of prescription glasses.

I have to wear mine all the time, and sometimes I just *want* new frames. When this happens, I take my old glasses to the optical shop and ask them to dye the glass dark so I can wear them for sunglasses. It costs about $10.

—Paulette Fordan
Ellensburg, Washington

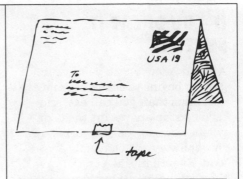

RETURN TO SPENDER

Dear Amy,

I used to send stamped, self-addressed envelopes (5¢? plus 29¢) when I requested responses. That meant sending a letter, too (4¢?), in an envelope (5¢? plus 29¢). Double postcards (sold by the post office) cost 38¢, a savings of 34¢ round trip, not to mention the amount of paper saved. You can make your own double postcards too, out of card stock and two 19¢ stamps.

—Malcolm Wells
Brewster, Massachusetts

(Double postcards look like two regular post office postcards that are attached at the top. To reuse, the recipient simply tears off the used side or flips the used side from the outside to the inside. FZ)

TAP TIP

Dear Amy,

I was medically advised to drink lots of water but grew weary of the chlorine taste from our tap water. I bought bottled water and investigated water filters.

Then I remembered what I read in an aquarium guidebook. I filled two jugs with tap water and didn't

cork them. The chlorine evapo-
rates out, and after two days I had
tasty water. This method has
served us well for two years now.

—Edgar and Denise Isaacs
  Pittsville, Maryland

A FRUGAL LESS-ON

Dear Amy,

I find frugal ideas pop up in the
strangest places. For instance, I
was in the park, walking the dog,
when I spotted a tiny yellow scrap
of paper saying "Less is more." I
took the paper home and propped
it in the kitchen alcove, and the
cogs in my brain started whirring.
This is what I came up with:

LESS junk food, MORE nutrients.
LESS car trips, MORE exercise.
LESS sweets, MORE weight loss.
LESS possessions, MORE space.
LESS self-pity, MORE happiness.
LESS presents, MORE appreciation.
LESS waste, MORE conservation.
LESS TV, MORE conversation.

I have since learned that the
"Less is more" card comes from a
packet of low-tar cigarettes. Less
tar is more flavor. So the mystery
of the inspiring card is solved.

—Mrs. M. Lockyer
  Camberley, Surry, England

NO COVER CHARGE

Dear Amy,

My sister made seat covers for
her Volkswagen bug from old
Levis that she bought at the thrift
store. These wear like iron and
haven't been replaced in ten
years. With a little creativity she
added pockets for sunglasses, etc.

—Erin Quinn
  Las Vegas, Nevada

NO-TOIL OIL

Dear Amy,

Most of us pitch the plastic bottle after putting oil in our car, but
did you ever think about the oil
left over in the bottle or can?

I saved 45 oil bottles until I
made a "dripper." Out of 45 bottles, I got ¾ of a quart. Based on
this I calculate 60 containers
would give you a quart.

That's a lot of oil when you consider it frequently ends up in the
water table.

Here's how to make a dripper:

Drill one ⅝ inch hole in a
garage stud on an angle. Drill four
or five one inch holes in a 1 ½ inch
pipe. Place the pipe in the stud
with the holes up, and put a screw
through the stud until it snugs the
pipe. You're all set.

—John T. Cant
  Blauvelt, New York

SAVINGS ON DISPLAY

Dear Amy,

Many stores, especially pharmacies, get many product displays every year, only to throw away later. I have a Dr. Scholl's rack for my LP's. A four-foot-tall Scotch tape rack is now an office basket. A brass and wood display holds my houseplants. I am hoping to bring home a bamboo-looking Hawaiian Tropic suntan lotion display to use for kids' books, stuffed animals, or an open dresser.

—Venus Weir
   Albuquerque, New Mexico

PITCH AND SWITCH

Dear Amy,

We needed a picture framed. To get it matted and framed at a local framing store would have cost nearly $100. One day I was in a discount department store and they were selling matted/framed posters for $15.99. This was exactly the size I needed for my picture, so I swapped the poster for my picture and got exactly what I wanted for $15.99.

—Ruth Campbell
   Rockaway, New Jersey

PINCH SITTER

Dear Amy,

A few years ago I joined a baby-sitting co-op. Participating parents were initially given 30 coupons (printed by one of our members). A coupon was worth one hour of child care, and this was how we paid each other. We used the co-op

to grocery shop, clean house, or have an evening out. Members were free to specify if they wanted to baby-sit during the daytime, evening, or weekends. One could always say "no" on an occasion that wasn't convenient. Our once-in-a-while meeting allowed us to meet new neighbors and keep up with how many coupons members had accumulated.

—Patty Kimmel
   Clarksville, Tennessee

CHEAP AND DIRTY

Dear Amy,

I needed some dirt to fill a hole in my yard. I thought: Where can I find some free? Who takes out dirt and can't put it back? Of course, the cemetery. They were glad to let me have all I wanted—free!

—Bill French
   Muscatine, Iowa

YOU DON'T HAVE TO BE A SOCKET SCIENTIST

GreenPlug sounds too good to be true. Plug this gadget, which is about the size of a pack of cards, into your wall socket. Then plug an appliance into it, and bingo: Your appliance works as well as it ever did, but it uses less power. As a bonus, says the company's literature, your appliance will last longer.

I was skeptical—at $35 (the local hardware store's price), would it pay for itself?

I'm no socket scientist, so we called Bill Howe. He is a researcher at E-Source, an independent energy-efficiency information service in Boulder, Colorado. Howe has done extensive tests on Green-Plug, and was generally positive about it. "It is a viable approach," he said.

GreenPlug saves energy two ways. First, if you receive high voltage in your home, GreenPlug reduces it to the minimum needed to run your appliance. Second, GreenPlug varies the amount of power it sends to your appliance's motor, depending on the load the motor is handling.

Howe says the payback time on a GreenPlug varies from 1 to 12 or more years. You're most likely to have a short payback time if all of the following apply to you:

1. You have high voltage. The voltage delivered to homes varies around the country from about 104 to over 130 volts. GreenPlug drops this to 106 volts, which is sufficient for all appliances.

Your utility company can give a ballpark estimate of your voltage. Or you can use a voltmeter (all electronics-repair people have them). If you live in a rural area, it's likely that you have high voltage, because utilities boost the power to send it down long, rural lines.

We interviewed several experts to determine whether running a refrigerator at 106 volts would prematurely wear out the motor. Opinion varied. A couple thought it might, most did not know, and several said it would be extremely unlikely.

2. Your utility rates are high. The national average is 8¢ per kilowatt-hour.

3. You use it on a constantly running, energy-*in*efficient appliance.

Generally, 1978 to 1985 refrigerators are the best bet. If yours is older, you will probably do better in the long run if you buy a new one.

One of the worst criticisms leveled at GreenPlug came in a November 1993 *Consumer Reports* article, which asserted that in some cases Green-Plug could make your refrigerator use *more* energy. But in my conversations with the makers of Green-Plug and with representatives of several utilities that had tested it, I learned that the device tends to make a refrigerator run a bit colder, and you don't realize energy savings unless you adjust the thermostat to bring the refrigerator back to its original temperature. I called *CR*'s researcher, Ed Growth, and learned that *CR* had not adjusted the thermostat, which makes its conclusions suspect.

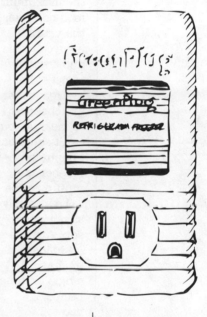

The maker claims that Green-Plug will help many motors run cooler and thus prolong an appliance's life. Though Howe hasn't done long-term testing, he believes that claim could well be true.

Using his voltmeter, my handyman husband, Jim, determined that our household receives 121 volts. That, plus the facts that we pay 12¢ per kilowatt-hour and have a 1982 refrigerator, has persuaded us to get one of these devices.

CREATE A BREAKFAST MUFFIN

As you read *The Tightwad Gazette,* you may notice that I don't print many recipes. Running recipes would be the easy (that is, lazy) way to fill the book, but blindly following recipes won't help you save the maximum amount on your food bill. Over the years, I have collected and created recipes that use foods that are cheapest to me, but you can't count on my pumpkin-blueberry muffin recipe to be a money-saver in Tucson, Arizona.

So instead of sharing a single muffin recipe, I wanted to

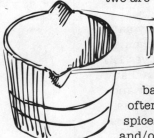

share the process of *creating* muffin recipes. This will allow you to use ingredients that are cheap in your part of the country, use up odd leftovers, and accommodate dietary restrictions.

So I made a big chart to compare the various components in 30 muffin recipes. Although no two are the same, the recipes all combine a grain, milk or juice, egg, a fat, a sweetener, baking powder, and salt. These basic ingredients are often combined with spices, fruits, vegetables, and/or nuts.

I studied these elements, came up with a formula, and made numerous batches over a period of weeks to make sure it worked. Now I've memorized the formula. I no longer need to refer to a recipe to make any kind of muffins, which saves me time.

The quantities listed are for a single batch of 12 muffins. To save energy and time, I always make a double batch. If your oven is large enough to allow ample air circulation, the tins can be placed side by side. If you have a small oven, place tins one over the other, and swap positions after ten minutes of baking.

To make muffins, combine dry ingredients, and then mix in wet ingredients until just combined; the batter should be lumpy. Grease muffin tin and fill cups two thirds full. Bake in a preheated oven at 400 degrees for 20 minutes (give or take 5 minutes).

The following ingredients are required:

Grain: Use 2 to 2½ cups of white flour. Or substitute oatmeal, cornmeal, whole-wheat flour, rye flour, or flake cereal for 1 cup of the white flour. Or substitute 1 cup leftover cooked oatmeal, rice, or cornmeal for ½ cup of the white flour and decrease liquid to ½ cup.

Milk: Use 1 cup. Or substitute buttermilk or sour milk (add a tablespoon of vinegar to 1 cup milk). Or substitute fruit juice for part or all of the milk.

Fat: Use ¼ cup vegetable oil or 4 tablespoons melted butter or margarine. Or substitute crunchy or regular peanut butter for part or all of the fat. The fat can be reduced or omitted with fair results if using a "wet addition."

Egg: Use 1 egg. Or substitute 1 heaping tablespoon of soy flour and 1 tablespoon of water. If using a cooked grain, separate the egg, add the yolk to the batter, beat the white until stiff, and fold into the batter.

Sweetener: Use between 2 tablespoons and ½ cup sugar. Or substitute up to ¾ cup brown sugar. Or substitute up to ½ cup honey or molasses, and decrease milk to ¾ cup.

Baking Powder: Use 2 teaspoons. If using whole or cooked grains or more than 1 cup of additions, increase to 3 teaspoons. If using buttermilk or sour milk, decrease to 1 teaspoon and add ½ teaspoon baking soda.

Salt. Use ½ teaspoon, or omit if you have a salt-restricted diet.

The following ingredients are optional. Additions can be used in any combination, up to 1½ cups total. If using more than 1 cup of wet additions, decrease the milk to ½ cup:

Dry Additions: Nuts, sunflower seeds, raisins, coconut, and so on.

Moist Additions: Blueberries, chopped apple, freshly shredded zucchini, shredded carrot, and so on.

Wet Additions: Pumpkin purée; applesauce; mashed, cooked sweet potato; mashed banana; mashed, cooked carrot, and so on. If using ½ cup drained, canned fruit or thawed shredded zucchini, substitute the syrup or zucchini liquid for all or part of the milk.

Spices: Use spices that complement the additions, such as 1 teaspoon cinnamon with ¼ teaspoon nutmeg or cloves. Try 2 teaspoons grated orange or lemon peel.

Jellies and Jam. Fill cups half full with a plain batter. Add 1 teaspoon jam or jelly and top with 2 more tablespoons batter.

Topping: Sprinkle cinnamon sugar on the batter in the tins.

Nonsweet Combinations: Use only 2 tablespoons sugar and no fruit. Add combinations of the following: ½ cup shredded cheese, 3 strips fried-and-crumbled bacon, 2 tablespoons grated onion, ½ cup shredded zucchini, 2 tablespoons Parmesan cheese. Spices could in-

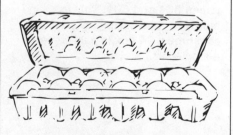

clude a teaspoon of parsley and a pinch of marjoram.

All this may seem a bit complicated to follow first thing in the morning. So, once you learn the possible variations, copy the following list of ingredients into your personal cookbook.

2 to 2½ cups grain
1 cup milk
Up to ¼ cup fat
1 egg
Up to ½ cup sweetener
2 teaspoons baking powder
½ teaspoon salt
Up to 1½ cups additions

Even including the "brain work" of creating a new recipe, I can get muffins in the oven in 20 minutes, and I take my shower while they're baking.

Muffins are a mainstay in our household; we eat them about twice a week. If made with nutritious ingredients and served with juice or milk, they make a hearty breakfast. Leftover muffins become snacks or are hoarded for future lunch boxes. Those who don't have six children can freeze the extra muffins for future breakfasts.

Though the cost varies depending upon the ingredients, I can make muffins for an average of about 4¢ each, including the cost of electricity to bake them. A breakfast of muffins costs our family between 50¢ and 60¢. This is a bargain, considering my tribe can consume a $4 box of cold cereal in a single sitting.

SAWDUST MEMORIES

Dear Amy,

Our neighbor had hired the tree company to cut down and mulch some trees. My husband asked the workers if they needed a place to dump the mulch (which they often do to go empty to the next job). They said, "Yes," and he had it dumped in our yard. We had enough to mulch our entire long driveway, and then some!

—Mimi Bock
  West Palm Beach, Florida

PICKUP TRICK

Dear Amy,

We live in a rural area, but our nearest neighbors are only about a mile away. We discovered that we each had only about one barrel of trash per week, so we decided to share a trash pick-up service, which is the same for two to three barrels. We take our barrels to their driveway, and both barrels are emptied there. This saves us $6 per month.

—Greta Goforth
  Loveland, Colorado

(To be completely ethical, I would check with the trash hauler to make sure this is okay. FZ)

ROLL REVERSAL

Dear Amy,

To use toilet paper for facial tissue, wrap the outside of the roll with wide tape and pull out the cardboard tube. Pull the tissue from the inside. I then put the roll inside a square, pop-up Kleenex box with the bottom cut out. Then pull the toilet paper through the slot. The box makes it look nicer than having a roll of toilet paper on the nightstand.

With toilet paper, you can take the exact amount you need: one, two, or more squares.

—Leanna Hawley
   Hales Corners, Wisconsin

THE GREAT LATE RATE

Dear Amy,

When going to the ballet, play, or symphony, buy "rush" tickets. These tickets are usually sold 15 minutes before the performance. In Atlanta, rush tickets are $5 for the ballet and $12 for the symphony. Normally, these tickets sell for $37.

—Walter Dowis
   Atlanta, Georgia

CHEAPER BY THE DOZER

Dear Amy,

Construction yards, brick companies, and lumber mills often have back areas where the public can pick through perfect-condition supplies and haul them away for next to nothing. I landscaped my entire yard with new brick costing from 10¢ each to nothing. Let people building those fancy new houses pay for your projects. The companies are glad to let you have their leftover materials in these days of rising dumping fees.

—Lindsay Amadeo
   Chanhassen, Minnesota

VOLUME DISCOUNT

Dear Amy,

Thinking about a set of encyclopedias for your children? Do not, I say do not, buy a brand-new set.

Five years ago, we bought a six-year-old set for $50 out of the newspaper. They were perfectly adequate as my sons went through their high-school years.

I'm selling them at my next garage sale for $35.

I have a friend who signed a $2,000 contract for a set at the same time I bought mine.

—Anne Husk
   Vista, California

LUMP IT AND LIKE IT

Dear Amy,

Since I sometimes need only ½ pound of ground turkey or two chicken legs, I don't freeze them in large, hard-to-divide lumps. I'll put the small amount of meat in the bottom of a bread bag, tie it off with a twist-tie, and then continue moving up the bag this way.

—Claudia Tomkiel
   Carlisle, Pennsylvania

(We do this. To avoid putting a long, greasy bag back into the freezer, we cut off each section as we need it. If using thin bags (for example, produce bags from the supermarket), double the bags to avoid freezer burn. FZ)

BE A SMART FISH

When Meg Downey of Boca Raton, Florida, sent me the following tip, it sparked an ethics debate among my staff. It's a perfect example of a type of ethics situation with which many people struggle.

"For a small fee (usually reimbursed) you can change telephone companies to take advantage of their generous offers. One month, I used Company A and got $35 in free calls (usually, you must sign up for at least two months). After 60 days, Company B offered the same deal, so I switched. Company C had a comparable offer, so I switched again after two months. All of the companies reimbursed me for the switch-over fees. I got $110 in free services over six months."

Based on letters from other readers concerning situations I have previously printed, I know many would think this is unethical. I don't, and here's why:

If you put a worm on a hook to try to catch a fish, would you think the fish was stealing if it snatched the bait without getting hooked?

Likewise, large businesses utilize highly sophisticated marketing strategies to separate you from your money. The companies (fishermen) know they will lose a small amount of money (bait) to a small percentage of savvy consumers (smart fish), but they are willing to take that loss because they will gain (hook) the business of a larger group of not-so-savvy consumers (stupid fish) in the long run. The small loss (a worm or two) is factored into their plan.

The success of such marketing is clearly evident just by looking at the stupid stuff most Americans buy. In fact, you could just as easily argue that it's unethical for businesses to utilize such sophisticated strategies to get your money.

I don't think smart marketing strategies *or* smart shopping strategies are unethical. I figure that's just part of free enterprise.

If a grocery store offers loss-leader sale items to lure you in, hoping that you'll spend lots of money on other products, it's ethical for you to buy the loss-leader items and nothing else.

If a time-share-condo company lures you to a sales pitch by offering a FREE CHEVY BLAZER, it's ethical for you to go, never intending to sign up for a condo, and accept the free jacket with the word *Chevy* printed on it. (This was a real offer.)

If a company offers you coupons, it's fair for you to combine these with sales and rebates to get free products and still not become a loyal customer.

Some readers have argued "What if everyone took advantage of the companies this way?" All successful businesses carefully monitor the profitability of their marketing strategies, and they withdraw any offers that lose money. As long as companies continue these offers, rest assured that they are still hooking customers.

So don't feel guilty about being a smart consumer. It helps to keep businesses more competitive and therefore to offer you lower prices in the end. And by taking advantage of the freebies that successfully lure naïve consumers, you may contribute to that company's withdrawing the offer, and consequently to sparing a few stupid fish from getting hooked.

NO STRINGS ATTACHED

Jim saw a television ad for a $9.95, solid-plastic replacement blade for a grass string-trimmer. The ad claimed it worked just as well as the string, but once you bought one of these you wouldn't have to buy the string anymore.

This commercial got Jim thinking, and he devised a way to make his own. He designed a plastic blade that could be cut from the lid of a plastic, 5-gallon bucket, the kind that holds paint or drywall joint compound.

Rotate the "tooth" shown at right around the bucket top, tracing around it each time with a felt-tip pen, until you have drawn a three-point star. It is easiest to cut out with a stationary jigsaw or band saw, but a hand-held saber saw also works well. If the lid has a natural curve or warp, cut the blade so that it curves up. Measure the spindle of your trimmer, and bore a hole exactly that size in the center of this star. Use two large-diameter washers (at least 1½ inches) to hold the star on the spindle.

As you use this, remember: This is *not* a string trimmer, which stings if it hits your leg. This thing will *cut* your leg.

But, on the plus side, Jim has used this to mow down brush that string could never conquer, including a patch of half-inch-thick raspberry canes.

This idea is particularly good to use on older trimmers, many of which are prone to hopeless string tangling. And string trimmers with broken or missing spools are dirt cheat at yard sales; this is an easy way to revive them. But note, this blade won't mount on trimmers with

trace this to make a pattern

cutting edge

nondetachable spools. Although we've found these blades won't break easily even if you whack them against a boulder, in time we did manage to break one. But it was no big deal. Jim can make a new blade in a couple of minutes.

MAIL TO THE CHEAP

When I asked readers to send me their favorite mail-order sources, I was skeptical. I have always believed that although there are some good deals through the mail, generally you can do better shopping locally if you wait for a sale.

By and large, I still feel that way, but after a great deal of research, we narrowed the field to just a few sources that we've determined really do offer good deals. Even so, you should still do local comparisons, because prices may vary in your area.

In some cases, we liked a source not because the prices were extremely cheap, but because it sold something unique.

BEDDING

Mother Hart's
P.O. Box 4229
Boynton Beach, FL 33424-4229
(407) 738-5866
Natural products for home and body.

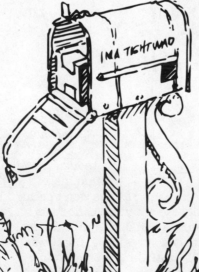

BOOKS

Christian Book Distributors
P.O. Box 6000
Peabody, MA 01961
(508) 977-5050
Twenty-five to 50 percent off Christian books and tapes.

Dover Publications
31 East 2nd St.
Mineola, NY 11501
(516) 294-7000
Amazing books and stuff for kids, like cut-and-assemble medieval castles.

Edward R. Hamilton Bookseller
Falls Village, CT 06031-5000
Discontinued books up to 90 percent off.

COMPUTER SOFTWARE

Reasonable Solutions
1221 Disk Dr.
Medford, OR 97501
(503) 776-5777
(800) 876-3475
"Shareware," inexpensive computer software.

HERBS AND SPICES

Let's Spice It Up, Inc.
P.O. Box 15
Highwood, IL 60040
(708) 433-6309 inside Illinois
(800) 659-6302 out-of-state
These prices beat my best local prices on herbs and spices by 25 percent.

HOSIERY

Legg's Brand Inc.
P.O. Box 748
Rural Hall, NC 27098
(919) 744-1790
(800) 522-1151
Fifty percent off name-brand hosiery.

POSTERS

Giant Photos, Inc.
P.O. Box 588
Rockford, IL 61105
(800) 826-2139
Posters and prints at reasonable prices.

RESTORATION SUPPLIES

Van Dyke's
P.O. Box 278
Woonsocket, SD 57385
(800) 843-3320
Hard-to-find parts for antique furniture restoration.

SCIENCE SUPPLIES

American Science & Surplus
3605 Howard St.
Skokie, IL 60076
(708) 982-0870
Optics, chemicals, science equipment—amazing stuff that makes great presents for older kids.

SEWING AND CRAFT SUPPLIES

Bee Lee Co.
P.O. Box 36108
Dallas, TX 75235
(214) 351-2091
(800) 527-5271

Kieffer's
P.O. Box 7500
Jersey City, NJ 07307
(201) 798-2266

TOOLS AND HARDWARE

Northern Hydraulics
P.O. Box 1499
Burnsville, MN 55337
(800) 533-5545

Constantine
2050 Eastchester Rd.
Bronx, NY 10461
(718) 792-1600
(800) 223-8087

Harbor Freight Tools
3491 Mission Oaks Blvd.
Camarillo, CA 93011
(800) 423-2567

VETERINARY SUPPLIES

UPCO
3705 Pear St.
St. Joseph, MO 64502
(816) 233-8809

R. C. Steele
P.O. Box 910
Brockport, NY 14420-0910
(800) 872-3773
Up to 50 percent savings, $50 minimum purchase.

WALLPAPER

American Blind and Wallpaper
28237 Orchard Lake Rd.
Farmington Hills, MI 48334-3765
(800) 735-5300

Silverwall Covering
3001-15 Kensington Ave.
Philadelphia, PA 19134
(800) 426-6600

Style Wall Coverings
P.O. Box 865
Southfield, MI 48037
(800) 627-0400

THE PANTRY PRINCIPLE

Generations of thrift writers have passed down certain "helpful household hints" for so long that they have become a sort of "Gospel According to June Cleaver." We hear them over and over and don't stop to wonder whether they really work.

Typical is the admonition to plan meal menus 30 days in advance and shop accordingly, never daring to veer from this carved-in-stone schedule. At the very least, we've been told, you should plan meals seven days in advance, working with what's on sale that week. You can even buy a computer program to prepare a shopping list based on your long-range meal plan.

Because I am the Grande Dame of Frugality and the World's Most Organized Human Being (read with tongue in cheek), people often assume that I plan meals days or weeks in advance. Wrong. In fact, planning meals far in advance is entirely backward. You should never decide first what you

WALLY, BEAVER, IT'S THE 17TH! WIENER-WRAP NIGHT!

want to eat and then go out and buy it, because:

• Your predetermined plan probably will not coincide with what's on sale, or with the very best sales;

• Stick-to-your-list thinking doesn't allow you to take advantage of the unadvertised deals;

• During the course of your long-range-plan period, you may discover you need to use up a perishable or clean out the leftovers from your crammed freezer.

Long-range planning probably evolved as the solution for the individual who habitually stops at the supermarket or fast-food restaurant on the way home from work to pick up the evening meal. This pattern is apparently pretty common, which is why people panic and empty store shelves before a snowstorm.

Although I agree that the long-range plan is better than the panic plan, it is far from the best solution.

A far more logical method is called the pantry principle, and Jim and I have successfully used it for years. (I first read about this concept in *Cut Your Food Bill in Half* by Barbara Salsbury and Cheri Loveless [Acropolis Books, 1983].)

Many families use this idea to some extent, but in my opinion, few take it far enough to save the maximum amount of time or money.

The basic premise is that you stockpile your pantry (and/or kitchen, freezer, basement, closet, and/or the space under your bed) with food purchased at the lowest possible price. The sole purpose of grocery shopping becomes replenishing your pantry, not buying ingredients to prepare specific meals. This is a subtle but important distinction.

To put the pantry principle into action, Jim and I scan the sale flyers each week for good deals. When the rock-bottom sale occurs, we inventory our supply and decide how much to buy. Unlike many families, we'll buy flour even if we have 20 pounds left—if the price is right.

Bulk-buying is not just for large families in large homes. Singles in tiny apartments can stockpile in accordance with their needs and available space.

We stockpile larger quantities of food that goes on sale less frequently (over time, you develop an instinct about this). Although we do most of our shopping once a month, when sales occur we make a point of picking up the items while doing other errands or by coordinating efforts with a friend. Because we buy in quantity, we don't have to take advantage of every sale.

Occasionally, we miscalculate and completely run out of 29¢-per-pound chicken. Nothing will

induce us to pay 69¢ per pound. We simply don't make chicken meals until we replenish our chicken supply. Instead, we eat other sale-purchased meals. By having a full pantry, we never need to plan our meals weeks or even days in advance.

Depending on your family's preferences, perishables may be handled differently. If you want to eat only fresh produce, you will have to shop for it every week. We buy fresh fruits at the beginning of the month, and as we run out, we gradually shift over to our supply of dried, frozen, and canned fruits and juices. If the fruit stand on my yard-sale route has good deals, I'll make a special stop. But I don't believe we'll die if there isn't fresh produce in the house.

Our meal planning works like this: Jim and I alternate washing the evening dishes. We have a rule that whoever washes the dishes plans the next evening's meal. During that 30-minute period, the designated meal-planner considers what type of meal we haven't eaten in a while, what we have a surplus of, what we need to use up, what the weather will be like (so we can make hot meals on cool days, and vice versa), what our schedule will be, who will be home, what garden vegetables are ripening, and so on. These and many other factors cannot possibly be known 30 days in advance.

Planning meals 24 hours in advance is ideal because many of our foods need to be thawed or dried beans need to be soaked. Meals to be prepared in a solar cooker or crockpot must be ready to begin cooking in the morning. And thawing foods in advance saves electricity because there is no need to microwave frozen foods. Although we have a repertoire of short-notice meals, the selection is much smaller.

A final note: This general concept applies to many areas of the frugal life. During the summer I stockpile yard-sale items I might need to replace during the remainder of the year, including lunch boxes, backpacks, sneakers, and clothing. I stock up on yard-sale toys for birthday and Christmas presents, and on sale-purchased gifts that would be suitable for my children to take to another kid's birthday party. Jim stocks up on sale-priced motor oil and oil filters, film, bolts, and hot-glue sticks.

When an unexpected need arises, we "go shopping in the attic." Consequently, we almost never make an emergency trip to the store. Whenever people complain to me that "I don't have time to do all of that frugal stuff," I wonder if they waste time running off to the store every time they run out of something. The pantry principle is one of many frugal practices that saves both money and time.

AVOID ANTI-SEPTIC PRACTICES

According to the U.S. Census Bureau, 22 percent of American homes use septic systems. According to several septic-system pumpers we interviewed here in Maine, at least 50 percent of people with septic systems don't know how to take care of them.

This can be expensive. Replacing a failed septic system generally costs about $4,000 and can cost as much as $10,000. On the other hand, properly maintaining a septic system costs only about $50 a year—plus a little common sense.

To research this, I spoke with septic pumpers, the local extension service, EPA Small Flows Clearinghouse (which specializes in septic-system information), and health-department officials in several states. I also read three books and six magazine articles. I was thorough because a great deal of information on septic-system maintenance is just folklore and anecdotes, and I wanted the informed, scientific viewpoint.

A septic system consists of two parts: a tank and a leach field. The solids settle to the bottom of the tank. The liquid drains from the top of the tank into the leach field, which is made of buried gravel.

Septic systems fail because the tank fills with solids, and these overflow and clog up the leach field. You'll know your system has failed if bad-smelling water leaks out above the ground, the plumbing in your house backs up, or both.

There are two basic things to remember if you want your septic system to last: Don't put the wrong things in it, and have the tank pumped at regular intervals.

These things should *not* be flushed or poured down the drain:

• Grease. To work properly, septic tanks need bacterial action to break down solids. Grease interferes with that biological action. Small amounts won't hurt, but dumping a pan full of hamburger grease into the kitchen sink is really rough on the bacteria.

• Colored toilet paper. The dyes in colored paper are also difficult for bacteria to digest.

• Garbage-disposal waste. This brings in more solids and grease. Use a compost pile.

• Excessive water. "A lot of people move to the country from the city, take an hour-long shower, and wonder why their system fails," says Steve Davis of Minot, Maine, who has pumped tanks for 20 years. "Septic systems won't take water continuously."

Aside from the shower, the other biggest wastewater producer in the average household is the washing machine. To make matters worse, its water contains harsh detergents that can block the septic tank's bacterial action. Davis says routing your washing machine's wastewater into a "dry well"—essentially, a hole filled with gravel—can extend the life of your septic field.

But note: All household wastewater aside from toilet water is known as "gray water." Laws vary on how gray water can be handled. In some areas, it *must* be routed into the septic tank. Check with your local codes-enforcement office before engaging in any creative plumbing.

Even if you follow all of the rules above, you must have your tank pumped at regular intervals. Some pumpers told us it should be done every two or three years, others said every three or four years. Ask around for an honest, reliable pumper, and when he arrives, ask his advice, based on what he finds in your tank. In Maine, pumping out a tank generally costs around $200. If it's done at four-year intervals, that works out to $50 a year. If you are lucky enough to have a place to dump the stuff, such as a big field, and local laws permit this, the pumping fee can be as low as $50, or $12.50 per year.

Try as I might, I was unable to find any independent source who believed additives could make pumping unnecessary. As far as I could learn, only the additive companies are making these claims. (And one company's additive package does say that you will still need to pump). The additive companies were unable to cite any independent studies to support their claims, whereas the independent sources said all the studies they had read indicate the additives were of little use, and that some could be harmful.

And even if it worked, the economic advantage of an additive is dubious. A spokesman for Rid-X, one of the best-known additives, told me that his product costs $48 annually. At that rate, it's generally cheaper to have your tank pumped.

Although most septic systems should be pumped every three years or so, it's possible to go much longer, depending upon many variables. Again, the best way to find out is to ask an honest pumper. In Maine, I've found that most pumpers are so busy they have little incentive to fabricate a short interval.

HOMEMADE GOO

Stephanie Sloan of Renton, Washington, sent in a recipe to make a substance that is like a cross between Gak and Silly Putty. I made up a batch of the stretchy stuff and let my children play with it. It provided hours of hilarious entertainment. It doesn't leave a residue or stick to anything but itself and will stretch to seemingly unlimited lengths. Its "disgusting" qualities make it a natural for Halloween entertainment.

8 ounces white or carpenter's glue
$3/4$ cup water
food coloring (optional)
1 teaspoon 20 Mule Team borax
1 to 2 tablespoons water

Combine the first three ingredients. In a separate bowl, combine the last two. Add the borax mixture to the glue mixture, stirring until a "blob" forms. Remove the blob from the mixture. Add a new batch of the borax mixture to the glue mixture. Repeat the process until the glue mixture is all gone. Knead all the blobs together. Store in an airtight container.

BEYOND BREAD-TAB EARRINGS

While I am a leading authority on frugal food and kid's clothing, and I know a dozen uses for dryer-lint mâché, inexpensive jewelry strategies are not my strong suit. So I asked readers to help. I specified that each idea had to be for something that Diane Sawyer would wear on prime-time TV.

About 75 readers responded. Most included samples. To narrow the field, I assembled a panel of seven staffers (of varying ages, tastes, and sexes) to judge the samples. Aside from fashion appropriateness, we also considered durability, how commonly available the materials were, price of materials, and how easily they could be made (we were particularly seeking ideas that required no talent or special skills).

Most of these jewelry ideas will require that you buy findings, stickpins, clasps, pin blanks, jeweler's pins, and/or a strong, clear-drying glue. This stuff is available by the bagful at craft shops and is surprisingly cheap. People who are allergic to inexpensive metal would need to buy gold or silver earring backs. A pair of needle-nosed pliers is also needed in making some of this jewelry.

One general idea first: Readers suggested picking up jewelry cheap from various sources and remaking it into new jewelry. Beth Dodd of Gainesville, Texas, pointed out that single earrings can be made into pins. Colleen Washburn of Newport News, Virginia, talks to the manager of an everything-for-$1 store and asks to buy broken jewelry. She buys a bagful for $1 and then repairs or remakes the pieces. Sherri Spare of Parsons, Kansas, picks through bargain bins for $1 jewelry. She paints the pieces with clear nail polish to prevent chipping and fading. Regard cheap or free jewelry from any source as raw material for your projects.

By far the most common idea that readers sent me was "button earrings." Any large buttons with a loop in the back can be made into very inexpensive earrings.

These might be metallic, mother-of-pearlish, or colored buttons. Many samples were surprisingly elegant. Susan Coy of Spring, Texas, wrote that she uses wire cutters to snip the loop off. She gently sands the remains of the loop smooth and attaches the earring back with glue. If you use pierced-earring backings, place them off-center so they don't twist or turn and so they set lower on your lobe.

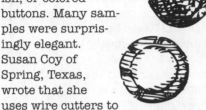

Lona Lockhart of Roxboro, North Carolina, pointed out that craft stores yield a variety of other items from which earrings can be made. Silk rosettes come in a range of colors. You can also find satin hearts (usually used for sweatshirts), tiny bows, and glass rhinestones. She uses hot glue to attach these to earring backings.

As a testament to how easy earrings are to make, ten-year-old Monica Madson of Minnetonka, Minnesota, sent in some of the loveliest pieces we received. She strings small, iridescent beads on jeweler's pins. She then bends or loops the pin ends to attach them to the earring findings. Kathy Littman of Santa Rosa, California, sent me

earrings made by the same method; however, she buys old necklaces at yard sales and thrift shops and takes them apart to salvage the beads.

All of these earrings can be made in fifteen minutes and cost between 15¢ and $1.

Susan Meyer of Beverly Shores, Indiana, sent me bracelets made from an unlikely item. Brass fishing swivels, which are used to attach fishing lures to the line, can be purchased in department or sporting-goods stores in bags of nine for about 47¢. She ties a swivel with a 1-inch section of gold wire, strings one to three beads on this wire, and attaches the other end of the wire to the next swivel. By continuing this procedure, she makes a chain. When it reaches bracelet length, you can attach the ends or add bracelet clasps. The samples she sent had wooden and stone beads.

Larrisa Stretton of Webster, Massachusetts, sent me her version of a pin she saw in a catalog for $29.95. She cut a small heart, about $1 \frac{1}{2}$ inches high, from white cardboard. Then she glued a selection of tiny buttons, beads, bows, lace, and silk rosettes to completely cover the cardboard, being careful to retain the overall heart shape. These items were white, gold, pink, or clear. I had seen this idea once before using all tiny gold items including tiny lapel pins (such as Masonic or high school ones). Larrisa prefers Tacky brand glue. Finally, she glues a pin blank on the back.

One reader sent a necklace made from 50¢ worth of black, blue, and silver "six-strand" embroidery floss. You could also use leftover yarn.

To make one, wind a total of 8 yards of floss around a large book or the back of a kitchen chair. Twist this big circle of floss tightly or loosely, depending on the style you want. Thread three 18-inch strands of floss through each of the loops at the ends of the twisted floss. Braid these strands tightly, and knot the ends of the braids.

Thread a tapestry needle with floss, and wind floss very tightly over the place where the braided and twisted floss joins together, overlapping each by about ½ inch. Knot the necklace in the center. Tie together the ends of the braided floss to form the necklace.

Debbie Sailer of Sooke, British Columbia, sent in a method of making beads from glossy magazine pages. As it happens, a staffer had recently picked up a 1950s crafts-from-trash book at a yard sale, and this idea was in it. I have been experimenting with this and have become addicted. To fully appreciate how nicely this idea works, you'll have to try making beads from several different pages. The final look of the beads depends on the color and composition of the art or photo of the magazine page. The beads have a Southwestern look. Part of the uniqueness of this technique is that ten or so beads that you make from a single page are "of the same family," meaning they look alike yet are individually unique.

To make these beads, cut long, triangular strips from a magazine page. I use an X-Acto knife (this tool is a must for crafts) and a metal ruler to do the cutting. You can also draw guidelines on the back side of the page and cut with scissors. At the wide end, the strips should be no wider than 1 inch (the width determines the final size of the bead). Cut the wide end so it has a shallow point. Starting at the wide end, tightly roll the strip on a small nail, making sure to get the strip rolling straight from the start.

Once the strip is completely rolled up, dab a small amount of glue on the end so it won't unroll. When the glue dries, slip the bead off the nail. Coat the beads with acrylic craft spray or shellac to make them weatherproof. The beads can be used to make a necklace by alternating them with other types of beads on a colored string. To make earrings, I would make dangling clusters of four or five beads per earring ring.

Jewelry making is an area in which my readers have taught me a great deal. I have very little personal need for jewelry and have relied on two pairs of earrings and a few pins to get me by. But from now on, I'll poke through those piles of yard-sale baubles and beads with a more discerning eye.

WANTED POSTERS

Dear Amy,

I was chatting with the manager of our local video store, and he volunteered that they regularly throw away the promotional video-release movie posters they get from the studios after about two weeks. I asked if I could have one (for a children's movie my kids love), and it made the perfect birthday gift. Since then, I've gotten several more and used them as gifts at birthday parties.

—Maria Hylton
  Evanston, Illinois

TWO-MINUTE WARMING

Dear Amy,

After years of feeling cheated by not being able to get that last little bit of solid antiperspirant deodorant out of the container, I finally decided it was time to try.

I dug all the remaining stuff out of the container with a knife and put it in a glass custard cup. I put it in the microwave for two minutes. Using a spatula, I scraped all the melted antiperspirant into an old container and let it cool. Four used-up antiperspirant containers filled a recycled container half full.

—Sally Ryan
  Black Hawk, Colorado

THE SUN ALSO DEFROSTS

Dear Amy,

I live in Vermont, where there's often frost on the car windows from October to April. To shorten both the length of time I must scrape snow/frost/ice from my window and the time I must run the defroster prior to driving, I always park my car facing east. This allows the warmth of the rising morning sun to melt most, if not all, of the snow/frost/ice from my car's biggest window.

—Susan DuBois
  Montpelier, Vermont

GET WELD SOON

Dear Amy,

A friend had a little bicycle just the size I needed for my son, only one pedal was broken off. Having it welded was the only way to fix it. After several frustrating trips and phone calls to welding companies (minimum charge, $15 to $40, one- to three-week backlog), I had a brainstorm. I called the welding department of our local technical college, and they were happy to fix it for me. A welding student did a super job in ten minutes, no charge! We wrote them a letter!

—Stephanie Sloan
  Renton, Washington

MARKER MAGIC

Dear Amy,

To reuse a highlighter pen, remove either the felt tip (the retaining pin must be pushed out) or the end plug, and add water. Better yet, add water mixed with food coloring. You can even make your own custom colors.

—David Stennes
  La Mesa, California

PICKUP PICK-ME-UP

Dear Amy,

The rusted wheels on our 1985 Chevy truck made it look dated and shabby although it functions well and is in good shape. We looked into replacing them and found, to our horror, it would cost $400.

Then we stumbled across a $5 can of "wheel spray paint" from an auto-parts store. Not only do we have "new wheels," but the whole truck looks more than presentable. Although this is only a cosmetic change, it extended the life of the truck in our eyes . . . my husband can't drive a broken-down-looking vehicle because of his business.

—Janet Steddum
    Raleigh, North Carolina

WASH AND CARE

Dear Amy,

This is a good idea if you know college students. We get a night of free baby-sitting for our two children (which would cost us $6 an hour for at least four hours) in exchange for letting the students use our washer and dryer. They provide their own soap, etc.

—Linda Smith
    Davis, California

THE FRUGAL BALANCE

Almost every time I give a speech or talk on a radio show, I hear a comment like this:

"My wife and I do many of the things you suggest to save money. Of course, we're just not as . . . er . . . well . . . as extreme as you are."

The notion that I am somehow too extreme is also reflected in a question journalists often ask: "Can you be *too* frugal?"

This sounds like a simple, yes-or-no question, but it actually requires this long answer:

Most people think of frugality only in terms of saving money. Under that narrow definition, the answer would clearly be "Yes, you can be too frugal." But if you look up *frugal* in the dictionary, you'll find it isn't defined specifically as having to do only with money. It's defined as "not wasteful," "economical," or "thrifty." These terms can apply to the expenditure of *any* resource.

All of us attempt to achieve the highest quality of life possible by balancing four basic resources: money, time, space, and personal energy. Because these resources are interconnected in an intricate way, frugality must encompass more than money; we must manage these four things in relationship to one another.

When people think of frugality run amok, they're usually reflecting on situations when these resources are out of balance and this imbalance hurts the quality of life.

There are limitless examples that I could discuss to illustrate this point. Let's focus on a common one that people sometimes mention to me: pack-ratting.

Typically, someone might say to me, "Yeah, my sister Thelma is really frugal. You can't move in her house because of all of the bread bags, Styrofoam meat trays, juice-can lids, egg cartons, broccoli rubber bands, and toilet-paper tubes. But I just can't live that way. I guess I'm not the tightwad type."

My response is that Thelma isn't being "too frugal;" rather, her frugality is out of balance. Her pack-ratting may save her money in small ways (if you have 600 bread bags in the closet, you don't need to buy plastic bags), but it costs her more in other ways:

• Because Thelma has to move piles of things to finish a sewing project, she wastes time and energy. Because she can't find her one good pair of scissors, she wastes time. Because she has to buy more buttons when she can't find the ones she saved, she wastes money.

• Because Thelma has limited space, she can't stock up on good deals on nonperishables at the supermarket. Instead, she buys only a few days' supply of food at a time and therefore wastes more time, energy, and money.

• Because Thelma has so much stuff saved, she rents a larger house—in addition to renting space in a storage locker. Aside from spending more money for rent, she also pays more to heat the larger space. Because she has to work overtime at her K mart job to pay for these additional expenses, she wastes more time and energy.

The result of this lack of balance is that Thelma's quality of life is diminished.

In contrast to Thelma, a shrewd, successful frugal person constantly monitors how much is stored, never keeping more than the maximum amount of bread bags or Styrofoam meat trays that might be needed at a given time. Pack-ratting, with organization and precision, is a huge money saver, especially when more valuable things are stored away. We have an abundance of children's clothing, lumber, hardware, and nonperishable food. However, I have exactly eight Styrofoam meat trays and four bread bags, and I can still move in my kitchen.

It's possible someone like Thelma may save more things than she needs, but because she has a surplus of space, stacks of meat trays might not cause her to be out of balance. Although she might not be saving money by keeping them, neither is she wasting other resources. It's also important to note that this lack of balance isn't a problem associated only with frugal people. Spendthrifts are frequently out of balance. If Thelma's brother doesn't have time to enjoy his new bass boat because he has to work overtime (at a job he hates) to pay for it, then he is out of balance as well. But people who aren't frugal can achieve balance. They might love their jobs, make loads of money, and spend a lot to buy things from which they derive great value.

In observing both the frugal and nonfrugal, this lack of balance is usually indicated by an expression of unhappiness or frustration about some aspect of their lives—when they complain about not being able to pay bills but aren't making adjustments in their habits. Regardless of their spending style, I don't worry about people when they and their families are clearly happy with the choices they've made.

When someone labels me "too extreme," it's usually because they've flipped through my books, picked out some obscure idea that doesn't work for them, and made a judgment about me. But I've never had a journalist come to my home, observe the obvious harmony, and write that I'm "too frugal." Although their values might be different from mine, they can't find fault with our choices.

Because we all have different amounts of money, time, space, and personal energy and different ideas about what constitutes quality of life, we each must find our own frugal balance.

If you think about frugality as I do, asking the question "Can you be too frugal?" is like asking "Can you be too happy?"

WHEN TO USE A COUPON

All of the books I've ever read on coupons focus solely on how wonderful they are. I have never read one that helps you figure out when coupons cost you money.

In many instances, a little quick in-the-aisles math will show

whether a name brand with coupon will beat the price of a store-brand equivalent.

But the waters get murkier when you use a coupon to buy a convenience food. When does the convenience food become cheaper than making the same item from scratch? To learn this requires that you make the scratch item, weigh or measure it, and carefully add up the cost of the ingredients used. When the final cost of the convenience food combined with coupons falls below this price, you should probably use the coupon. (I say "probably" because many of these foods are highly packaged, highly processed, and lack the nutrition of the scratch versions.)

Unfortunately, no one ever takes the time to figure this out. So I decided to break some ground in the Wonderful World of Coupondom and provide you with a list of rules of thumb. Because there are thousands of products at your supermarket, this list is incomplete. To be really accurate you should figure prices based on ingredients available to you, but if you don't want to take the time, this list should help.

Many of the prices on my list are based on previous articles I have written. In many cases, the recipes appear in my books. I've provided a per-ounce figure as well as a per-package figure. I rounded the numbers to the nearest penny, which accounts for any discrepancies.

Here's how low the price with coupons must be for each of these products to be a good deal:
Baked beans: 1¢ per ounce or 33¢ per 28-ounce can.
Cake mix: 2¢ per ounce or 25¢ per 15-ounce box.

Chili: 4¢ per ounce or 54¢ per 15-ounce can.

Chocolate syrup: 3¢ per ounce or 72¢ per 24-ounce bottle.

Cookies: 40¢ per pound for sugar cookies and 60¢ per pound for oatmeal cookies.

Hot cocoa from mix: 7¢ per 1-cup serving or $1.12 per 16-pack box.

Chicken Tonight: 4¢ per ounce or 99¢ per 23½-ounce jar.

Cold cereal: 7¢ per ounce (as compared to other breakfast options).

Corn-muffin mix: 3¢ per ounce or 22¢ per 8½-ounce box.

Cream of mushroom soup: 4¢ per ounce or 43¢ per 10½-ounce can.

Frosting: 3¢ per ounce or 48¢ per 16-ounce can.

Granola (without nuts): 6¢ per ounce or 48¢ per 8-ounce box.

Hamburger (or Tuna) Helper: 75¢ per box.*

Jell-O Snack Paks: 2¢ per ounce or 35¢ per pack of four 4-ounce containers.

Jelly and jam: 3¢ per ounce or 42¢ per 16 ounces (as compared to homemade with home-grown fruit).

Microwavable pancakes and waffles: 10¢ per 2-ounce serving.

Microwave popcorn: 2¢ per ounce or 8¢ per pouch.

Onion-soup mix: 33¢ per ounce or 66¢ per two-envelope package.

Pancake syrup: 3¢ per ounce or 66¢ per 24-ounce bottle.

Pizza (frozen): $1.25 per 15-inch cheese pizza.

Popsicles: 3¢ each or 60¢ for a 24-count box (as compared to homemade from apple juice).

Pudding snack packs: 7¢ per ounce or 44¢ per pack of four 4-ounce containers.

Ramen noodles: 5¢ per ounce or 17¢ per package.

Rice-A-Roni: 28¢ per cup. Box contains 1 cup.

Italian salad dressing: 3¢ per ounce or 45¢ per 16-ounce bottle.

Tomato soup: 5¢ per ounce or 53¢ per 10½-ounce can, as compared with homemade from tomato paste.

Seasoned salt: 14¢ per ounce or 49¢ per 3½-ounce container.

Spaghetti sauce: 45¢ per quart (as compared to homemade with homegrown vegetables).

Stove Top Stuffing: 46¢ per cup or $2.76 per 6-cup package.

Taco seasoning: 14¢ per ounce or 21¢ per 1½-ounce package.

TV dinners: 50¢ per dinner.

Yogurt with fruit: 14¢ per 8-ounce container (as compared to homemade with a tablespoon of jam added).

*Recipe from *Cheaper & Better* by Nancy Birnes.

IS THERE A GELATIN IN YOUR CLOSET?

When most people think of gelatin, they're really thinking about Jell-O: They don't know there's any other way to make a gelatin dessert. I never buy Jell-O because it's basically nothing more than unflavored gelatin, sugar, and Kool Aid powder. In short, it provides no nutrition other than an insignificant amount of protein from the gelatin. Instead, we buy bulk, unflavored gelatin for $5.33 a pound at our health-food store and use this to make our own fruit gelatin. This is by far the cheapest way to buy unflavored gelatin; a four-packet, 1-ounce box of Knox unflavored gelatin costs 95¢, which works out to $15.20 a pound. Unflavored gelatin keeps indefinitely, so there is no advantage to buying smaller quantities.

A tablespoon of unflavored gelatin combined with a cup of cold liquid and a cup of boiling liquid will make solid gelatin. You can make your own version of Jell-O by using Kool-Aid for this hot and cold liquid. This will cost about 18¢ per four $1/2$-cup servings. A box of Jell-O makes the same amount, but costs 44¢ a box. Royal gelatin is 33¢ a box.

I prefer to use fruit juice to make a healthier gelatin. Apple juice, for example, with a little food coloring (brown gelatin doesn't cut it) works well. At a cost of 32¢ for four $1/2$-cup servings, this is still cheaper than Jell-O or Royal gelatin.

Obviously, it's easier to just drink juice than make gelatin out of it. But fruit-juice gelatin is a handy way to suspend frozen fruits (like blueberries, strawberries, or blackberries), which are hard to convert to "lunch-box food." I can make pies or crisps to use up my supply of berries, but my family has to eat lots of sugar and fat to get a little fruit. Fruit gelatins are a form of lunch-box fruit that I can make using a little sugar and no fat. I also use fruit gelatin to suspend overripe banana chunks.

After some experimentation, I've progressed to a speedy method to make fruit gelatin that uses frozen fruit (which we either grow or pick from wild bushes) and no juice (which I would have to buy). Here's how I do it:

I thaw a quart of frozen berries and whiz it in a 5-cup-size blender. If I'm using blackberries, I then strain out the seeds and pour the thick, pulpy juice back into the blender. I add 2 tablespoons of unflavored gelatin and ½ cup of sugar and fill the blender with hot water. I blend this mixture, pour it in a bowl, and chill.

Blender gelatin has one important advantage: The gelatin always mixes completely. I find if I simply stir the mixture, my gelatin might have chewy gelatin "seeds."

Blender gelatin also becomes foamy, and as it jells, it tends to separate to form a light-colored foamy layer and a dark, clear layer. These layers are interesting if we're making parfaits.

Aside from using less fat and sugar, fruit gelatins require much less energy and time to make than other scratch desserts like pies and puddings. And, for some reason, homemade gelatins seem to hold up better in lunch boxes on warm days than Jell-O does.

Another quickie lunch-box treat is "jigglers" or "Knox blocks," a sort of gelatin finger food. To make them, simply double the amount of gelatin or add 1 tablespoon of gelatin per cup of liquid. Combine in a bowl using a whisk. Recently I made jigglers with lemonade and pink food coloring. I poured 6 cups of gelatin/lemonade mixture into a 9-inch-by-13-inch Pyrex baking dish and chilled it. Once jelled, this can be cut into cubes or, for fancier shapes, cut with cookie cutters. These were hugely successful with my kids and made fashionable, fake-looking, sort-of-healthy lunch-box food.

FACTORY FINDS

Dear Amy,

My husband gets our firewood (oak, untreated) for $10 a truck-load from leftovers at a local log-cabin manufacturing plant. I get new material (many pieces over 1 yard) for $2 per large box from remnants from a local sewing factory. These make great curtains, pillows, and kids' clothes. Check your local factories. Many have materials to be given away.

—Cynthia Hale
　Clay City, Kentucky

SMEAR TACTIC

Dear Amy,

A plastic surgeon friend said to use Crisco shortening on my dry lips rather than anything else. It works well!

—Tina Schneider
　Oceanside, California

MICKEY MISER

Dear Amy,

As soon as you make your plans to visit Disneyland/World, shop at garage sales for souvenirs. I was able to stockpile Disney hats, T-shirts, coin purses, waist bags, and stuffed characters for $4.70. The retail for these items was $114.05. These were doled out over the course of the week as the "I wannas" struck.

—Kathy Gervasio
　Mendham, New Jersey

FIND IT AND BIND IT

Dear Amy,

Since I love trying new ideas and foods while cooking, I have ended up with at least a dozen cookbooks that I use for only a few recipes. Now, I go to the library and check out cookbooks instead. I look for and copy recipes that I like or will use, insert them into a plastic sheet protector, and organize them by category (i.e., seafood, salads, chicken, etc.) in a binder. I also use this idea to keep track of home projects, articles, crafts, etc. I'm on my fifth binder, and my total cost so far is less than one cookbook.

—Deborah Holtzer Potter
  Vineyard Haven, Massachusetts

CITRUS SYRUP

Dear Amy,

After making the candied orange and grapefruit peels (see page 198), I found that you can use the syrup in which you boil the peels on pancakes and waffles . . . the peels give it a nice flavor. This brings the cost of the candied peels down to the energy cost of using the stove.

—JoAnn Sprague
  Three Lakes, Wisconsin

KILL A WATT

Dear Amy,

A friend of mine discovered a unique way to cut down on her electric bill. Instead of having her high school–graduate son pay rent, she made him pay the elec-tric bill. Once it became his responsibility, he ran around turning off lights and appliances that weren't being used. Her bill was cut by almost 30 percent! She not only saved energy, she taught her son a valuable lesson.

—Robin McFetridge
  Jonesboro, Georgia

DECIDE TO DIVIDE

Dear Amy,

When your physician prescribes medicines, ask what milligram sizes the medication comes in. If he, for example, plans to order 5-mg. tablets and the medication also comes in a 10-mg. size, and the cost is the same, ask him if he will prescribe the larger size. Then cut them in half. Tablets are often scored and easy to break in half.

—Harriet Reisman
  Port Jefferson, New York

(I asked my physician about this, and he agreed it was a good idea because the larger sizes may cost the same or only slightly more. There are a few exceptions to this practice. Coated tablets should not be broken. The coating makes the medication dissolve more slowly, often when it reaches the lower intestine. A broken, coated tablet would release the medication too quickly. And don't do this with unscored tablets, unless you have the device mentioned in the following letter. FZ)

SPLITTING PAIRS

Dear Amy,

I use a pill splitter for dividing both scored and unscored pills of any size. Theoretically, it could also be used to halve each half. This is useful for people with arthritis, unsteady hands, or poor eyesight.

—Beatrice Slamavitz

(A pill splitter costs $4 at drug-stores in my area. FZ)

GOWN ABOUT TOWN

Dear Amy,

We celebrate our wedding anniversary by donning our wedding outfits and doing something cheap but fun. This year, we rode the bus and stopped at a garage sale. I also wore it to teach preschool the day we learned the letter *W*. Kids came from the other classrooms to gasp. Tim and I decided I'm having too much fun with my wedding dress to sell it. The ad would read: Wedding dress, size 8, worn just 7 times, $50.

—Mary Nelson-Smith
  Billings, Montana

LUCK-KEY LUGGAGE

Dear Amy,

My wife, Carolyn, found a used, Samsonite, hard-shell, 26-inch luggage piece with wheels at a thrift store for only $7 (comparable new retail pieces are $90 to $120). The only thing wrong with it was there was no key to the locks. Carolyn merely called Samsonite at (303) 373-2000 and gave the name of the model, located inside the suitcase. The rep sent her two free keys.

—Don Reeves
  Nashville, Tennessee

HOMEWARD BOUND

Dear Amy,

In my car's glove compartment I keep a spiral-bound 6-inch-by-9-inch notebook and a small stapler.

When friends and relatives give me directions to their homes, I staple them into my book.

We travel a lot, and this handy idea saves us phone-bill money.

—Louise Cady Fernandes
  Lexington, Massachusetts

PACK IN THE BOX

Dear Amy,

Don't buy those outrageously priced boxes to store clothes. Go to your grocery or liquor store and ask for the boxes they are throwing away. The liquor-store boxes have convenient, built-in compartments to store breakable items.

—Sharon Dahlmeyer
  Durham, Connecticut

THE 95¢ QUILT

My first exposure to quilting occurred when I moved to Leeds six years ago. Here, women from ages 25 to 85 gather twice a month at the church to make quilts to raise money.

The quilts are beautiful, but I was surprised to find they are made from all new materials. Lois Hathaway, a professional quilter and instructor, told me why:

• Maine laws restrict the sale of quilts with used batting.

• Used fabrics may not be as durable as new ones, and so are not desirable in quilts for sale.

• Used fabrics are more time-consuming to work with, so they aren't cost-effective for quilts to be sold. There is generally a limited amount of the same type of fabric, it's harder to find the grain, and it may be hard to identify cotton/synthetic blends (these stretch more than 100 percent cotton does when sewing).

My theory is:

• Quilting from used fabrics may have fallen out of favor when frugal quilters attempted to use garish fabrics from the sixties and seventies . . . big green polka dots, purple polyesters, and orange plaids.

But Lois agreed that used materials *can* work well in quilts for personal use—and that the original purpose of patchwork quilting was to use up leftover fabrics. A quilt made from used fabrics also has an appealing sentimental value: Each time you see it, you'll remember "those were Brad's toddler pants, that was my maternity top," and so on.

And, naturally, sewing with scraps is a money-saver. Professionally made quilts cost a minimum of $200. New fabrics alone cost $50 to $100. But by using secondhand materials, you can easily make a quilt for under $5.

To learn more I visited 82-year-old Louise Grant, one of the few quilters in my area who sews with scraps. Although she uses no secondhand fabrics, she makes quilt tops from factory scraps, fabric-shop samples, and extra material from other quilters. She also buys scraps and partially completed quilts from an antique dealer, who obtains them when cleaning out attics. Louise has about ten quilts in progress, awaiting scraps to finish them.

As we chatted in her fabric-crammed workroom, I came to understand her feeling about quilt making. She knows that using scraps won't produce the most beautiful quilts conceivable, as compared to using entirely new and expensive materials. Instead, she enjoys the challenge of using the discards of others to make the most attractive quilt that she can within that limitation.

Quilting from scraps means that you accept what one of my art teachers termed "accidental quality." The results aren't always perfect, but you kind of like that. Accepting this less-perfect result is actually liberating. Louise says she doesn't "fuss" about combining different prints and colors. And it's obvious that making a quilt from near-free fabrics is less intimidating than making one with a $100 investment.

Although you can make totally random designs, Louise suggests settling on a basic design and color scheme and sometimes having a lot of one common, plain fabric to separate printed fabrics. She showed me a variety of examples of how using this method produced attractive quilts that looked "planned." To illustrate one solution, here's how I recently completed my first quilt for—get this—95¢.

Four-year-old Rebecca and eight-year-old Jamie share a double bed in their Pepto-Bismol–pink room (the supreme act of maternal love is to let kids choose their room color). I gave them a set of dark pink sheets (which were given to us). Unidentified culprits soon cut a hole in one pillowcase and stained the bottom sheet with play makeup.

These ruined sheets and an old, torn, store-bought, twin-size comforter became the beginning of the girls' new quilt. I decided to cut up the ruined pillowcase

and sheet to make patchwork pieces and use the one good sheet for the quilt backing.

I thumbed through a stack of *Country Living* magazines specifically looking for examples of quilts made with scraps. Then, after doodling on graph paper, I designed a square that would be easy for my first quilt, consist of 50 percent pink fabric, and lend itself to the randomness needed for used fabrics. The shaded

areas represent the solid-pink fabrics and the white areas represent printed fabrics. I designed it so that when the squares were sewn together, they would create diagonal patterns across the quilt, as shown below.

I purchased four items of cotton clothing with a variety of pink flowery prints for a total of 85¢ at yard sales. I sacrificed a stained, pink-printed dress and a pink-printed blouse that I didn't like, providing two free items. I cut all of the items at the seams and pressed the sections flat. Using cardboard templates for the square and triangle pieces, I marked and cut this fabric.

I machine-sewed the squares. No two pieces of printed fabric were alike in each square. This ensured I would have fewer leftover pieces and I could make future repairs with fabric that didn't match precisely.

I used up many of my spools of odd-colored thread to sew the squares, and "borrowed" pink thread for the more visible top stitching from a friend with whom I have a mutual-mooching relationship. I bought a ball of embroidery cotton for 10¢ at a yard sale to "tie" the quilt.

The old comforter required special preparation. The batting in store-bought comforters is rolled under at the edges before it's sewn, making a bunchy edge that is hard to work with when re-covering. I slit the edges and pulled this batting out flat. I also smoothed out lumpy batting and used batting scraps (from the ladies at the church) to repair holes and thin areas. I added a section of batting and scrap fabric (from a light-colored baby comforter) on one side to make the comforter full-size.

When assembling the layers of sheet, old comforter, and quilt top, I duct-taped corners to the floor to assure there were no wrinkles while I pinned it. Then I trimmed, tied, and hemmed the layers.

I had enough remaining pink material to make a new pillowcase and a matching, ruffled throw pillow.

This project required roughly 60 hours spread over six weeks. A "cutting wheel" (looks like a pizza cutter), knowledge of time-saving techniques, and experience would reduce these hours significantly.

After completing this quilt, I did some research to determine whether used fabrics really are cheaper than other options. I am working on my next quilt (design shown on page 188), which needs 3-inch square pieces almost exclusively. I used this dimension for my calculations:

A yard of fabric (36 inches by 45 inches) would yield 180 3-inch squares. You can buy a yard of dirt-cheap remnant material for $1.25 at a fabric store.

I went to a nearby bedding-factory outlet and bought ½ pound of sheet-fabric trimmings for $1. This yielded 196 squares. Because these were long strips there was some waste, but not as much as with smaller pieces. So purchasing fabric this way roughly equals 92¢ per yard.

I bought a boy's size-14 dress shirt for 25¢ at a yard sale. This yielded 90 squares—plus buttons. So purchasing fabric this way roughly equals 50¢ per yard, even less for adult-size clothing.

I went to a nearby thrift shop that has some boxes of quilt scraps containing both new and used fabric. I picked out what I could use in this next quilt and bought 3 pounds (half of a grocery sack) for 50¢. Because these are smaller pieces there will be far more waste. Figuring there will be a pound of waste and that ½ pound of fabric roughly equals a yard, I got 2 pounds, or 4 yards of usable fabric for 50¢. So buying fabric this way roughly equals 13¢ per yard.

But the great advantage of quilting from scraps is that you

can use clothing that is torn, stained, and otherwise unusable, as long as the fabric isn't too worn, so the material is free. In addition, once people learned I'm now working on a blue quilt, I've had two offers of free blue fabric.

Prices will vary depending on the resources in your area, but remember that sale-purchased new fabric will probably not be the cheapest.

The real surprise to me was not how cheaply quilts could be made, but that this is an ideal hobby for people with limited time and space. Because you sew a few squares at a time, quilt making can be squeezed into the tiny chunks of time we all have. Then all the pieces can be stored in a small box until the next fragment of free time. The handwork can be done while watching TV. I found it was stress-relieving to sew at the end of a one-step-forward-two-steps-backward type of day. This is a terrific example of a productive hobby that can be combined with quality family time. My children were fascinated. I discussed the process and design with them. They helped iron squares and clip threads, and ten-year-old Alec is working on his own quilt design (for me to sew).

I also learned why quilting can become a lifelong hobby; the combinations of designs, colors, and patterns are unlimited.

I made a quilt with minimal knowledge, but a stack of library books on quilting techniques and designs will be useful and a source of inspiration for most beginners. They can, however, be overwhelming. As I did, you should choose simple designs for your first venture into quilt making.

I'M DREAMING OF A TIGHT CHRISTMAS

During a rare speaking engagement I briefly addressed our culture's tendency to wrongly associate frugality with poverty. I pointed out that because frugality is incorrectly perceived as "poor person's behavior," many people are embarrassed about being frugal.

As I chatted with audience members after my speech, a woman said my comment was exactly right. She admitted that last Christmas she had spent more on her nieces and nephews, because they were from an affluent family, than she had spent on her own children.

Her story powerfully illustrates the fact that many frugal people allow themselves to be pressured into overspending during the holidays. Readers frequently tell me that they have similar problems at the workplace: pressure to chip in on birthdays, to buy candy bars to support the soccer teams of coworkers' children, and to exchange holiday gifts.

If you give in to the pressure to buy expensive gifts despite your wishes, understand why you are doing this; and why you lack the courage to say no. You may believe people perceive inexpensive gifts as signs that you are "poor," "cheap," and/or "thoughtless." Self-esteem becomes entangled with gift giving.

In addressing the perception of being "poor," consider that inexpensive gifts are often a sign of different values and priorities. You *can* afford the expensive gifts, but you prefer to spend your money on things that have a higher priority for you. Or you prefer to work fewer hours so that you can have more quality time with your family.

If you fear people will think you are "cheap" or "thoughtless," ask yourself if you would be happy with the quality of the gift you're giving. If you buy yourself expensive goods from Bloomingdale's, people will justifiably feel that it's inconsistent for you to buy them bargains from the dollar store. In contrast, if you always seek out bargains for yourself, others will be far more likely to accept them as presents from you.

Having a clear vision of your financial goals and making sure that frugal gifts are consistent with your whole lifestyle provide the self-esteem that's essential in dealing with those who make expensive demands of you.

Once we gain the confidence to say no, we further desire that our coworkers, friends, and family will accept, and perhaps even adopt, frugal gift giving themselves. There are two ways I know to achieve this:

THE UP-FRONT PLAN

Talk about it.

Your first inclination may be to hold the discussion on Christmas day, since everyone is in one place, but that isn't the best time. People could easily interpret what you say as a rejection of what they just gave you. Bring it up at a graduation party, a summer reunion, or some gathering that's at least a couple of months from Christmas.

You may be surprised to find how receptive other people are to the idea. Many people feel that Christmas is too commercialized, but they believe *other* people like it that way.

If you all agree that gift-giving has gotten out of hand, the next step is to decide on an alternative.

Many of these may sound familiar, but you can use this list as a tool to guide the discussion.

1. For acquaintances and friends who have become distant geographically, you might simply decide to exchange cards rather than gifts.

2. Draw names within families or between extended families, rather than buying for and receiving from everyone.

3. Shift to "household" gifts, rather than gifts to everyone in a household.

4. Try alternative gifts. Make a rule that only food can be exchanged. Suggest more swapping of services such as baby-sitting. Money that would be spent on gifts could be used to take a family trip or donated to a charity.

5. Set a spending limit, say $5, and then challenge yourselves to see how wonderful and creative you can be within that price range.

It's important that this talk be an exchange, not a lecture. Make it clear that all comments are welcome, and no point of view is "right."

As you move toward a decision,

it's also important to emphasize that it need not be permanent. If one of the strategies doesn't work, try a different one next year.

THE COVERT PLAN

If it's too late to discuss the problem with your family this year, or if you are sure the discussion would be fruitless, try *showing* them.

Although extravagance has seldom been a problem in my family, if it were, I would regard frugal gift giving as my mission to show others how much more fun inexpensive gifts can be. Here are some examples of my successes:

When Jim visited the home of a distant Navy friend during the summer, he was surprised to see the clever tag I made to go with our Christmas gift, "Jim's Homemade Wild Grape Jelly," still prominently pinned to their bulletin board. My mother has kept my homemade Christmas cards on display in her home for months. One aunt, who watched my delighted kids open their top-quality yard-sale presents as I whispered the cost of the gifts to her, laughed and said, "Gee, next year I'm doing all my shopping in Maine."

If you choose the covert plan, consider these points:
1. To successfully convert people, your gift giving must be excellent. Gifts that are inappropriate or poorly made will fail. Frugal gift giving usually requires more time and/or thought. Let your desire to prove your point drive your efforts. If those on your gift list think inexpensive equals inferior, make an extra effort to "bowl them over" with your cleverness.
2. Start slowly. In some families,

where extravagant, commercial holidays are deeply entrenched, change can require several years. One friend, who can afford the extravagance of her family but dislikes their lack of imagination, has still continued to spend in the expensive tradition but has also begun to sneak in clever, homemade gifts, a first for her family. Each tiny success will slowly erode their prejudice.

3. Provide information. Although it's generally considered tacky to divulge the cost of a gift, it's essential if you want to educate the receiver. I *always* tell my children, usually at a later time, that a toy came from a yard sale. I tell them how much I paid and how much the new equivalent would have cost. If a friend thinks my homemade gift is store-bought, I "accidentally" let it out of the bag that I made it. If she really loves the gift, I might also share how easy the gift was to make, how much the materials cost, and offer a set of instructions.
4. Be confident. Never apologize for the "humbleness" of your gift. Don't even let the thought enter your mind. If you think giving your children gifts from yard sales is a sign that you are "poor," they will pick up on your feeling and believe the gift is inferior. This is also true when giving to adults. The way you feel about the gift will, to some degree, be reflected by the recipient.

In attempting either the up-front plan or the covert plan, it helps to explain why you want to save money. If you choose the up-front plan, this reason should be a part of your discussion. If you choose the covert plan, frequently mention your financial goals to those around you. If you let everyone know you are saving for a down payment on a house, what reasonable person could fault you?

But if others still see your frugal gift giving as "poor," "cheap," and/or "thoughtless," use . . .

THE BUZZ-OFF PLAN

It's unreasonable for others to expect you to spend in accordance with their values.

And it isn't written anywhere that the cost of your gift has to match the cost of theirs. In some cases, both parties can be comfortable with the "inequity."

But even if you do encounter hostility, consider this to be their problem, not yours. If everyone had the courage to ask for a change, Christmas could be transformed from a marketing opportunity to the holiday it was meant to be.

WRAPPING IDEAS

When you buy wrapping paper on those wide, wide rolls, it's easier and less wasteful to use if you cut through the entire roll one third of the way down, using a sharp razor blade or bread knife. The smaller roll is then just right for wrapping smaller boxes, and the larger roll is perfect for shirt boxes, and so on. (Muriel Kupper, Downers Grove, Illinois.)

Wrap awkward-shaped gifts in a Rudolph bag. To make one, take a brown paper bag. Fold down the top, folding in the sides so the top is triangle-shaped. Cut antlers out of brown paper, and tape or glue to the bag. Add eyes and a red nose with crayon, marker, or even a red pom-pom. (Vicki Fisher, Ogden, Utah.)

Use leftover trick-or-treat candy from Halloween for gift-decorating presents. You can make a neat bow from gum sticks . . . leave them in the wrappers, put a small dab of Elmer's glue on the centers, and arrange in a star shape. Put an old button in the center. (Donna Watkins, Lucedale, Mississippi.)

Make a simple, decorative box from any kind of heavy paper, such as old greeting cards, wallpaper, or old calendars.

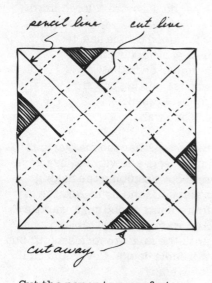

pencil line   cut line

cut away.

Cut the paper to a perfect square. To establish the center point of the paper, draw a pencil line from corner to corner on the reverse side. Fold a corner to the center point. Fold this fold line to the center point, lining it up with the pencil line. Repeat with the other three corners.

Cut the paper on the fold lines as shown.

To make the box, fold the corners of the two wider sides to the center point. Then fold the remaining two corners in to the center point. A dab of glue under each corner will secure the box.

To make a matching box to fit

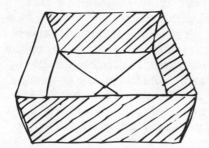

inside, repeat the process with a paper square that is ¼ inch narrower and shorter than your first square. If making boxes from greeting cards, use the "word side" for the inside box. (Jackie Wood, Gordon, Georgia.)

Enhance your scaled-down gift giving through creative "mystery wrapping." This is an especially good strategy if a family member has an annoying talent for guessing what's in a present before he unwraps it. For example if you're giving him a new belt, you could wind up the belt, put it and three marbles in a glass jar, and wrap. Or you could insert the belt into a long wrapping-paper tube and wrap. You could bend a coat hanger into a circle, wind the belt around the circular hanger, and wrap the present so it looks like a doughnut.

Cut an apple in half vertically, dip in acrylic paint, and stamp it on the inside of a cut-up paper bag. Then paint on brown seeds and green stem. Other fruits, such as lemons or oranges, could also be used. (Shawn Philley, Colville, Washington.)

FOOD FOR THE FESTIVITIES

All of the recipes in this section will make terrific gifts. You could make gift baskets with a selection of goodies. Decorate small bags with ribbon and "glitter stars," and include a homemade ornament.

In each case we tested the recipe and figured the cost (including energy for baking) and the preparation time to help you decide whether you want to try it.

STAINED-GLASS COOKIES

The original recipe, which came from a library book, frustrated my crack recipe tester so much that we initially rejected it. But her failed cookies so fascinated my children that I decided to experiment and alter the recipe to make it work. After many attempts, I finally had success.

This is a wonderful project to do with children. However, it's a bit finicky. I strongly suggest you try one cookie first, to be sure your oven times are the same as mine.

The recipe requires about 2 hours (less if you don't have help from kids) and makes about 20 cookies for $2.41.

You will need:

½ cup softened margarine
1 cup sugar
1 egg

1 teaspoon vanilla
½ teaspoon baking soda
½ teaspoon salt
2½ cups unsifted flour
1 pound assorted colored hard candies
2 foil-lined cookie sheets
heavy, clear plastic bag
hammer or mallet
wooden cutting board
yellow #2 pencil
cotton swab

Blend together the margarine, sugar, egg, and vanilla. In a separate bowl combine the baking soda, salt, and flour. Add the dry ingredients to the sugar mixture. Add water, about 6 tablespoons, until the mixture forms a stiff but workable dough. Cover and chill for 1 hour.

Unwrap and sort candies by color into separate bowls. One at a time, put each bowl of candies into the plastic bag and crush with a mallet. The final texture should include granules and small chunks. Return crushed candies to their separate bowls.

Preheat the oven to 350 degrees. Flour your hands, and roll a small piece of dough into a rope exactly the thickness of a pencil. Shape the ropes into holiday designs on the cookie sheets. Chanukah designs could include a dreidel, a Star of David, or a menorah. Christmas designs could include a Christmas tree, a star, a bell, or even a stained-glass church window.

If you want to make cookie ornaments, shape with a loop on top. For strength, this loop should be made from the middle of a long rope that forms a larger design— not added on afterward. To be sure that your loop doesn't close up during baking, test the size with the pencil. The loop hole should be slightly larger than the eraser tip. To join the ends of the dough pieces, dab with a wet cotton swab.

Prebake the cookies for 10 minutes or until lightly golden. Remove them from the oven. Fill the cookie sections with crushed candy. The depth of the candy should be the same as the thickness of the dough. Although you can mix colors for special effects, avoid mixing "color opposites" like red and green or yellow and purple, which, when blended, turn brown or gray.

Bake about 4 minutes, watching carefully. Remove cookies as soon as the candy melts. The candy can be lumpy or smooth, depending on your preference, but it should not cook until it bubbles.

At this point you can leave the cookies plain, or you can further decorate them by immediately pressing uncooked candy chunks into the melted candy. In this way you can add "colored lights" to your Christmas trees.

Let the cookies cool completely before carefully peeling them off the foil. If your cookie loop breaks easily, you might not have prebaked the dough shapes long enough. If you want these to work as ornaments, the final cookie should be so hard that only a kid would want to eat it.

BISCOTTI

These cookies have a grown-up taste that would go nicely with a special tea. My kids were excited only about the ones that were dipped in chocolate. The recipe requires 45 minutes of preparation time and yields 16 ounces for $2.32. A pound of Stella Doro biscotti costs $3.84, and a pound from a specialty shop costs $20.

½ cup sugar
¼ cup margarine
2 eggs
1 teaspoon almond extract
¼ teaspoon anise extract
1¾ cups flour
½ cup ground almonds
¼ teaspoon salt
1 teaspoon baking powder

Mix the first five ingredients with a mixer. Combine 1½ cups of the flour, ground almonds, salt, and baking powder. Add to the egg mixture, beating well. Stir in remaining ¼ cup flour. Cover and chill for two hours. Coat two sheets of heavy-duty plastic wrap with cooking spray. Divide dough in half and shape each half into a 12-inch log using the plastic wrap. Remove the wrap and transfer the logs to a cookie sheet coated with cooking spray. Flatten the logs to a ¾-inch thickness. Bake at 350 degrees for 20 minutes. Put the logs on a wire rack to cool. Slice diagonally into ¼-inch slices. Lay slices flat on a cookie sheet, and bake at 300 degrees for 15 minutes. Turn the slices over, and bake an additional 15 minutes or until dry. Once cooled, the top edge of the cookies can be dipped in melted chocolate chips. (Monique Van Hoek, Charlottesville, Virginia.)

CANDIED ORANGE PEEL

This is classically tightwaddy, as its main ingredient is something that is usually thrown away. Assuming the peels are free, it costs 52¢ to make 20 ounces. If you figure in simmering time but not drying time, this requires 1½ hours. These are pleasantly bittersweet.

Peels from 3 large oranges or
    grapefruits
¾ cup water
2 tablespoons corn syrup
2¾ cups sugar

Cut the peel on each fruit into quarters. Pull the peel off in these quarter sections. Slice peel into ¼-inch-wide strips. Put them in a 3-quart saucepan (not aluminum), and add water. Bring to a boil, reduce heat, and simmer 15 minutes. Drain. Boil the water, syrup, and 2 cups of the sugar. Keep stirring until the sugar dissolves. Add the peels. Simmer 40 minutes, stirring occasionally. Remove the peels with a slotted spoon, then put on a rack over a baking pan. Drain for 5 minutes, separate peels, and dry for another hour. Toss the peels into a plastic bag with the remaining sugar. Allow to air-dry 3 more hours, then store in an airtight container. Keeps one month, or can be frozen.

TOFFEE

Candy making scares some people, so this simple, delicious recipe might be a good way to begin. You can make 1¼ pounds for $2.20. Almond Roca, which tastes almost exactly the same, costs $3.99 for 7.05 ounces. Preparation time is 21 minutes.

1 cup chopped walnuts
¾ cup packed brown sugar
½ cup butter or margarine
½ cup semisweet chocolate chips

Butter an 8-inch square pan. Spread the chopped walnuts in the pan. Heat the butter or margarine and sugar, and boil over medium heat in a 1-quart saucepan, stirring constantly. Do this until the mixture darkens and just begins to smoke, about 7 minutes. Immediately pour the mixture over the walnuts. Sprinkle the chocolate chips evenly over the hot mixture, and put a cookie sheet over the top to hold in the heat so that it melts the chips. Spread the chocolate with a knife. If desired, sprinkle ground walnuts on the melted chocolate. Score into 1½-inch squares while still warm. Refrigerate. Break into squares when cool.

CHRISTMAS CHEESE BALL

A plain, 12-ounce cheddar ball from Hickory Farms costs $3.99. This recipe makes an 11-ounce ball for about $2.80 and requires 20 minutes of preparation time. If you mass-produce these using a food processor, you can save more time. The festive look and tangy taste make this recipe a winner.

2 ounces cream cheese, softened
1 teaspoon minced onion
2 teaspoons chopped pimento
dash garlic salt
2 tablespoons mayonnaise
¼ cup chopped green pepper
8 ounces grated cheddar cheese
½ cup chopped walnuts

Combine the first seven ingredients, and form into a ball. Roll the ball in the chopped walnuts so that the outside is completely covered. (Cindy Alldredge, Allen Park, Michigan.)

WHOLE-WHEAT CRACKERS

If you're making cheese balls for gifts, you might want to bake a batch of homemade crackers to go along with them. This recipe, a personal favorite of my recipe tester, is similar to a recipe I published a few years ago, except it's less crumbly. It requires 35 minutes of preparation time and makes 20 ounces for about 88¢. A 12-ounce box of Nabisco Wheat Thins costs $2.79.

1½ cups whole-wheat flour
1½ cups white flour
¼ cup sugar
1 teaspoon salt
½ teaspoon baking soda
½ cup margarine
¾ cup buttermilk
¼ cup wheat germ

Sift the first five ingredients together. Add the margarine and process in food processor. Add the buttermilk, and process until it forms a ball. Set it aside for 10 minutes. Cut the dough into four parts. Grease cookie sheets and sprinkle them with wheat germ. Roll each dough piece out on a cookie sheet. Sprinkle with salt. Cut into diamond shapes with a pastry wheel. Bake at 350 degrees for 20 to 25 minutes. Cool and put into a covered container.

PUPPY CHOW (FOR PEOPLE)

A staffer made these for us last year, and I asked her for the recipe for publication. If you don't have double coupons, the Crispix cereal will be the expensive ingredient. This recipe requires 20 minutes and makes 8 cups. Without coupons, the recipe costs $3.94, or 49¢ per 1-cup gift.

1 cup chocolate chips
1 stick margarine
1 cup peanut butter
8 cups Crispix cereal
2 cups powdered
    sugar

Melt the first three ingredients together in a saucepan, and pour over the cereal. Put the powdered sugar in a large plastic bag, and add the coated Crispix. Toss until evenly coated with sugar. Dry on foil, and store in an airtight container.

SOUTH OF THE BORDER SALSA

A quart of homemade salsa, a huge bag of taco chips, and a 2-liter bottle of soda make a flavorful and appreciated gift.

4 cups canned tomatoes with juice
1 large onion, diced
1 small, fresh jalapeño pepper,
    seeds and all, minced fine
    (adjust the amount depending
    upon the spiciness desired)
¼ teaspoon garlic powder
Salt and pepper

Cook all the ingredients in a large saucepan for 20 minutes. Pour into hot, sterile quart jars, and seal. Process in a pressure canner for 25 minutes. (Peggy West, Cleveland, Ohio.)

TREES FOR FREE

Residents of college towns should note that students leave for home between December 10 and 15 and leave the curbs strewn with perfectly good, discarded Christmas trees waiting to be rescued and recycled. (Corinne Kinane, Syracuse, New York.)

There's no law dictating that a Christmas tree must be a dead evergreen. You can decorate an orange tree, ficus, or other indoor treelike plant that you already own. (Carolyn Richards, Pepperell, Massachusetts.)

A good, sentimental tree skirt is an old quilt. This solves the problem of what to do with a really old, worn textile that you don't want to pitch but can't otherwise use. (Susan Morgan, Ballwin, Missouri.)

In some areas, the U.S. Forest Service sells a permit for about $8 that allows private citizens to select and cut one Christmas tree from a national forest. Forestry experts advise taking small trees that are within 10 feet of another small tree, as this "thinning" can help the forest. (Valerie Campbell, Calhan, Colorado.)

If you get all gooey about the ritual of tree decorating, this idea may seem *too* efficient, but you can save lots of time, energy, and money by buying an on-sale artificial Christmas tree, decorating it with lots of sale ornaments and lights, and storing it, complete with decorations, in the basement. Protect it with two garbage bags: one over the top, the other pulled up from the bottom, and seal the seam with duct tape. (Andi Hart, Camas, Washington.)

NOT NECESSARILY HALLMARK

This is a well-known tightwad tip, but it bears repeating just in case you don't know it: You can cut off the front half of a used Christmas card to make a Christmas postcard.

Kids enjoy making cards. Just supply them with green construction paper, gold paint, and red glitter. But they may tire before they produce the desired volume of cards. You can mass-produce their artwork as follows: Have the kid draw a picture on a Styrofoam meat tray, pressing hard enough to make an impression. Then use a hard-rubber roller (available at art-supply stores) to roll ink on the meat tray. Lay a piece of paper over the inked tray, and rub lightly with a spoon.

Paste a wintertime picture of your home on a piece of plain paper, leaving a 1-inch margin at the bottom. Using calligraphy, write something like "Holiday Greetings from the Swartz Family." Photocopy the card onto some colored paper (white paper might give better results with some photos). Then fold and trim to fit the envelope. (Ron Swartz, Sharon Springs, New York.)

GIFTS FOR GROWN-UPS

Make a jewelry purse for frequent travelers. As I made samples to test this idea, my small daughters were quick to claim them. Cut one 13½-inch and one 11-inch circle from paper to use as patterns. Cut two circles of each size from lightweight fabric. Cut a 5-inch circle from a piece of noncorrugated cardboard or, if you want the purse to be washable, use the plastic lid from a margarine tub. Stitch the "right sides" of the large fabric circles together with a seam that is about ¼-inch from their edges, leaving a 1-inch gap in the seam. Do the same with the small fabric circles. Turn the fabric circles inside out, press, and hand-stitch the gaps closed.

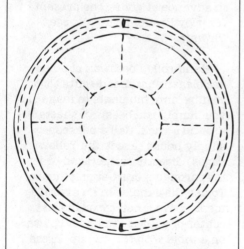

Place the two fabric circles on top of each other with the cardboard in between and pin to secure all three pieces. Sew around the cardboard circle. Fold the 11-inch paper circle into eighths, and use the fold marks as a guide to divide the smaller fabric circle into eight sections. Mark the sections with

pins. Sew eight seams from the edge of the cardboard circle to the edge of the smaller fabric circle.

Sew two seams around the larger fabric circle, one about ½-inch from the edge, and the second ½-inch inside the first. Cut two slits between these two seams on opposite sides of the purse. (To prevent fraying, these slits can be coated with "Fray Check," or you can sew buttonholes in these places before the larger fabric circles are sewn together.) Using a large safety pin, thread two drawstrings through these slits.

When the drawstrings are pulled, the purse has an area in the center for large pieces of jewelry and eight pockets for earrings and other small items.

If you have extra fabric, you might stitch some matching drawstring bags to hold shoes. (Meg Winfield, Columbia, Maryland.)

Copies of old photographs, such as grandparents' wedding pictures or Mom and Dad's baby portraits, make wonderful gifts for grown family members. Photo stores can charge as little as $3 to make a negative, and 30¢ for each 3½-by-5-inch copy. Extra touches, such as sepia toning, can cost a bit more. If you don't own family heirloom photographs, borrow them, and make an extra photo for the lender to show your appreciation. These can be given for years, as you work back through parents, grandparents, great-grandparents, and so on. (Karen Humiston, Sheboygan, Wisconsin.)

Check to see if local, nonprofit agencies are offering items. For instance, a local group raising money to renovate low-income housing is selling cedar ornaments at $5 each. A purchase like this contributes to a good cause and provides a gift that could be given to a boss, and so on. (Joan Brown, Lake Lotawana, Missouri.)

For elderly relatives who find shopping difficult, stock up on the foods and products they like as they go on sale throughout the year. At Christmas, you'll have collected enough to fill a carton, which you can decorate for their Christmas present. While it is not an "exciting" present, it is sure to be appreciated. (Camille Hawthorne, Munchen, Germany.)

Make a home-made bird feeder: Take a hardwood branch that is about 12 inches long and 3 inches in diameter. With a drill or hole saw, cut two holes about 2½ inches apart as shown. About ½ inch below the large holes, drill another hole about ½ inch wide. Cut two ½-inch dowels, or twigs, about 6 inches long, and insert them into the ½-inch holes. Glue into place. Cut the top of the

branch at a slight angle so water will run off. Put an eye bolt in the top center of the log, thread with cord, and hang from a tree.

Fill the two large holes in the bird feeder with birdseed mixture. Be sure to include this recipe with your gift:

2 cups shortening
1 cup peanut butter
1 cup cornmeal
1 cup oatmeal or flour
1 cup birdseed

Melt the shortening with the peanut butter in a large saucepan. Add the cornmeal and mix well. Add the birdseed and mix well. Pour into a rectangular baking pan or cupcake pans, and let set overnight. Pack into holes in the bird feeder with a spoon or your hands. Can be made months in advance of giving the present. (Shirley Braden, King George, Virginia.)

Hand-rolled beeswax candles are elegant handmade gifts that require only moments to make . . . you simply roll beeswax sheets around a wick. Call a beekeepers' supply house (check the Yellow Pages) directly rather than ordering through a craft-supply house. To use the candles in an arrangement, drive a nail through the center of a juice-can lid and place on a table with the nail up. Press candle on the nail to secure it. Arrange several candles together, and put the flowers or greenery around the base. (Sharon L. Crow, Klamath Falls, Oregon.)

For a "homemade" gift that requires only shopping skills, put together your own version of the overpriced food baskets sold by Hickory Farms and similar companies. For example, there is a gift pack with five 2-ounce packages of flavored coffee for $18.99. At a gourmet coffee shop, they can be purchased for $1.49 each, totaling $7.45. At the grocery store, they can be purchased for 99¢ each, totaling $4.95. Use decorative baskets or tins, and fill with gourmet coffee, homemade spiced-tea mix, homemade cookies and candies, mixed nuts (bought in bulk), and/or home-canned jam or jelly. Add some fresh fruit and a personal touch, such as a homemade Christmas ornament. (Angela Birchfield, Warner Robins, Georgia.)

Certificates for services are always appreciated. "One night of baby-sitting" is common, and a welcome gift to parents. More creative alternatives include "One year's worth of mending," which is especially appreciated by college students. Other ideas could include snow shoveling, changing oil, or home repairs. (Jody Grage Haug, Seattle, Washington.)

The Lentil-Rice Casserole (page 151) works well as a gift. Put raw ingredients in a 1-pint canning jar. Put a pretty piece of fabric over the top before screwing on the band. Make a label that says "Tightwad Casserole" and provide cooking instructions. (Kirsten Melton, Pleasant Hill, California.)

A hot-glue gun is a gift that every young parent should have . . . handy for toy repairs, Halloween-costume creation, and general crafts. (Dr. Richard Sonnenfeld, San Jose, California.)

If you own a camcorder, make videotapes of your adult children. Each year, give them a videotape featuring them and their families. (Joyce Bant, Hazelhurst, Wisconsin.)

Have a contest to see how many gifts a husband and wife can buy for each other for $10. Requires ingenuity, and makes for a special Christmas morning. (Vivian Walker, Markham, Ontario, Canada.)

Make it a rule that only consumable, "festive" items can be exchanged. Examples (many of which are homemade): flavored salad vinegars, honey, spices, candies, and fancy jams and jellies. You may also specify that less exotic items are okay, such as cotton balls, soda, tissues, soaps, pens, lightbulbs, and so on. Add quips such as "Do you know how to tuna guitar?" to a can of tuna. (April Passofaro, Prior Lake, Minnesota.)

Give a "soup of the month." Make a double batch of some special soup once each month, and give half to the gift recipient. This gift enhances your own menus as well. The same idea could be used for breads. (Pat Miller, San Antonio, Texas.)

If the recipient has freezer space, make several batches of slice-and-bake cookie dough, which can be frozen in rolls and wrapped attractively. This allows the recipient to have cookies after the holiday glut has passed. Recipes can be found in *The Complete Make-a-Mix Cookbook* by Eliason, Harward, and Westover. Order it through interlibrary loan. (Rebecca Novakovich, Cambridge, Massachusetts.)

If you have an excess of family photos, recycle them into mini photo albums made from 5-inch-by-7-inch pieces of construction paper. Put yarn through holes punched in the left side, and add clever captions. (Wanda Owen, Wexford, Pennsylvania.)

For a gift for a grandparent, have a child put her hands on a copy machine at the edges of the markings for a regular-size sheet of paper. Either put a photo of the child between the hands, or leave blank if you have a photo you want to paste in. A note under the photo or just a signature with the date and/or age of the child finishes the gift. If these are given each year, they can be collected into a notebook. (Mary Lou Fisher, Redmond, Washington.)

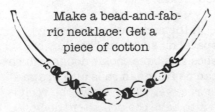

Make a bead-and-fabric necklace: Get a piece of cotton

or cotton-blend fabric, 36 inches by 3 inches. Fold in half lengthwise. Sew down the long edge with a ¼-inch seam allowance. Turn in-side out. Alternately insert large beads into the tube, and string smaller beads on the outside of the tube. Make about 8 inches of beadwork. Adjust all to the center of the strip. Knot each end of the beadwork. Tuck in a half inch of each end of the fabric tube, and stitch closed. (Rhonda Monden, Moore, Oklahoma.)

GIFTS FOR KIDS

This Christmas section would not be complete without a plea for restraint when it comes to toy buying, which is where Christmas becomes the most crazy and materialistic. So here's a letter that makes some excellent points:

I am approaching my first tight-wad Christmas with three sons (ages thirteen, ten, and five) who have seen only spendthrift Christmases. I was worried about how well my resolve would hold out as the shopping season approached, so I went into the boys' rooms and made lists of last year's gifts (those that were still around), writing down the cost of each and estimating the time each had been played with. Some (jigsaw puzzles and board games) proved to have been good buys. Unfortunately, in other cases, my estimates showed that my husband had worked more hours to pay for a toy than my children had played with it!

Armed with last year's list, I made my first Christmas-shopping trip last weekend. After slowly touring every aisle of one of the largest toy stores in Wichita, my cart held only two modest gifts. I looked at everything, considering the probable play value of each item. I discovered there really are not many good ideas in toys and games. In many cases, the good ones have been around since my childhood. I am no longer worried that I will spend too much this year. Rather, I am worried that it may prove hard to find gifts that meet my new criteria. (Jane Kelly, Wichita, Kansas.)

Begin stockpiling yard-sale toys in May. New-looking toys selling for less than one tenth of their original cost are common at yard sales. Also, for older kids, check out the used sporting-goods stores that are popping up all over the country.

A month or so before Christmas, take books you no longer need to a secondhand bookstore. Trade them for "new" children's books. (Marie Davies, St. Louis, Missouri.)

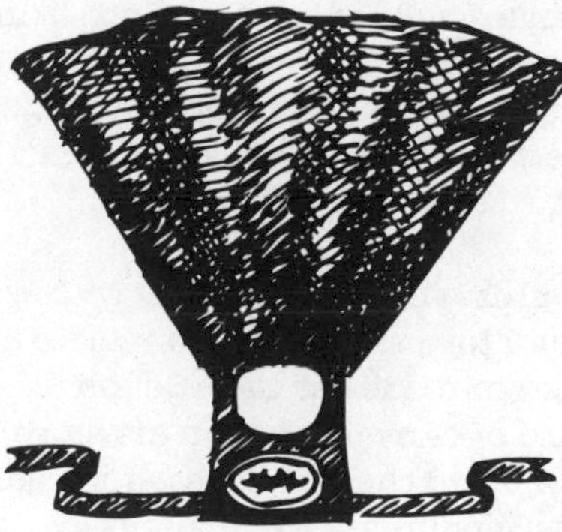

Make a superhero cape from fabric scraps. Cut two chest pieces, then cut out pieces for the logo. Adhere the logo to the front, chest piece with fabric glue and a zigzag stitch. Make two long strips for tying on. Attach these when you are sewing the chest pieces together. Attach the cape at the shoulders. (Cindy Alldredge, Allen Park, Missouri.)

Make an Indian teepee. Cut triangular shapes for the height wanted. Sew together, making a casing at each seam. Put PVC pipe through for poles, about a foot taller than the top of the fabric. Tie poles together at the top, and secure with hot glue. Paint on Indian designs if desired. Similar teepees sell in catalogs for $59.95. (Cindy Alldredge, Allen Park, Missouri.)

One of the best kid-gift concepts is "gathered presents." Assembling these requires skilled scrounging and advance planning, but they make wonderful, creative gifts. These include:

Doctor's office: Bag (black canvas or vinyl purse with white cross and "M.D." written on it), eye dropper, syringe (no needle), small scissors, adhesive tape, swabs, cotton balls, tongue depressors (cleaned popsicle sticks or ask your doctor for a few) bandages, gauze, small cups, plastic gloves, sling, mirrored headband, name tag, stethoscope (can be made from wire coat hanger, black electrical tape, adhesive tape, and a juice-can lid), X ray (black paper with a white drawing of skull or bones), small skeleton model, skeleton chart (copy from reference book), eye chart, clipboard, prescription pad, office-hours sign.

"Crimebusters": Magnifying glass, flashlight, gloves, binoculars or periscope, camera, decoder, invisible writing pens, handcuffs, I.D. with badge, signs for office, attaché case, small tool

kit, safe, crime-scene reports, evidence bags, money, CRIME SCENE — DO NOT CROSS banner.

School: Chalkboard, chalk, eraser, pointer, spelling tests, report cards with envelopes, write-and-wipe calendar, markers, roll book, bell, flag and stand, U.S.A. map, puzzles, whistle, clock, hall pass, stamps or stickers that say "excellent," "well-done," and so on, awards, reward jar with treasures, red pen, pencils.

Crafts: Feathers, sequins, construction paper, yarn, beads, colorful macaroni, mini-clothespins, paints, markers, dowels, confetti, glue, scissors, pipe cleaners, doilies, buttons, pom-poms, moving eyes, metal brads, idea book, carrying case.

Other possible gathered-present themes include: café, office, travel, veterinarian, learn-to-read, and theater. (Debra Posthumus-Forbes, Kalamazoo, Michigan.)

Make Christmas "treasure boxes." Cut long strips of the colorful Sunday funnies, and put in a box. Bury within this assorted candies, and, for girls, a pretty lipstick holder, a pink, folding comb, inexpensive, colorful earrings, and other small yard-sale treasures you've collected over the year. This is a nice idea for mailing to distant relatives, when you don't know their children well enough to know what they like. (Laura Henning, Flushing, New York.)

Metal riding horses on spring frames are often inexpensive at yard sales because they have worn paint. You can repaint one with a variety of colors . . . you can even paint it to match the colors of the child's favorite "My Little Pony." (Lauren Wahl, Miami, Florida.)

Babies love a simple Christmas rattle made from a large, metal "jingle" bell (at least 1½ inches in diameter) attached to a short length of brightly colored ribbon. (Letty Bernard Steckler, Morgan City, Louisiana.)

Kids who enjoy playing with small toy cars might appreciate a custom-made car mat. Get one yard of canvas from an art store, sew down the raw edges, and use fabric paint and permanent markers to make streets, stores, Dad's work, our house, the library, the local sports stadium and McDonald's (for spendthrift families) or the thrift shop (for frugal families). (Mary Nafis, Chino, California.)

HOLIDAY TRADITIONS

If your child constantly asks "How many days until Christmas?" try this variation of a Cherokee ceremony for children: Tie knots in a rope, one for each day remaining until Christmas, and hang it on the child's doorknob. Each night, untie one knot. This can become a much-loved family tradition. (Jennifer Pounds, Dawsonville, Georgia.)

Ask older children to take on a service project, such as helping in a food drive for the homeless, in place of a gift to their parents. On Christmas, have them report on what they did as they open their gifts from the parents. (Sharon Ditto, Hixson, Tennessee.)

Insert "work chores" and "fun chores" into red and green balloons. Examples: "Help clear the table, and share a favorite Christmas memory," "Serve the dessert, and kiss the neighbor on your left," "Take extra chairs back to the kitchen, and tell about your best Christmas ever," and "Relax, put your feet up, and take a nap." Blow up balloons and tape them overhead at Christmas dinner. Have long, curly ribbons hanging from each one. After dinner, each diner pulls a ribbon, bursts the

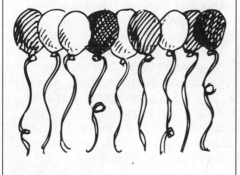

balloon, reads the note, and does what it says. Children and adults both love this, and it can become a family tradition for Thanksgiving as well. (Jean L. Winteringham, Farmington, Michigan.)

Make an Advent candle from 11-inch to 12-inch candles, which can be purchased on sale for as little as 20¢. Mark them into 24 sections with acrylic paint, then number each section, starting with 1 at the top and 24 at the bottom. Each night at dinner, burn down one section. (Vicki Fisher, Ogden, Utah.)

THE MOMMY STORE

For families with several young children, pick up inexpensive gifts at yard sales . . . a typical price is 25¢. During the holiday season, allow kids to do special chores in exchange for "Mommy money." Just before Christmas, set up "store," setting out gifts you have preselected for one child at a time. The kids come and buy using "Mommy money." Little kids enjoy earning and giving gifts, older kids enjoy saving money, and parents enjoy the extra help they get from kids. (Susan Dransfield, Nampa, Idaho.)

A homemade "Christmas Book" can be made from yard-sale stuff, including a three-ring binder covered with a scrap of Christmas fabric. Put dividers inside labeled: STORIES, RECIPES, GIFTS TO MAKE, DECORATIONS TO MAKE, and so on. Cut out stories, recipes, and craft instructions from Christmas magazines purchased at yard sales or fished from recycling bins, and put them in their proper places in the book. Get the book out the day after Thanksgiving, and use it regularly up until the big day. (Vickie Jackson, Lubbock, Texas.)

DECORATIONS FOR THE HOME

The decorative border on some Christmas cards makes a perfect mat for framing holiday photographs. Just cut out the center of the card with an X-Acto knife so that the border remains intact, then trim the edges so it will fit in a yard-sale frame. (Karen Jones, Lovettsville, Virginia.)

Luminarias, made with paper bags, sand, and candles, can be difficult to light in windy weather. Gallon plastic milk jugs, cut off so that they are about 8 inches high, provide a similar look, but with more manageability and safety. (Carol Leppert, Erie, Michigan.)

Luminarias can also be made of tin cans. Fill a can with water

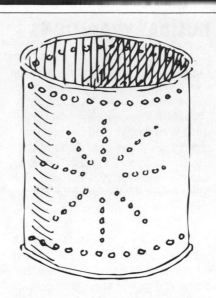

and freeze, then punch holes with a hammer and nail to form a picture or abstract pattern, such as a Christmas tree, snowflake, or Star of David. The frozen water inside keeps the can from bending as you punch it. (Jay-Niles Memorial Library, North Jay, Maine.)

You can add sparkle to old-fashioned pomander balls by alternating the cloves with silver studs . . . the kind kids stick on jeans. (Ruth Sutton, Porterville, California.)

Christmas placemats can be made with old Christmas cards. Choose the part you want to show . . . either the cover, the inside scripture, or a warm, handwritten thought. Remove the protective backing from a sheet of clear contact paper, and lay it down with the sticky side up. Arrange the card pieces on it, face up, in the composition desired. Then carefully place a second piece of clear contact paper atop the first. Cutting the edge with pinking shears creates a nice effect. (Dan Steinbeck, Canton, Missouri.)

Children who are too young to light Chanukah candles can "light" the candles on a menorah wall hanging made of felt. The "flames" are attached with Velcro backing, so that one more can be stuck on each night. Ready-made, store-bought versions of this cost $25, but materials for a homemade version are under $2.50. (Celeste Leibowitz, Brooklyn, New York.)

Make an Advent calendar from poster board, construction paper, and glue. You can make a Christmas-tree shape of green paper, and cut pictures from holiday catalogs or Christmas cards. (Barbara Durmick, Alexandria, Virginia.)

Here is an inexpensive Christmas potpourri:

peels from 2 apples, dried and
    broken up
1 cup or less orange peel, dried
    and broken up
2 tablespoons whole cloves
1 cinnamon stick, broken into
    small pieces

Mix and store in a jar or paper bag. Simmer in a pot for a wonderful aroma. (Rene Miles, Lake Jackson, Texas.)

Use what you have, creatively. For example, collect a half-dozen stuffed bears, tie inexpensive plaid ribbon around their necks, and arrange them on a cleaned-up child's sled to make an attractive indoor display. (Jane R. Gilson, Denville, New Jersey.)

Make decorative "snowflakes" from six-pack rings. You can obtain these without buying the soda by speaking with the vending-machine stocker at your place of business or the manager of a convenience store.

To make one you'll need 20 six-pack rings, a small stapler, thread, and white yarn or narrow ribbon.

Place two rings together, and staple together at points 1, 2, and 3. This makes one "pair" with a "front and back section." Repeat until you have ten stapled pairs. Fold the end of each of the 20 rings, and staple at points 4, 5, 6, and 7.

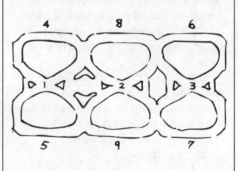

To attach the ten pairs together, staple point 8 in one pair to point 9 in another. Attach both the front and back sections in this way. You now have one long piece.

Run a piece of thread through one end of front sections. Repeat with the back section on the same end. Pull these threads tight to form the center of the snowflake. To complete the snowflake, staple the remaining points 8 to the remaining points 9.

These can be left as is or decorated with "spray snow." Hang with yarn or ribbon.

By cutting the rings and experimenting with different combinations, you can make different sizes and designs. (Norma Kelly, Huntsville, Alabama.)

Make "grapevine" wreath ornaments from the hanging branches of weeping willow trees. Gather branches while they are still soft and pliable, wrap them to form a circle and fasten with wire. Set them aside for a few days to dry, then decorate with a small bow. Small ones can be used to decorate wrapped packages, larger ones can be hung on the wall. (Christine Summers, Levittown, Pennsylvania.)

Beat-up artificial Christmas trees can be recycled into permanent wreaths . . . just remove the limbs and bend onto green floral wire. Hot-glue holly, bells, and other decorations to the wreaths.

Use sheets of foam packing material to make snowmen cutouts to hang in windows. These also make great ghosts for Halloween. (Teresa Huebener, Ottumwa, Iowa.)

Put several mason jars on a sill, and stuff an equal length of inexpensive twinkle lights in each jar. (Mary Christensen, Larson, Wisconsin.)

Pine-cone Christmas trees are an excellent project for large groups of children. Spray-paint large pine cones green, then have kids decorate them with glitter and top them with stars. (Larada Lynn Read, Oxford, Georgia.)

EASY AND INEXPENSIVE ORNAMENTS

Recycle scratched glass ornaments. Remove the metal neck and hanger. Soak the whole ornament, inside and out, in bleach for 5 to 15 minutes. Use a cotton swab or child's toothbrush, if needed, to carefully scrub the inside. Rinse it, dry it, and stuff it. Use feathers, tinsel, potpourri, confetti, or anything colorful. Replace neck and hanger. The outside can also be decorated with feathers and lace. The sample sent in to me is attractive enough to make a nice gift. (Fran DeChane, Eastpointe, Michigan.)

Make woven hearts: Cut two 7-inch-by-2-inch pieces from different-colored paper or felt. Fold each piece, round the end, and cut strips as

shown. Put strip A through strip 1, then continue in an "around, through, around, through" pattern. Slide strip A up and resume weaving with strips B, C, D, E. Make a handle with a 7-inch-by-½-inch strip of paper or felt, glued or stapled to the top-centers of the heart pieces. (Jay-Niles Memorial Library, North Jay, Maine.)

Glitter stars are among the simplest ornaments to make, yet they are strikingly pretty. Use white craft glue (such as Tacky, Sobo, or Elmer's, which works best) in a bottle with a tip. Simply "draw" a star shape on wax paper. (Aluminum foil worked better for us.) The shapes can be solid or a ¼-inch line. Don't try to make the star shapes too perfect. Sprinkle the glue with glitter, making sure it is completely covered. Let the stars dry for 4 to 24 hours, depending on the type of glue. Carefully peel the wax paper or foil away from the back, working in from each point. Hang on your tree, or use to decorate presents. Use this same idea to make hearts for Valentine's Day. (Rhonda Cliett, Belton, Texas.)

Put a cheap paper plate and water in a blender, and process on "liquefy" for one minute. Press the pulp into a cookie mold, and let dry until hard. Decorate with gold glitter, and hang from a loop of gold thread or an ornament hanger. (Barbie Murray, Sterling, Virginia.)

The pattern to make this paper dove comes from *Better Homes & Gardens* magazine. Start by making this pattern out of cardboard:

Fold a heavy piece of white paper in half. Line up the top edge of the pattern with the fold, and trace. Cut out the paper bird. Glue the two halves of the head together with a drop of white glue . . . put on a paper clip to hold it together as it dries.

Once dry, insert each wing through the slot from the inside outward, as shown. Make a hole in the bird's back, and hang with a loop of string.

AFTER THE HOLIDAYS . . .

About a month after Christmas, visit any large cemetery. You'll find the caretakers have piled big heaps of ornaments and decorations ready for trash pickup. It's easily possible to collect several bags of decorations. If you have a problem with this hint, ask yourself this question: Why is a landfill a more sacred and respectful destination than your home?

This seems incredible to those of us who live up north . . . but apparently, in Southern areas, the weekend after Christmas is the best time of year for yard sales, as that is when many people get rid of unwanted gifts. This is an excellent time to pick up brand-new gifts for next Christmas.

Save gifts that you cannot use to give to someone else next year . . . for example, if you don't drink and are given liquor, pass it along next Christmas. Be sure to put a tag on it noting who gave it to you, to avoid major embarrassment. (Anna Weisend, Cleveland, Ohio.)

PICTURE PERFECT

Dear Amy,
    I have a tightwad *perfect* gift suggestion when you are the mothers of the bride and groom. Moms get together and swap pictures from birth—match age to age—Cub Scout to Brownie, cheerleader to Little League, whatever. Place in a collage and have a *keepsake* gift for the couple.

—Deb Palka
  Peoria, Illinois

A FINE LINE

Dear Amy,
    I don't use clothespins to hang up my shirts. Instead, I hang them on plastic hangers, and put the hangers on the clothesline. I can fit more clothes on the line this way, and taking them down to put them away is much quicker.

—Ellen J. Urbina-Martin
  Salem, New Hampshire

ISN'T THIS GRATE?

Dear Amy,
    Our grocery store sells blocks of cheese for about $3 per pound. The same store has a salad/taco bar, which features, among other items, grated cheddar cheese. The items in this salad bar sell for $1.99 a pound. Most of the time, when we want cheese we want it in grated form, so buying our cheese from the salad bar saves both money and the work of grating.

—Susan Schubel
  Fredericksburg, Virginia

SCRAP HAPPY

Dear Amy,

For cheap or free fabric, contact a custom drapery shop. My husband installs draperies, and the drapery workroom has tons of remnants from lace to heavy fabrics. This has been a big savings on dresses and craft materials for my family.

—Marlene Albers
Katy, Texas

WEAR AND SPARE

Dear Amy,

I used to feel that waiting a week to ten days, then doing six to eight loads of laundry, was cost-efficient (because the loads were full) and energy efficient (my energy, that is) in that I would save on trips to the various areas where the folded clothes were kept. But I suddenly realized that if you wash more frequently, you can have fewer clothes and need less storage. In my limited-storage home, that's a larger saving.

—Lynn Golson
Tucson, Arizona

(I realized this years ago. Because I wash every day, it's possible for a boy to squeak through a school year with two good pairs of jeans. FZ)

EARN DOCKET CHANGE

Dear Amy,

By appearing in court to "explain" a traffic violation, you can save money.

I neglected to renew my tags, and the original fine was $133 (stated on the ticket). In court I explained this was an oversight. The judge reduced the fine to $75. That saved me $58. It would have been a greater reduction if I hadn't been five months expired. *Oops!*

—Kathleen Sconce
Evans, Washington

NEWS YOU CAN USE

Dear Amy,

Encourage your local paper to start a reader exchange. Our weekly town paper just started one, and it has been a big hit. People can call in their requests for hard-to-find items or offers of free items. People call in their replies, which are printed the following week. We already have acquired some nice things for free.

—Kimberly Frodelius
Solvay, New York

UNITED WE SAVE

Dear Amy,

I wanted to make my own price book for over a year but could not seem to make myself spend the time or effort. Finally, I made up a list of regular grocery items and then photocopied the list and distributed it among friends. Each person did a price survey of a different store in our area in the same week. I compiled the results and distributed these to each participant. Now I have a price book, and it took only one week to put together!

—Eve Burch
Claremont, California

VAPOR VALUE

Dear Amy,

To get "free" distilled water, save gallon jugs and use water from your dehumidifier during the summer months. Use it for your iron or vaporizer.

—Amy Guenterberg
Madison, Wisconsin

TEST-TUBE TIGHTWADDERY

Jim's guffaw boomed from the laundry room where he was changing Brad's diaper. "Come on, Amy, don't you think bread-bag plastic pants is a bit over the edge?" Although my long-suffering husband of 12 years has become used to such oddities, it still caught him off-guard to unsnap

his son's pants and read "Butter-Top Wheat Bread."

This particular experiment came about because our plastic-pants supply was low and our bread-bag supply was high. I had remembered the early disposables, which were held with pins, and wondered if a slit-open-and-flattened bread bag could work with cloth diapers in the same way. It did work reasonably well. Although I've never used the idea again, I've always known it could serve in a pinch.

Scoffers will rightly accuse me of being nutty if I ever advocate bread-bag plastic pants as a permanent solution. However, I proudly defend my actions in the larger context of tightwad scientific experimentation. The person who is willing to try new ways of doing things will have some failures, but also have infinitely more successes than the person who is unwilling to try at all. It's the constant, creative experimenting—"tweaking" to make adjustments—that helps you save an extra 5 percent or 10 percent more than the less adventurous tightwads.

But often people don't experiment because:

• They figure that Heloise, or I, or some other domestic genius must have already figured out the best way. But in consumer reporting, complex information is often distilled into very simplistic answers that work only for the average person in an average place with average resources. It's a sure bet that you don't fit that description.

• They have complete faith in the way they've always done things. But think back to all those scientific facts that have been disproved: The world is flat, the earth is the center of the universe, and man can't fly. Given that these immutable facts have been disproved, how do we know that freezing panty hose makes them last longer, anyway?

• They're afraid they will be ridiculed if their experiment fails. But don't think of ideas that didn't work as failures. When Thomas Edison was asked about his 1,000 failed experiments in an effort to perfect the lightbulb, he said he didn't regard these experiments as failures, he had merely learned 1,000 ways it wouldn't work.

I see this experimental mindset in "black-belt" tightwads who send me all sorts of unconventional ideas. However, one failing I frequently observe is a lack of true scientific methodology—specifically, the failure to test the idea against a "control group." To be purely scientific, you need to compare results of the experimental method to the results of the conventional method.

One experimental-versus-control-group test I plan to try involves an old tightwad theory: If you put iron-on patches on the inside knees of new pants, the pants will last longer. Although this sounds logical, I have wondered whether it would make sense for yard-sale pants in good condition. If I buy these pants for 50¢, would it be worth it to iron on $1.25 worth of patches?

In the past, I've found that though the patch holds up, sometimes the area around a patch wears faster. So I plan to iron a patch on one knee and see how much longer the patched knee lasts compared to the unpatched one.

Like Edison, I've tried experiments that didn't work. I wondered if small amounts of leftover casseroles could be saved in a muffin cup to make "leftover muffins." It didn't work.

I knew you could substitute a heaping tablespoon of soy flour and a tablespoon of water for an egg when baking, and I knew you could substitute an equal amount of applesauce for cooking oil in baking. So I wondered what would happen if I used soy flour *and* applesauce in a drop-cookie recipe. The cookies, after a much longer-than-normal baking time, just sat there and got harder; they never expanded and melted the way regular cookies do.

I concluded that in most baking, recipes need some fat to work.

But I have also had successes. Last year I made sauce from the small, sour apples of neglected, nearby trees. The resulting dark applesauce was so sour the children wouldn't eat it. So I tried the applesauce in place of pumpkin purée in pumpkin pie. Applesauce pie was a great success.

Similarly, one day Jim started making bread-crumb cookies (from the first book) and realized he hadn't allowed enough time in his schedule to bake them. So he spread the chocolaty dough in a Pyrex cooking dish and baked it. The result was respectable bread-crumb brownies.

Aside from determining whether an experiment actually works, I often note how long an idea took to execute and whether that justifies the savings. For example, I experimented with methods to repair torn plastic pants. Hot glue worked, but melted when the pants went through the dryer. Then I successfully stitched the tears on the sewing machine in seconds. But I also learned that if tears are due to long-term aging, within a few wearings the pants will simply tear again next to my repair. In contrast, I've learned it *is* worthwhile to stitch ragged diapers; it takes a minute, and they last for another year.

Sometimes before you actually invest money and time in an experiment, you might gather data for months. When his household knives became too dull to sharpen with his diamond-dust rod, a friend embarked on a search for a cheap alternative. Each time he visited a friend or relative's house, he asked how

knife sharpening was done there. He *tried* the method on the spot and judged how well it worked.

After a year (during which the toughest meat his family ate was hamburger/TVP meat loaf) he determined that the only sharpening tool that met his exacting standards was a $75 motorized gizmo. But he noticed the stone it used was of the same grit as a $2 grinding wheel for an electric drill. He bought a wheel and tried it on his dull knives. It worked perfectly. (If you try this, hold your finger on the blade to make sure it does not overheat. This could make the blade lose its "temper.")

Of course, there are a few areas where you should not experiment. Readers keep asking for a home-made contact-lens solution or, at least, a method for using less store-bought solution. And other readers have sent me a few ideas. But, sorry, I can't recommend creative ocular hygiene. Stick to the wide range of everyday activities with which you can experiment safely.

Finally, you ask, what's this about freezing panty hose? Supposedly, if you freeze new panty hose, they last longer. Since *The Tightwad Gazette* has a blue-jeans-are-fine dress code, it would take me years to test this theory. But it could be done by purchasing two identical pairs of panty hose, freezing one pair, then cutting one leg off each pair, combining the remaining prefrozen and not-prefrozen hose to make one pair, and then wearing them to see which leg lasts longer.

But what if your office desk tends to snag one leg more than the other? Then forget cutting the legs off: Buy two pair, and wear prefrozen and not-prefrozen hose on alternating days.

But does the freezing technique work differently on different brands? And does it matter if it's winter or summer?

If anyone figures this one out, let me know.

HOP, SCRIMP, AND JUMP

My daughter Jamie reminded me of the amazing entertainment possibilities of scrap paper when she taught herself to make an origami hopping frog. Although this works best with a 3-by-5 index card, she amused her siblings for a good hour making scores of frogs from scrap paper. I couldn't step anywhere without squishing one. She learned that the smaller the frog, the bigger the jump. One ¼-inch frog hopped as high as a flea.

If an hour's worth of free kid entertainment doesn't impress you, think back to how long your children really played with those "Happy Meal" toys.

A parent, with practice, could entertain birthday-party attendees with a repertoire of a few dozen origami creations, as well as provide take-home gifts for nearly nothing. Special origami papers are nice, but not necessary. For advanced origami, you'll want to check out a library book.

In the meantime, save those abundant lime-green school notices, and on the next snow day show your kids how to make hopping frogs.

As you follow the directions, note that a line of dots means to fold up to make a "valley" and a line of dashes means to fold down to make a "mountain."

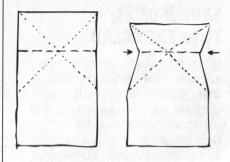

Fold and reflatten paper.

Push in at the sides, and fold down to make a triangle shape.

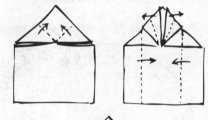

Make folds as indicated. Then turn over and draw eyes and a nose.

To make the frog jump, push its back down and slide your finger off. Hold frog races and jumping contests.

SAVE MONEY; TOSS THE SALAD

When it comes to produce, our ancestors ate seasonally. When their gardens were producing, they ate greens, cucumbers, and tomatoes, but during the winter they ate sweet potatoes, carrots, and butternut squash because these would keep without freezing or canning. Now, with modern transportation and food preservation, seasonal eating is almost

nonexistent. Beyond this, we've come to believe that expensive wintertime salads are essential for good nutrition.

But are they? In general, fresh produce begins to lose vitamins the moment it's picked. So fresh, in-season produce that comes from your garden or from a local grower is superior. But the so-called "fresh" produce shipped from Florida and Mexico in January is often six to ten days old by the time it gets to the market. Ac-

cording to the produce manager at a large chain supermarket, produce can sit on the shelf for another ten days before it's sold. Then, it may reside in your refrigerator for seven more days. In short, store-bought "fresh" produce can be almost four weeks old before it's consumed.

So the question is: How does fresh supermarket produce, which loses nutrition through aging, compare to canned and frozen vegetables, which lose nutrition through processing? There are many variables, but in one study, conducted by the University of Illinois, flash-frozen green beans lost 17 percent of their vitamin C content due to processing, but seven-day-old fresh green beans picked from the same vines at the same time lost 60 percent. According to registered nutritionist Liz Ward, home-canned foods also retain most of their nutrition, but commercially canned foods, which generally have added sodium, are regarded as the least nutritious alternative.

It's true that some fresh produce can be consumed without the cooking that would cause some further loss of nutrients and fiber. But given the possible age of fresh produce, processed and cooked vegetables can still have equal, if not superior nutrition.

Then where did we get the idea that we need to eat salads all year long? Most of us are recalling our mothers' admonition to eat dark green, leafy vegetables to get vitamin A. So, lucky for us that they ship all of that iceberg lettuce north, right?

Wrong. Iceberg lettuce is a "head" lettuce, not a leafy lettuce, so it's not a good source of vitamin A; a serving provides only 2 percent of the Recommended Daily Allowance of A. In fact, it provides so little nutrition overall that it's never a good value. Leafy lettuces are better, providing 20 percent of the R.D.A. of vitamin A. Spinach provides 35 percent.

But dark green, leafy vegetables aren't the only sources of vitamin A. Deep yellow and orange vegetables and fruits (except citrus) are even better. The real vitamin A powerhouses are carrots, at 330 percent of the R.D.A. per serving, and sweet potatoes, at 520 percent per serving. Other candidates include cantaloupe, tomatoes, butternut squash, pumpkin, and apricots, which provide between 30 percent and 140 percent of your daily need for vitamin A.

Vitamin C also has its share of mythology. While an orange provides 110 percent of your daily need for C, you don't need to eat citrus fruit every day. Look at the amount of C provided by other produce: A serving of tomato has 40 percent, potato has 50 percent, cabbage has 70 percent, cantaloupe has 90 percent, cauliflower has 110 percent, kiwi has 115 percent, a bell pepper has 130 percent, strawberries have 140 percent, and broccoli—wow—provides 240 percent!

(These percentages are based on a broad sampling of fresh supermarket produce and are intended only as a general guideline. Nutrition calculation is a fuzzy science, as actual nutrition may vary due to many factors.)

The nutritionists I interviewed all agreed that the exact form of produce (fresh, frozen, canned, or dried) was a minor concern. Instead, they stressed volume and variety. Eat a minimum of five servings of fruits and vegetables daily, including some that are high in A and C. Eat cruciferous vegetables (cauliflower, brussels sprouts, cabbage, and broccoli) several times a week. Several studies have shown that these help to prevent cancer.

So, you wonder, just what is the cheapest way to buy fruits and vegetables? Because of the variables in season, region of the country, and type of produce, I can't offer hard-and-fast rules. You need to do the homework by calculating the cost per serving. For example, notice how many meals you get from $1 worth of frozen broccoli versus $1 worth of fresh. Also compare how many servings you get from a head of cabbage versus cauliflower, and lettuce versus frozen spinach. Vary your strategy accordingly. The bottom line: Although fresh, green salads *look* more nutritious than cooked vegetables, they may not be. If you prefer them to sweet potatoes, or if you prefer fresh over cooked, you can opt to pay a premium price for them in the winter. But if you want to save money and still eat nutritiously, shift your diet to frozen out-of-season produce and to fresh, low-cost winter vegetables. Your family may balk for a while, but most people come to enjoy a different food as it becomes more familiar. And it won't become familiar if you don't serve it.

SHOOT, I FORGOT

Dear Amy,

In response to your article on winter vegetables . . .

People forget about sprouts. They are very easy to grow at home, take only a few days, are a perfect substitute for lettuce in sandwiches and pack a powerful nutritional punch. A creative sprouter can grow a wider variety than is available at the supermarket. Sprouting how-to's can be found in vegetarian cookbooks.

—Madeline Sobel
Westport, Connecticut

DAYS OF OUR SOAPS

Dear Amy,

I always mark the date on certain products. I stick on a piece of masking tape and mark the first day of use on it. It gives me incentive to beat the number of days I can make the product last. Examples: dish soap, dishwashing detergent, shampoo, and so on.

—Suzette J. Lucas
Hightstown, New Jersey

RETURN TO VENDOR

Dear Amy,

Although I've taken steps to decrease my junk mail, I still get some. If the mail contains a new business-reply envelope marked "postage paid," I sometimes stuff all the junk mail (including the used envelope it came in) into the envelope and send it back to the company. I *never* hear from them again!

—Virginia Scharf
Adamant, Vermont

(Living in an area where I must pay to dispose of trash, this idea is especially appealing. And what a thoughtful gesture: That company saves money by taking you off its mailing list. FZ)

FROM-SCRATCH PATCH

Dear Amy,

In "Test-Tube Tightwaddery" (page 214) you talked about denim iron-on patches, which cost about $1.25 to repair two knees. You can make your own iron-on patch from a scrap of fabric and Wonder-Under fusible webbing. It costs about $2.50 per yard (20 inches wide) . . . or as little as $1 per yard on sale. You iron the Wonder-Under to the fabric scrap, cut it out, pull the paper off the Wonder-Under, then iron the patch to your pants. It works great for appliqués, too. Other manufacturers make a similar product, but I find that Wonder-Under works the best.

—Cindy Cousineau
Appleton, Wisconsin

PRIME CUT RATE

Dear Amy,

I have discovered an excellent way to get high-priced meats at a 75 percent savings. Every Monday at my local supermarket, the meat department marks down all the meat dated for the following day. I buy in quantity and freeze that day. Sometimes stores don't display marked-down meat in the meat case . . . you must ask.

—Erin Goodwin
East Bridgewater,
Massachusetts

HOW TO CUT YOUR DRY-CLEANING COSTS

When I requested tips on saving money on dry cleaning, I expected the result would be a short article. But there was more to learn than I imagined. I soon had a two-inch stack of letters from readers.

I concluded that it is possible to save on dry cleaning, but that one must be careful. Many of the tips readers sent seemed risky, so I ran them past Norman Oehlke, director of information services at the International Fabricare Institute, and a dry cleaner for 35 years.

He pointed out that among the tips were several common myths. You may disagree with some of his conclusions, but I felt it was important to include the "official" viewpoint:

Myth #1. "Dry cleaning will wear out clothes quickly." No. According to a University of North Carolina study, dry-cleaning solvents will not damage fabrics. Soil is what prematurely wears fabrics.

Myth #2. "Most fabrics were around long before dry cleaning was invented, so consumers have been duped into believing they can't hand-wash 'dry-clean only' clothes." No. It's true that dry cleaning has been around only since the 1800s, when Parisians used kerosene, benzene, and gasoline to remove soil from clothes, but many fabrics have been developed since. In some cases the fibers may withstand hand-washing but the dyes will not. Fabrics that were not preshrunk and some interfacings and linings may not fare well when exposed to water.

But it's true that a 1984 FTC ruling allows manufacturers to list only one laundering method on garment tags, and most choose the more cautious method. Oehlke says that if the garment says "dry-clean" instead of "dry-clean only," there is a slightly greater chance it will withstand home laundering. But because of the range of types of fabrics, it's impossible to give concrete rules as to ones that can be hand-washed. Even among wools, some can be hand-washed and some can't. You can ask your dry cleaner for an opinion, though. It's also wise to test the garment in an inconspicuous place for colorfastness. This, however, may not determine whether the garment will shrink.

Myth #3. "You can use solvents, such as lacquer thinner, to remove spots." No. Any solvent residue remaining in the clothing will make your clothes more flammable, and fumes in your clothes aren't good for you. Likewise, you shouldn't use professional dry-cleaning fluid. Dry cleaners have methods to remove the solvents after they clean the clothes. Instead, use the spot removers sold in drug and department stores designed for "dry-clean only" clothes.

Myth #4. "Instead of dry-cleaning, simply have garments pressed and save two thirds the cost." No. Oehlke says the heat from pressing, as well as from fluffing clothes in a hot dryer, could set dirt and stains in clothes that haven't been cleaned. Not all dirt is visible.

Myth #5. "Women get charged more than men for cleaning shirts, so specify that your shirt is a man's to save money."

This one may actually have some truth to it. Oehlke says dry cleaners press a large volume of shirts on a shirt-pressing machine. This machine will accommodate only a certain size range. Any smaller (or much larger) shirt, regardless of gender, must be hand-ironed, which costs the cleaner more money. Along with being smaller, women's shirts tend to have more pleats, darts, ruffles, and delicate fabrics than do men's. In short, he says it's the extra labor that causes the price difference, not a gender-based price gouge.

On the other hand, several readers told me that a Chicago television station did an intensive investigation and found that many Chicago-area cleaners charge far more for shirts labeled "women's" than for those labeled "men's," though the shirts were exactly the same. I tried to track this down but was not successful; apparently, this investigation took place several years ago. Other readers told me that they personally knew of instances in which women were overcharged for shirts that required no extra work to clean or press. The bottom line: If you find a cleaner who seems to be overcharging you for no reason other than gender, ask the manager why you can't have the man's rate. (I don't recommend saying that the shirt is a man's. As our mothers correctly pointed out, two wrongs don't make a right.)

Myth #6. "All clothing that goes to a dry cleaner is dry-cleaned." No. Men's cotton shirts for example, are laundered. Ruth Miller of Valatie, New York, a dry cleaner for eight years, pointed out that about 35 percent of clothes brought to a dry cleaner don't need to be dry-cleaned.

Myth #7. "Same-day cleaning and clothes left at a 'drop shop,' which sends them for cleaning elsewhere are subject to extra charges." Oehlke said this isn't generally true, although there may be exceptions. Check just to be sure.

Myth #8. "Budget dry cleaners, which charge by the pound or offer very low prices, and do-it-yourself machines at laundromats do just as well as expensive dry cleaners." No. Depending on the method, your clothes will receive little or no finishing, nor expert stain removal. But if the lesser service meets your needs, the savings can be significant. Sally Kirby

Hartman of Norfolk, Virginia, says her off-price cleaner charges $1.79 per piece, no matter what it is. The full-service cleaner charges $7.50 for a dress and $8.85 for a coat.

Oehlke's general advice is to follow the manufacturer's instructions, unless you're willing to risk ruining the garment. Obviously, as a professional, he tends to stick to the industry's viewpoint.

So let's move on to the tightwad mind-set. If you buy a blouse for 25¢ at a yard sale, you are more likely to "wash dangerously." As Jane Paulson of Seattle puts it, "Since most of us reading this publication buy our clothes at thrift stores, laundry roulette is a game we can afford to play."

Reader after reader reported success with home laundering "dry-clean only" clothes, and very few cited ruined garments. They generally suggested hand-washing or using the gentle cycle with cold water and mild detergent, then laying the garment flat to dry.

By *far*, the most common suggestion we received was "Don't buy stuff that needs dry cleaning." Obvious, but it bears repeating: When you buy, take the laundering advice into account.

Here are some of the tips from readers with which Oehlke agreed:

1. Wear underarm shields to protect clothing from perspiration. (Debbie Halvorson, Somerville, New Jersey.)

2. For men's silk ties, spray with a fabric protector. If you get a spot, simply wipe it off with a damp cloth. Fabric protectors work best on tightly woven fabrics like silk, chintz, etc. (Joyce Whatley, Atlanta, Georgia.)

3. Compare prices for a suit versus a blazer and skirt. Sometimes it's cheaper to have individual items cleaned. (Lisa Romano, Cedar Grove, New Jersey.)

4. A down coat can be washed alone, using the gentle cycle, in cold water with Woolite. Rinse several times. Place in the dryer with a pair of clean sneakers. (Linda Krupa, Fairport, New York.)

5. Leather-goods stores sell something called "Suede Bar and Brush" for about $4.50. This makes suede jackets look new. Cleaning by professionals costs from $25 to $40. (Margaret Maloney, Casper, Wyoming.)

6. Use a non-terrycloth dishtowel as a press cloth when ironing hand-washed "dry-clean only" fabrics. Iron when fabrics are still slightly damp, except for wool, which should be dry to avoid shrinkage. Use lower temperatures for silk, higher for linen. Rayon needs medium, and wool can take medium-high. (Lori Stahlman, Fort Collins, Colorado.)

7. You can have clothes dry-cleaned, but press them yourself. The pressing of a professional cleaner can be approximated with pressing boards, sleeve rolls, and so on, from a sewing-supply store. (Janet Campbell, Houlton, Maine.)

8. Or if you're brave, wash wool blazers and skirts in Woolite and cold water, then have the dry cleaner press them. This can save two thirds of the cost over dry cleaning and pressing. (Linda Bennett, Farmington Hills, Michigan.)

9. Some cleaners will accept competitor's coupons. Look for specials in newspapers, coupons in telephone books, and "entertainment bargains" books. (Hedwig Blaser, Lakewood, California.)

10. Many cleaners offer a small amount per wire coat hanger that you return. (Dawn Katzoff, Orem, Utah.)

11. Point out and identify various stains to your dry cleaner. Food, blood, and mud require different chemicals. (Albert Gatica, Atlanta, Georgia.)

12. If a woman's suit needs cleaning, consider having only the jacket cleaned. Hand-wash the skirt, which is easy to press yourself. Again, this depends on your confidence that the skirt can be hand-washed, (Nancy Roebke, Stuart, Florida.)

13. Avoid buying "dry-clean only" clothes that are worn next to the skin. Layers of clothing, such as a T-shirt and dress shirt, catch the perspiration that would soil a suit. (Betty Alsberg, Astoria, New York.)

14. If you sew your own clothes, buy ¼ yard of extra fabric and wash the fabric before cutting out the material. This way you know delicate fabrics will survive home laundering. (Deborah Ronnie, Tucson, Arizona.)

15. Dry-clean only the parts of clothing that require it. Remove zip-out linings, belts, and detachable collars. Some cleaners charge $2 just to clean a belt. (LaDonna Jewson, Wasaba, Minnesota.)

16. Avoid buying "dry-clean only" clothes with pleats, beadwork, and other adornments that drive up pressing costs. (Sandy Croslow, Vincennes, Indiana.)

17. Check your pockets. Forgotten money is treated as a tip by dry cleaners. Oehlke says the common industry practice is to keep small change, but to return any paper money. (Frederick Young, Newton, Massachusetts.)

THE GREAT MOTOR-OIL DEBATE

We received about 50 letters in response to our newsletter solicitation for readers' experience with synthetic motor oil.

There was a wide range of opinion. Much of it was positive. For example, a reader said his salesman-father's synthetically lubricated 1980 Chevy was nearing 300,000 miles when he sold it. He changed the oil twice a year, or about every 12,000 miles.

But other readers reported excellent luck with high-quality, standard mineral oils and had also accumulated impressive mileage. Because top-quality standard oils are about one third the price of synthetics, they can be changed (by the car owner) three times as often for the same price.

Confronted with these diverging viewpoints, we called the Society of Automotive Engineers, *Nutz & Boltz* (an automotive consumer newsletter), the American Automobile Association, the technical editor of *Star* (the magazine of the Mercedes Benz Club of America), the technical director of Blendzall Corp. (which makes racing-car oils), and representatives of Amsoil and Mobil 1, the two largest synthetic-oil manufacturers. We also reviewed articles and surveyed technical data.

The result? There's no dispute that synthetics lubricate somewhat better than regular oils. But most of these experts questioned whether the average motorist would see a benefit that justified the extra cost.

It's true that synthetics cost no more if you extend the drain interval beyond what your car manufacturer recommends, but most of these experts agreed this is a bad idea. *Any* oil will still accumulate acids, condensation, and dirt. The experts added that although the base stock of synthetic oils lasts longer, the additives in both kinds of oils wear out at about the same rate.

Further, extending the intervals of oil changes will almost certainly void your car's warranty. Amsoil says you can extend the interval to 25,000 miles and guarantees to replace any parts that have failed as a result of poor lubrication, and they say they have never had a claim. Skeptical experts pointed out that it would be difficult to establish that a specific part wore out due to the oil's condition. Thus, it might be impossible to prove your claim. David Solomon, editor of *Nutz & Boltz* and a former "direct jobber" for Amsoil, said that he personally diagnosed engine failures that resulted from poor lubrication when customers followed the 25,000-mile recommendation. He added that he didn't know whether Amsoil honored the claims.

To add one more note of caution, reader Stanton Sittser of Gresham, Oregon, said several years ago he exactly followed a synthetic-oil maker's instructions to change the filters and oil, except he changed the oil every 20,000 miles instead of every 25,000. The engine failed at 51,000 miles. His mechanic said it was no wonder, as the oil he drained was like mud.

On the other hand, there *is* evidence that drain intervals can be stretched with synthetic oil, particularly if high-quality air and oil filters are used and changed regularly. The synthetic manufacturers are quick to provide their own "conclusive" test studies to "prove" this (the experts I consulted were skeptical of these tests). Solomon, former owner of an oil-analyzing company, said analysis of 1,000 synthetically lubricated engines showed that, at 12,000 miles, still-viable oil was the rule, not the exception. But it's important to note that Solomon was the only knowledgeable, independent source that I could find who supported extended change intervals. He recommends changing synthetics at 12,000 miles or once a year, whichever comes first. He endorses only Redline oil.

Now, suppose you decide to use synthetics *and* change your oil at the car maker's recommended intervals because, though it costs more, you feel your car will last longer. The experts we interviewed knew of no independent studies that conclusively prove that your engine will last longer. They agreed that synthetics may marginally extend the life of your car, but there's no way to know whether this benefit will offset the extra cost of the oil.

Likewise, it's uncertain whether the improved gas mileage, which is claimed by some synthetic-oil makers, would offset the cost. Some readers said they got better mileage with synthetics, and others said their mileage was the same. Either way, one expert pointed out that some standard oils also improve gas mileage.

There was also disagreement between these experts as to whether synthetics and standard oils could be mixed, and whether it was a good idea to switch an older car to synthetics.

One area of universal agreement was that synthetic oils are particularly beneficial in extreme cold (like Alaska), in extreme heat (like Death Valley), and in industrial applications (like pulling house trailers). But most passenger cars aren't exposed to these conditions.

The bottom line? If experts who live and breathe cars can't agree on this one, I can't make a final determination. At the very least, a good case can be made for either high-quality standard oil that is changed every 3,000 miles, *or* synthetic oil that is changed at the car manufacturer's maximum recommended interval (usually, about 7,500 miles). If you follow the latter course and you change your own oil, using synthetics will cost about $250 more every 100,000 miles. Because this extra cost, spread out over several years, is fairly low, even one of the skeptical experts used synthetics to hedge his bet.

David Solomon is a certified master mechanic in every aspect of auto repair with an impressive list of credentials and 30 years of experience. I don't know enough about auto mechanics to endorse his publication, but if you would like a free sample, write to:
Nutz & Boltz
Butler, MD 21023

STUBBORN DIAPER PINS

Dear Amy,

I use cloth diapers on my baby. I used to stick pins in a bar of soap to lubricate them so they would slide easier. But the bar of soap broke up after a few months. I figured there must be a better way. So I melted paraffin in a tuna can and now stick the pins in the hardened wax. When the wax breaks up, I remelt it.

—Lorie Slater
Pittsburgh, Pennsylvania

(Stubborn pins can be enough to discourage people from using cloth diapers. I solve the problem another way. I run the pin under my hair, along my scalp. The natural oil lubricates the pin. FZ)

FREEZING RAIN CHECKS

Dear Amy,

Living in a tiny one-bedroom apartment, I found everything else was scaled down to size, especially my freezer, which is one of those tiny, flimsy, tin ones inside the refrigerator. I learned to go to the grocery stores on the last day of a sale and get a rain check for frozen sale items that they were out of and I didn't have room for. Then, a week or so later when I have more freezer room, I go back and pick them up. Some rain checks are good for 30 days.

—Jon Juliot and Tina Triebs
  Eau Claire, Wisconsin

A FARE TO REMEMBER

Dear Amy,
  For urban dwellers, many employers now offer transit subsidies for employees who use public transportation, but it may be up to the employee to investigate it. For example, I receive a check for $15 per month from my employer, which must be used for mass-transit costs. Also a group of employees in my office teams up to purchase large quantities of mass transit passes and receives a 5 percent discount.

—Lori Kier
  Philadelphia, Pennsylvania

FLIGHT OF THE TIGHT

Dear Amy,
  My husband and I love to backpack in the West but seem to have less and less time to drive. Now, we call our travel agent with the dates and ask for the cheapest flight *anywhere* west of, and including, Denver. We also ask for the cheapest mileage-included rental car. When we've found a cheap flight, we can almost always find a wonderful backpacking

venue within a half-day's drive. We have flown for less than it would have cost to drive.

—Kathryn Paul,
  Bloomington, Indiana

METER MATTERS

Dear Amy,
  You once wrote that you really couldn't get an exact wattage use on a bread machine. You might try checking at a utility company and asking for a "check meter." It is an actual meter in a "box." You plug an appliance in it and voila: exact usage. We did this on an old freezer and were horrified at what it was costing. We replaced it.

—Valaree Stodola
  Shellsburg, Iowa

(I am aware of these, however when I called my utility several months ago, they didn't know such a thing existed. You can buy your own [through a mail-order company], but the cost exceeds that of a new freezer. FZ)

WINNER TAKES ALL

Dear Amy,
  Never, ever refuse anything that someone wants to give to you . . . even if you have to haul it directly to the dump. If you say no, they may never offer anything to you again . . . and next time, they might have something quite useful or valuable that could be sold at a garage sale. Some things that people have given me over the years include: two bushels of zucchini, a workshop cabinet, a metal shelv-

ing system, a deluxe baby buggy, 50 pounds of carrots, stone-tumbler equipment, a microscope, six Styrofoam coolers, a terrarium, countless broken tools, and a 9½-pound lobster that was breathing its last.

—David Currier
  Orlando, Florida

QUICK QUIP

Dear Amy,

I came across this recently and thought you'd enjoy it:

Sign in store window: Use our easy credit plan . . . 100 percent down, nothing to pay each month.

—Henra Trent
  Irving, Texas

100-YARD STASH

Dear Amy,

Birthday gift wrap is expensive, and you don't get much of it. So during the Christmas season I look for 100-yard rolls of Christmas paper that would double as all-occasion wrap. I usually get one roll for adults and one for children.

—Pam West
  Batavia, Illinois

(Great tip for those after-the-holidays sales. FZ)

LET'S GO SHOPPING WITH JIM

Whenever I discuss our frugal accomplishments, nothing impresses people more than the fact that we feed our family of eight for under $180 a month. To be specific, from January 1992 through December 1993, we averaged $175.60 a month.

This figure represents only the cost of food and gardening and canning supplies. We never eat out or buy hot lunches at school. It doesn't include things like toothpaste and toilet paper. I figure it this way because comparing "grocery" budgets has become extremely difficult as you can now buy motor oil in the supermarket and snacks in the autoparts store. In theory, you could artificially lower your grocery budget by eating out more, buying school lunches, and buying personal-care items in the drugstore. By defining the food budget as the cost of feeding a family, you can compare more precisely.

Our monthly budget for personal-care and cleaning supplies is about $25. We also spend $30 to feed a big cat that requires an expensive diet, and a big dog.

We achieve our low food budget through a combination of scratch cooking, gardening, semivegetarianism, *never* wasting food, and other strategies (17 in all; see the first book).

But if I had to list one tactic as the most crucial, it's smart shopping. By using our price book to compare deals at local stores, we realized it's possible to buy many foods for half of what most people pay, if we buy them at the right place and the right time.

For most of our 11-year marriage, Jim has done the grocery shopping. In the early days, it was because the stores were on his commuter route. Now it's because he's the "homemaker."

So let's go shopping with Jim and see how our system works. We followed him on September 6, 1993. Jim went, as usual, to Lewiston/Auburn, a metropolitan area of 30,000, to do our big, once-a-month, stock-up shopping expedition. This is where our closest supermarkets are located, 15 miles or 30 minutes away. As usual, he took the two-year-old twins, Brad and Laura.

This trip always takes place near the sixth of the month so that it coincides with dropping off the *Gazette*'s newsletter paste-ups at the printer. A basic principle of the frugal life is to combine errands. *Never* make a special trip.

The first stop was Myer's Country Cupboard, a natural-food store in the small town of Greene, which is about midway between Leeds and Lewiston/Auburn. Myer's specializes in bulk natural food; it's where we get nearly all of our spices. But we didn't need spices that month. Jim bought cocoa, soy flour (which we use one tablespoon at a time as an egg substitute in baking), and sunflower seeds.

The next stop was Marden's. This "surplus and salvage" chain sells everything from aluminum siding to odd lots of food to zippers. On Saturday, the fourth, I had stopped by (it's on my yard-saling route), scouted the offerings, and bought a box of "Maizoro" (Mexican-made) sugar-frosted cornflakes. The price worked out to 5¢ per ounce, about

one fifth the usual price for sweetened cold cereal. I had taken it home and tested it on my kids, and they were pleased to find it just as disgustingly sweet as the more popular brands. So Jim bought 18 boxes, a six-month supply for us. This was our first purchase of presweetened cereal in five years.

The next stop (after dropping off the paste-ups) was the Country Kitchen Bakery Thrift Store. Jim bought twelve 20-ounce loaves of bread at 50¢ a loaf.

Then he headed to Shop 'n Save. This New England supermarket chain is remarkable for its large selection of high-quality store brands. Everything Jim got there was on sale or a store brand.

Finally, Jim got the big-ticket items at Wholesale Depot, a warehouse store. He bought a lot of tomato paste because it was spaghetti-sauce-canning season.

The price book is handy when deciding whether to buy something at a supermarket or a warehouse store. For example, supermarkets usually beat warehouses with "loss-leader" sales, particularly on meats, but flour and cheese usually cost less at the warehouse. A 25-pound bag of "Robin Hood" flour is $5.98 at Shop 'n Save, versus $3.88 at Wholesale Depot. Mozzarella cheese is $11.90 for 5 pounds at Shop 'n Save, versus $8.99 at Wholesale Depot.

Altogether on this trip, Jim spent $124.77 on food items. Clearly, the list of items purchased doesn't represent a balanced diet; it's simply what we needed to buy that month. We were loaded with garden surplus. We already had some fruits and meats, and bought more at supermarket sales in the middle of the month. These later-in-the-month excursions are always combined with other trips.

We also shop by cooperating with friends. If anyone within our circle of tightwads finds a great deal, he or she calls around to ask, "Do you want me to pick some up for you?" Such relationships will help your budget.

Although I've provided a list of our prices (unit prices are rounded to the nearest penny), don't use these as your guideline. Maine prices tend to be slightly higher than those in many areas of the country. And we have since purchased some of these items for

less. We recently found tuna at 39¢ a can; we bought a lot.

Because of odd great deals that pop up, and because our surplus waxes and wanes, our actual monthly outlay for food over the past two years has ranged from $89.43 to $296.59. But the average is under $180.

You may have noticed Jim didn't use coupons. An effective coupon shopping system relies on access to double-coupon stores, a large number of free coupons (usually obtained by collecting a dozen Sunday-paper inserts from friends), and shopping at several stores each week to combine coupons with sales. We don't have double-coupon stores, and only 16 big-city newspapers with coupon inserts are sold in our town of 1,700 people each week (most people buy the local paper, which has no coupons). By calculating the true savings, I've found I usually can't recoup the cost of the paper through coupon use.

I do agree that coupons can be beneficial, but be careful of overuse. Two coupon experts, who have appeared on national television demonstrating amazing shopping trips with savings up to 95 percent by using coupons, shared their real grocery-bill averages with me. Both spend more on groceries for smaller families than I do.

Now, here is the point that I want to emphasize about our shopping system. Many people resist frugality because, as they put it, "I don't have time to drive all over the state hunting down bargains." We have carefully kept track of the total amount of time we expend on shopping per month. The major expedition chronicled above takes four hours, including nonshopping errands. The side excursions we make during the rest of the month easily take less than two more hours. So we do a month's worth of grocery shopping in under six hours. Although we shop this way because of the distance we drive to large stores, it's an excellent strategy for people with limited time.

Finally, for those who are wondering how Jim handles the challenge of shopping with toddler twins, the answer is: immobility. He keeps one twin in the backpack and the other in the kiddie seat of the cart at all times. He stays near the center of the aisles and extends his arm fully to take things from the shelves. "As long as my arms are longer than theirs, we won't have any problems," he says.

Store	Item	Price
Myer's Country Cupboard	Cocoa, 1.78 pounds at $2.18 per pound	$3.90
	Soy flour, 1.93 pounds at $1 per pound	$1.93
	Sunflower seeds, 2.18 pounds at $1.39 per pound	$3.03
	Total	$8.86
Marden's	Sugar flakes, 18 boxes at 50¢ per 10-ounce box	$9.00
	Total	$9.00
Country Kitchen Bakery Thrift Store	Whole wheat, six 20-ounce loaves at 50¢ per loaf	$3.00
	Oatmeal, six 20-ounce loaves at 50¢ per loaf	$3.00
	Total	$6.00
Shop 'n Save	Macaroni and cheese, 8 boxes at 25¢ each	$2.00
	Dry milk, 20-quart size	$8.49
	Tea bags, 100	$2.29
	Brown sugar, 2 pounds at 59¢ per pound	$1.19
	Tuna, 5 cans at 53¢ each	$2.65
	Powdered sugar, 2 pounds at 59¢ per pound	$1.19
	Celery, one bunch	$ .59
	Bagged apples, 3 pounds at 33¢ per pound	$ .99
	Total	$19.39
Wholesale Depot	Raisins, 6 pounds at $1.42 per pound	$8.54
	Shortening, 6 pounds at 76¢ per pound	$4.58
	Tomato paste, 36 12-ounce cans at 69¢ each	$25.14
	Brown sugar, 4 pounds at 56¢ per pound	$2.24
	Powdered sugar, 4 pounds at 56¢ per pound	$2.24
	Ketchup, two 40-ounce bottles at 4¢ per ounce	$2.98
	Salt, 5.5 pounds at 36¢ per pound	$1.97
	Shredded mozzarella, 5 pounds at $1.80 per pound	$8.99
	Cream cheese, 6-pack at 87¢ per pack	$5.25
	Colby cheese, 2 pounds at $1.99 per pound	$3.99
	Monterey jack, 2 pounds at $1.93 per pound	$3.86
	Onions, 10 pounds at 39¢ per pound	$3.98
	Flour, two 25-pound bags at 15¢ per pound	$7.76
	Total	$81.52

PEANUT-BUTTER SNACKS

Dear Amy,

I have a quick and easy recipe that my kids love in their lunch boxes:

½ cup honey
½ cup peanut butter
¾ to 1½ cups dry milk

Combine all the ingredients and roll into small balls. Roll the balls in coconut, sunflower seeds, or nuts.

—Teresa Duncan
  Marion, North Carolina

(This was a big hit in my home. If it seems too sweet, you can experiment with less honey. FZ)

BUDGET BREW

Dear Amy,

While stationed in Germany, we found that European coffee is ground almost to a talcum-powder fineness, which makes it possible to use much less. Now I buy extra-fine grind and regrind it to a powder at home before using it in my machine.

—Ruth Campbell
  Comox, British Columbia

HAIRDO-IT-YOURSELF

Dear Amy,

I'm proud to announce that I've mastered giving myself a permanent. A year ago I would have sworn I would *never* get it, but I shut myself in the bathroom early one Saturday morning and really set myself to the task. Once you decide you *will* learn to handle hair, end papers, and rods, you will get it.

—Beth Wright
  Union City, Tennessee

(When I was at a book-signing I was approached by a handsome, 50-ish couple—the kind who look like they have a yacht and a summer home. The wife proudly told me she saved money because her husband had learned to give her a permanent. Her husband blushed, but his wife looked wonderful. FZ)

AX THAT TAX

Dear Amy,

My son recently bought a new truck at a city dealership. The dealer charged him at the sales-tax level within the city, though we don't live in that city. A friend of my son's worked at the dealership and caught this error. She then figured out the correct sales tax for the area where we live. She found that the dealer had over-charged him $156. The dealer had to pay us back the money. We were told that dealers do this everywhere.

—Mona Breaux
  Livingston, Louisiana

ROWS OF ROSES

Dear Amy,

When my sister was married last year, I took the half-dead roses from her bouquet after the ceremony. At home, I rooted them by cutting off the heads, making a clean cut on the bottoms, dipping the fresh-cut bottoms in a rooting hormone, and putting them in a pot that was half Perlite and half soil. I kept these moist until rooted and then planted them in a shaded location in my garden. This year, on her first anniversary, my sister received a gift that could never be replaced: 12 rose bushes from her wedding bouquet.

—Kimberly Hill
Warren, Michigan

FEE FREEBIE

Dear Amy,

When moving to a new home or apartment, investigate using the former dweller's phone number. This will save you the $40 to $50 usual hookup fee for telephone service and instead cost you less than $10. The phone company will call the former dweller to ask permission (because if he moved nearby, he may still use the same number). You will have to put up with wrong numbers for a short time.

—Judy Davies
Mystic, Connecticut

(Undoubtedly, phone company policies vary around the country, and you should check with your local company. I called mine and learned their policy:

The regular installation charge is $44.75. If you know the previous tenant well and just want to change the name on the account, the charge is $6.74.

But if you don't know the previous tenant, and your move doesn't coincide with the end of the billing cycle, there's a third option. For $18.70 you can get a transfer of service: You keep the old tenant's number but you can specify when this bill ends and when yours begins. By doing this, you can't get stuck with his unpaid bills.

These last two prices apply only if you plan to keep the exact same service options that the previous tenant had. FZ)

GAIN SOME GROUND

Dear Amy,

Adjacent to our backyard is a large, vacant piece of land. I approached the owner last fall about using a portion of it in the spring for a garden. He was willing, because I would be clearing it of weeds and he wouldn't have to worry about the city weed ordinance for the part I cleared. Now I have a garden of over 1,000 square feet and lots of fresh vegetables every year.

—John Mauro
Wheat Ridge, Colorado

THREE STEPS TO A FRITO-FREE CHILD

After "How do you pronounce Da-cyczyn?" perhaps the most fre-quent question I get is "Don't your children feel deprived?"

Because I'm asked this so often, my antenna is always up looking for signs. I even interview my kids on this subject. The fact is, our children rarely complain of any gap in material goods.

The objections are so rare that when they arise, they surprise me. Such was the case when Neal,

then five, asked, "How come we don't have 'good food' like other people?" I pressed him for specifics and learned he wanted store-bought snacks in his lunch box like most of his kindergarten classmates had.

Many frugal parents would give the simple answer "We can't af-ford it," presuming small children can't comprehend the complexi-ties of money. But this unfortu-nate response leads children to conclude that their family is "poorer" than other families who do buy those things, and therefore frugal alternatives are second-rate.

I do believe children can under-stand, and I explain why our choice is "smart." Here's how I handled this situation:

Step 1. I had a conversation with Neal to explain:
1. If you do the math, you find it's not worth the money. I pointed out real fruit costs 25¢ to 50¢ per pound, while fruit-chewy things cost about $5 per pound. So, pound for pound, we can buy ten times more apples than Shark Bites. If he had wanted juice boxes, I might have explained that the juice in-side costs 10¢, and the package costs 20¢. Then I would have asked him whether he would throw two dimes in the trash. I might also have used a calculator to show that over the school year, one juice box per day times three kids would add up to $100 wasted.
2. Store-bought snacks often have artificial ingredients and less nu-trition. Although fruit-chewy things are made with some fruit juice, they're so overprocessed that the nutrition label shows an almost total lack of vitamins. I ex-

plained that children need good nutrition to do well in school. (Subsequently, Neal noted he was the smartest in his class in math, and he theorized his homemade snacks were the key. It was tempting to let this slide, but I did explain that the relationship might not be so direct.)

3. Store-bought snacks are usually worse for the environment. We had a kid-level conversation about the trees that are chopped down to make packaging, the pollution produced by factories, and the mountains of trash that result when people throw this stuff away. I said even recyclable trash requires energy to recycle. Kids learn about "saving the earth" in school, and they need to know their family's behavior does make a difference. I told Neal that the "dump guy" said he couldn't think of another family that brought as little trash as we do. I said we could be proud of that.

4. Without discussing the finances of a specific family, I stressed that people who buy store-bought snacks aren't necessarily "richer" than we are. The children he envied might have been from families that are deep in debt, whose parents work multiple jobs to keep up with their bills, or perhaps even receive public assistance. I explained that some families make different choices; they spend money on lots of little things to make them feel good for a short time now, instead of saving for something bigger that will make them feel good for a long time, like a nicer house or a parent who can stay home with children.

Step 2. I improvised. Although I always try to make sure that our frugal alternatives satisfy the children, if a kid raises an issue, I step up my creative efforts. In this case, I made an extra effort to create homemade snacks with a higher "wow" factor, such as fruit-juice jigglers, whoopee pies, cinnamon rolls, popcorn, trail mix, pies made in tiny aluminum pie tins, and so on. Victory occurred when Neal reported a friend asked to taste a jiggler.

I am one mom with six kids, so I have to focus my attention on the specific areas in which the kids express concerns. Neal has never fretted over his yard-sale clothes, but he does care about his snacks. So I spend more time on snacks than clothes.

Children don't need exactly what their friends have, as long as they feel that they have some things that are as good.

Step 3. I asked him to earn it.

Usually, steps 1 and 2 work for my children, and they worked with Neal for a year. But he raised the question of store-bought snacks again the next year. I repeated steps 1 and 2, but I knew this alone would not satisfy him.

So, I had Neal do a special 15-minute chore to earn 25¢. The next time I was in the store, I bought a small bag of corn chips with his quarter to put in his lunch box. Neal was excited about the chips but has not asked for them again in the year or more that has transpired.

When I shared the corn-chip story during a radio interview, a woman called in and said having kids earn money for food, even junk food, was near-abusive. "After all, it cost only 25¢," she said. I argued that it wasn't the question of a single bag of chips. We're establishing a pattern of dealing with money that we hope will carry us through the age when their wants escalate to stereos and cars.

Having children earn money for extras not only saves the parents money; it also provides these benefits:

1. It slows their rate of consumption by 90 percent. Kids rarely want anything enough to work for it, and if it's not important enough to them to work for it, why should I?

2. It empowers them. Kids gain the ability to satisfy their wants on their own. Most children get what they want by whining, complaining, and making their parents feel guilty, and this pattern continues through the teenage years. My children *never* whine for anything.

3. It teaches children that money is the relationship of effort to stuff. A six-year-old can understand that taking three buckets of food scraps to the compost pile equals a bag of corn chips. This is a very important concept, one that has escaped many adults. By always being paid in increments of 25¢, my children can easily compute the relationship of effort to stuff.

4. It teaches them, early on, one of life's most important lessons— that what they covet isn't worth their hard-earned money. Jamie didn't ask for a school lunch until the third grade. Our school-lunch deal is that we will split the cost with the children. After careful consideration, she chose a pizza lunch. When she got home that day, I asked about her lunch. She shrugged and said, "I like Dad's

pizza better." She hasn't bought any more lunches.

5. If they use their own money to buy toys, they take better care of the things.

6. It teaches them to save. As your children get older, they will sock away money for larger items. Alec, who is ten, recently saved $14.50 and bought a well-made toy crossbow with suction-cup darts (to be used only with adult supervision). Although he could have, he didn't spend a cent on store-bought snacks. Alec got his bow within days of when Neal got his corn chips. I asked Alec if he would rather have his bow or 58 bags of chips. "The crossbow!" he exclaimed, as if this were obvious.

These strategies have been part of our kids' lives from the start. But if you're making a transition from a spendthrift way of life, it's important to sit down with your older children and explain the new rules. Point out that it's okay to express a want, but begging and whining will be treated as misbehavior.

If these three steps fail—your child doesn't accept your explanation, is not satisfied with creative frugal alternatives, and is unwilling to work for the stuff he wants, remember that families are not democracies, and that you should stand firm. You are the adult and are better able to judge how your money should be used.

20-20 TELEVISION

It always amazes me how many people have come to regard cable TV as a necessity. I can think of only one situation in which it might be needed: if the reception in your area is so poor, it seems to be the only way your picture can rise above "fuzzy blob."

But if this is your situation, there may be other options. You can put a big antenna on your roof, but this is impractical for those who are transient or live in apartments. So I was pleased to learn about a bit of "intermediate technology" that could solve the problem: powered rabbit ears, also known as amplified indoor antennas.

There are several varieties, ranging in price from about $30 to over $80. How to choose?

Start by heading down to your local Wal-Mart or Radio Shack and buying the cheapest set of powered rabbit ears you can find. Powered versions can be identified because they brag about their levels of "db gain" on the box. Be sure to keep the receipt. Try them out. If they don't work well enough to suit you, return them and buy the second-cheapest set, again, keeping the receipt.

Keep going through this process until you find some that meet your needs. One of my staffers who did this discovered that a set called Recoton TV500 improved his reception by about 50 percent, allowing him to double his available channels (from two to four). These cost $29.

We talked with Frank Rodriguez, the antenna's inventor. He said Recoton boosts the signal "gain" about ten times as much as a nonpowered indoor antenna and draws less than 1 watt per hour. At the national average of 9¢ per kilowatt-hour, it would cost less than 6¢ a month to operate.

Though my staffer settled on the Recoton, we aren't recommending any particular brand. The point is to "seek the minimum level" or find the cheapest satisfactory solution.

POST-JERSEY PJ'S

You can make toddler pajama pants from hubby's old knit or velour shirts. Reader Alicia Lopez of Torrance, California, says they can be completed in 30 minutes or less.

Turn the shirt inside out and lay it flat. Use a pair of your toddler's pants as a pattern and trace onto the shirt allowing extra for seams and the waistband.

Cut the two pant legs out. Sew up the side of each. Put one leg inside the other, right sides together. Pin and sew the crotch.

To finish, sew waistband down, to form casing for elastic, leaving a 1-inch opening for insertion. The elastic can be scavenged from old panty hose.

SWAP TILL YOU DROP

Reader Carol Parker of Oakland, California, writes, "I would like to join a bartering network. How do I know which ones are legitimate and legal?"

Back in my graphic-design days I joined two trade exchanges, also known as bartering networks. I observed a curious contrast: some members thought these were a scam, other members loved them. After some thought, I've come to some conclusions about exchanges.

First, some facts. A trade exchange is a group of businesses (usually between 300 and 3,000) that trades goods and services. When one business sells to another, it's credited with "trade dollars," which have the same value as cash dollars and can be traded with any other member. Typically, exchanges charge an annual fee of $100 to $800, and collect a 10 percent cash or trade-dollar fee on all transactions.

This modern form of trade exchange has been around for 15 years, and there are over 150 nationwide. Over time, exchange owners have learned better methods of operation. If you had a poor experience ten years ago, you might fare better today.

Frugal people are attracted to trade exchanges because they're accustomed to saving money through informal swaps with friends. But a trade exchange is actually a miniature economy. One of the major ways in which it differs from personal barter is that trade dollars are reported to the IRS as earnings. Like cash, trade dollars spent in the operation of your business are tax-deductible, but trade dollars spent for personal use aren't. So when you spend 100 trade dollars at a hair salon, remember that you paid Uncle Sam (about) $25 in cash for taxes. You must also factor in materials and exchange costs. Don't think of exchange goods and services as free.

Although most exchanges are legal, some have serious management problems. If you're considering joining an exchange, learn the following:

• Whether there have been any complaints filed with the Better Business Bureau or the National Association of Trade Exchanges (27801 Euclid Ave., Cleveland, OH 44132; [216] 731-8030).

• How many members it has. A good exchange will show you a directory of all members. Call several members for references.

• How long it has operated.

• Whether it complies with IRS laws.

• Whether members trade 100 percent. A 50 percent cash/50 percent trade-dollar policy may mean members aren't confident they can spend trade dollars.

An exchange, like any business, is only as good as its owner. If the owner creates trade dollars out of thin air for personal use, inflation occurs. Members become overloaded with trade dollars and are unwilling to accept more. When you call members for references, ask how easily they can spend their trade dollars.

Any exchange that meets all the above criteria is probably first-rate. However, don't discount one that doesn't. A "lesser" exchange can be beneficial under the right circumstances.

Beyond determining whether the actual exchange is good, decide whether your business is right for an exchange. Consider an exchange if:

1. You own a service business or sell a product with a minimum 40 percent profit margin. If you have a small profit margin, you won't recover out-of-pocket cash costs.

2. Your business has slow times. A business that's *always* busy should avoid exchanges, as real cash is easier to spend than trade dollars. But if your hair salon is slow on Wednesdays, or if your carpentry business slows during the winter, you can specify that you'll accept trade dollars only at those times.

3. Your business is in a heavily populated area. Exchanges in large cities offer dramatically better trading opportunities than those in small cities.

4. You offer something many people want. If you're a hypnotherapist, there may be few members who want your services. You may not recoup your membership fee.

There are also personal qualities that lead to successful trading, such as:

• A yard-sale mentality. If you can always find a bargain at a yard sale, you'll like exchanges. People who prefer the predictable selection of department stores will be disappointed.

• Realistic expectations. Some businesses acquire more trade dollars than they can use. I knew one member who amassed thousands of trade dollars to pay for a house addition, only to find that the building contractor dropped out. If you're saving for a large trade, work closely with the exchange and the other business to avoid nasty surprises.

• An awareness that "lesser" exchanges primarily trade services rather than goods. The better exchanges have an abundance of goods; lesser exchanges have few or none.

• Creative trading skills. Some businesses allow employees to use trade dollars as a benefit or bonus. My baby-sitter agreed to accept trade dollars as payment. I made the arrangements, and she got haircuts at a member salon.

Clearly, trade exchanges are more complicated than dealing with cash. So why would anyone bother? Because the exchange funnels work to you that you might not get otherwise. Exchanges are good for new businesses, as word-of-mouth from members may eventually bring in cash customers.

Initially, I belonged to a poorly run exchange, then I joined a lesser exchange. Even so, I successfully traded for a pawnshop microwave and VCR, restaurant meals, auto repair, furniture refinishing, chair cushions, upholstery cleaning, dental work, hair care, new encyclopedias, a clown/magician for a birthday party, and small items for gifts.

To learn whether there is a trade exchange in your area, look in the Yellow Pages under "barter and trade exchanges," or contact N.A.T.E.

FASTER THAN A SPEEDING BREAD MACHINE

Our favorite complement to quick-but-humble leftover soup has been popovers because of their speed, tastiness, and elegance. But move over, popovers. Sarah Severns of Kensington, Ohio, sent me this recipe for "Cuban Bread." Aside from eye appeal and great taste, it has one remarkable feature that sets it apart from other yeast breads: It takes only an hour and 15 minutes from start to finish.

5–6 cups all-purpose flour (you can substitute whole-wheat flour for 1 or 2 cups)
2 tablespoons dry yeast
2 tablespoons sugar
1 tablespoon salt
2 cups hot water (120–130 degrees)
1 tablespoon sesame or poppy seeds

Mix 4 cups of the flour with the yeast, sugar, and salt. Pour in hot water and beat 100 strokes, or 3 minutes with a mixer. Stir in the remaining flour until the dough is no longer sticky. Knead 8 minutes.* Place the dough in a greased bowl, and cover with a damp towel. Let rise

15 minutes. Punch down. Divide into two pieces. Shape into two round loaves, and place on a baking sheet. Cut an X ½ inch deep on top with a sharp knife. Brush with water, and sprinkle with seeds. Place on the middle shelf of a *cold* oven. Place a cake pan of hot water on the lowest shelf. Heat the oven to 400 degrees. Bake 40–50 minutes until deep golden brown.

*If your food processor has a dough blade, you can avoid the hand-kneading: Combine dry ingredients in the processor. As the machine is running, drizzle in water until the dough forms a ball. Spin the ball 20 times.

WHAT TO DO WITH . . .

Gunky White-Out. Instead of buying expensive White-Out brand thinner, thin it with a few drops of nail-polish remover. (Chris Rogers, Madison, Illinois.)

Empty Match Folders. Make into sewing kits for traveling. Needles and pins can be stuck into bottom fold. Various colors of thread can be wrapped around the back of the folder. (Wanda Good, Mount Joy, Pennsylvania.)

A Band-Aid Box. Make a soap holder for showering when camping. Poke drain holes in bottom. Attach a string to hang around your neck. (Carolyn Marck, Seattle, Washington.)

A Milk Jug. To make a great berry-picking bucket, cut the top off a gallon-size jug, put a strip of rope or cloth through the handle, and tie it around your waist. Can also be used to carry clothespins or nails. (Sally Kirby Hartman, Norfolk, Virginia.)

Newspaper. Dampen and use in place of masking tape when painting windows.

A Record Player that spins but doesn't play. Use for art projects. Place paper plate in the middle, and hold markers or paintbrushes against the spinning plate. (Mary Kay Carney, Minneapolis, Minnesota.)

A Paper Clip. Use as a "buttoner" if you have arthritis in fingers. Mail-order version costs $4.49. (Abraham Landsman, Madison, Wisconsin.)

A Dead Lawn Mower. Remove engine and bolt a board to the base. Use for carting heavy items. (Charlene Rasmussen, Milwaukee, Wisconsin.)

Carpet Scraps with attached foam padding. Fold with foam side out. Clamp with a clothespin to make a touch-up paintbrush.

Dented Ping-Pong Balls. Put them in boiling water to pop the dent out. (Peter Baylies, North Andover, Massachusetts.)

 Soda-Can Tabs. Use to make replacement clips for elastic bandages. Clips aren't sold separately. Attach two tabs with a rubber band. (Leonard Duane, Newport, Maine.)

Margarine-Tub Lids. Make playing-card holders for children. Place two lids with flat sides together. Staple together in the center and put a sticker over the staples. (Sue Quinlan, Rosemont, Minnesota.)

Old Socks. Make a mop head for the old clamp style mops. Stitch toes together and clamp as many pairs in the mop as will fit. (Gertrude Roll, Forestville, New York.)

Old Metal Shower-Curtain Rings. Use to make homemade space-saving hangers. Put the ring over the neck of a hanger, then hang a second hanger from the ring. (Robin Gauthier, Halifax, Massachusetts.)

Marker Caps from kids' dead markers—the long kind. Use to make pencil extenders, so you can use too-short-to-hold pencils. (Theresa Stafford, Albany, Georgia.)

Styrofoam Peanuts. Use as beanbag-chair refill after original Styrofoam pellets pack down. Some nursery and grammar schools have beanbag chairs and might appreciate your donation. (Debbie DeLost, Santa Ana, California.)

LAUNDRY QUANDARY

When we buy laundry detergent, Jim and I usually don't strain our brains. Years ago at a warehouse store, we bought the 4¢-per-load, weird-brand powdered detergent in the 50-pound bucket, but it irritated the kids' skin. So now we buy jumbo boxes of 12¢-per-load, name-brand powdered detergent at the warehouse. We've always bought powdered because sometime in my early tightwaddery I determined that, on average, the per-load cost was about half that of liquids.

But last year a rare thing happened. I found myself in possession of several high-value coupons and rebates for liquid detergents. So I ventured into the detergent aisle at a local supermarket to see if these would bring a liquid down to a competitive price, and I realized why so many readers have asked for an article on this subject.

Unlike powdered detergents, only two off-brands of liquid detergents had loads-per-container information on their labels. Most label instructions say to add a "capful," but only 5 out of 24 brands said how many ounces were in a cap. The caps vary in size because the detergents vary in concentration. The stores offer a per-quart unit price,

but this is useless when trying to compute price per load.

So, without a calculator (I was cursing myself for not bringing it) I tried to figure the loads per bottle by guessing that the cap looked like, say, a ¼ cup measure. After ten dizzying minutes I found one brand, with coupon, that I guessed would equal my regular warehouse price.

Back at home, I learned that even this calculation was flawed. The caps to liquid detergents have an inner rim that extends down into the bottle, so you can't accurately compare cap sizes in the store. In short, it's near impossible for shoppers to make an informed choice.

Why do manufacturers go to such lengths to muddle the number of loads per bottle? We called several and got weasel-worded responses. So we were surprised when a Procter & Gamble representative told us frankly that if the information were listed, "People would find that liquids are generally more expensive."

So, why bother with liquids? Some people prefer that they can easily be poured directly on stains, and people with exceptionally hard water may find that powders don't dissolve completely. Finally, if you can calculate the cost per load, there are cases in

which liquids can be cheaper than powders.

So, since the manufacturers would not, I decided to provide you with a way to calculate the cost per load for liquid detergent. At first I tried to do this by simply buying various detergents and measuring how much the caps hold. But after finding many confusing, odd measurements, I decided to call the manufacturers themselves. I learned that they're in the process of concentrating their products. This makes the situation even more confusing for a number of reasons:

• The manufacturers use the terms "concentrated" and "ultra" inconsistently. "Ultra" usually means the product is concentrated, but not always. Fab Ultra has been concentrated and is now called Fab Ultra Power. So it's hard to figure out whether you're buying the old regular product or the new concentrated one.

• None of the "with bleach" versions say they're concentrated, although many clearly are.

• Even if you call the manufacturers to get information on cap sizes, you can't be certain that the representatives are always right. When I called Dial Corp. to learn cap sizes for Purex, the representative didn't even know that Purex was available in Ultra Concentrated.

• The manufacturers are downsizing differently. Colgate-Palmolive is downsizing from 4-ounce to 3-ounce caps. Lever is downsizing from ½ cup to ¼ cup, but their "with bleach" version is ⅓ cup—which results in an odd-ounce size. Procter & Gamble has the most confusing measures. Their representative told me their caps hold 98 milliliters, except for their Tide "with Bleach Alternative," which holds 125 milliliters, but she didn't know how many ounces these numbers equaled. So, unless you know how to convert ⅓ cup to ounces, and milliliters to ounces, you can't figure ounces per load.

• In this downsizing process, some manufacturers are staying with the old 32-, 64-, and 128-ounce bottles, while others are changing to 50-, 100-, and 150-ounce bottles.

I also observed other potential fiscal hazards.

• The cap sizes often aren't exactly what the manufacturer claims. I amplified the disparity by dumping four caps of water from each brand into a Pyrex measuring cup. I found, for example, that 4-ounce caps from different brands could vary by ½ ounce. This sounds insignificant, but if you compared 128-ounce bottles,

this difference would equal 4½ loads, or about $1 of detergent.

• The "fill lines" in the caps are a problem. In some cases the words "fill line" or the line itself could not be seen without holding the cap up to a bright light. Some caps didn't have the words "fill line" or an actual line; I presumed I was supposed to fill to where the "ridge design" ended. The fill lines varied from ⅛ inch to ⅞ inch from the rim of the cap. So, one could easily use too much detergent.

• It's hard to get all of the detergent out. Liquid-detergent bottles have a recessed plastic-spout-thing into which the cap screws. Because it's recessed, the spout can retain between 1 and 3 ounces of detergent. You could get this out by filling the bottle with water, shaking, and dumping the water into your washer, but chances are many people wouldn't realize so much is still in the bottle.

Given these problems, I have three solutions to offer:

• If you're a math wizard who loves to combine sales, coupons, and rebates, you might regard an evening spent in the detergent aisle with a calculator to be a thrill. If so, you'll need the specific cap sizes:

Arm & Hammer's "double power" PowerFresh is 2 ounces.

Colgate-Palmolive's "Ultra Power" versions of Ajax, Fab, and Dynamo are 3 ounces. The unconcentrated versions are 4 ounces. This company deserves credit for being the only major manufacturer that prints cap sizes on the labels—though you must hunt for this on the back of the bottle.

Dial's Ultra Purex is 3.5 ounces. The unconcentrated Purex and Purex "with Bleach Alternative" are 4 ounces.

Lever's "Double Power" All, Wisk, and Surf are 2 ounces. The "with bleaching action" versions are 2.7 ounces. The unconcentrated versions are 4 ounces.

Procter & Gamble's Bold, Cheer, Era, Gain, Ivory Snow, Solo, and Tide are 3.3 ounces. Its Tide "with Bleach Alternative" is 4.2 ounces. These products are usually labeled "Ultra" and/or say "Super Concentrated" on the cap.

To calculate ounces per load, first determine your after-sale, after-coupon and/or after-rebate cost (remember to factor in postage). Divide that by the number of ounces in the bottle to determine the price per ounce. Multiply that by the ounces per load to determine the cost per load.

Because you can often get a better deal using a coupon or rebate on a smaller product with a higher unit price, you'll have to do this calculation with several bottle sizes in each brand that you're considering.

• If you're not a math wizard but still want to use your coupons and rebates to buy name-brand liquids, try to get them for half price. We found that the cost per load for name-brand liquids varied from 18¢ to 28¢, so at half price they cost the same as powders. Also investigate store brands, which cost as little as 12¢ per load. We found one on-sale off-brand called Xtra that cost 9¢ per load.

One reminder: Ignore the manufacturer's suggested retail price printed in the flashy starburst on the label; it usually varies from the store's actual price.

• There are about 25 brands

available in my area, and each comes in three or more bottle sizes. Of these brands, there are seven different cap sizes. This is simply ridiculous. If this makes your brain hurt, simplify your detergent shopping by boycotting any detergent, be it liquid or powdered, that doesn't include loads-per-container information on the label, and report this decision to the manufacturers. Here are their numbers:

Arm & Hammer: (800) 524-1328
Colgate-Palmolive: (800) 338-8388
Dial: (800) 457-8739
Lever: (800) 598-5005
Procter & Gamble: (800) 846-7669

"WHOOPEE, WE CAN SPEND AGAIN!"

Roseanne is in its seventh season on TV, but old shows are syndicated nightly in our area. I caught few of the weekly episodes when they first ran, but I'm catching up, fast-forwarding through the past 6 years of the Connors' lives. A fascinating aspect of this show is that it's one of the few sitcoms featuring a family with financial problems. Specifically, the show's creators have perfectly depicted the feast-or-famine spending style of most American families.

Dan is frequently unemployed, and Roseanne works dead-end jobs. Money is tight. When an unexpected lump of money not only allows them to catch up on bills but actually yields a surplus $50, Dan and Roseanne vow to save it. But Roseanne secretly purchases a $50 bottle of perfume, while Dan secretly buys a $50 bell for the

boat he is building in the garage. Another show was devoted to their misadventures when their power was cut off because they couldn't pay the bill. Yet, in good times, there is always money for beer, soda, and bowling. When the family goes to the mall and daughter Darlene wants money, she holds out her hand. Dan and Roseanne oblige.

You may feel that your income isn't cyclical because you don't have seasonal, iffy employment like Dan, a building contractor. But there are many kinds of employment cycles. For some, the cycle is annual. For others, it is linked to the performance of the national economy, which may take a decade to shift from boom to recession.

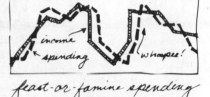

feast-or-famine spending

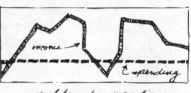

tightwad spending

In any case, at the first sign of a personal economic improvement, we celebrate. We saw this whoopee-we-can-spend-again syndrome during the 1993 Christmas-shopping season. With November and December reports that the economy was improving, retailers experienced an "up" Christmas. There was a direct relationship between the drop in unemployment figures and the rise in gifts under the tree. In fact, frugality and bad economic times are so closely associated that I can actually gauge the severity of a drop in the G.N.P. by the boost in the number of media inquiries I get.

People spend lavishly during good times because they believe that it's better to have splurged and gone bust than never to have splurged at all. Even the semiresponsible admonition to always save 10 percent of your income essentially endorses the constant contracting and expanding of family expenditures.

But surprisingly, life is easier and more enjoyable if spending, particularly in "lifestyle" areas (food, gifts, clothing, entertainment, and so on.) always stays, on average, at a modest level.

Let's look at some of the problems that arise from the feast-or-famine spending style.

• It leaves you with little to survive the times when your income drops. If, as my chart demonstrates, you save money during good economic times, you can survive the bad, often without scaling down your lifestyle.

• Continually changing rules create stress. Adjusting to a tighter budget is hard for parents, but it's even harder for kids. And their unhappiness, moping, and arguing make the unemployed parent feel guilty and inadequate. Kids are happiest when the rules are constant. If their allowance changes from 50¢ to $5 and back to 50¢, the happiness over the $5 allowance will be more than offset by the unhappiness over a return to 50¢.

• Although some frugal activities can be quickly adopted in times of famine, others can't. A garden might take a year or two before it produces well. It might take more than a year to stockpile enough yard-sale clothes so that you rarely have to buy new again. It takes time and patience to convert uncooperative family members. Many skills, from

bread-making to oil-changing, require much practice before you can perform them quickly and skillfully enough to make them practical.

• When frugality is practiced only during unemployment, it acquires a stigma. Family members associate meatless meals and yard-sale clothing with bad times. Often, the terror of unemployment isn't about not having enough to eat or losing a house, but about having to do all that "low-class" penny-pinching stuff. Conversely, when frugality is practiced even in good times, the family learns to enjoy it and stretch the possibilities with their creativity.

A tightwad tends to be fearless in an uncertain economy. He knows that as long as there is enough money for basic needs, he can live quite happily without luxuries. He knows that there will always be Christmas because he can create it from nothing. He knows he can wring more miles from his old car. He knows he can feed his family well from his extensive repertoire of hamburger recipes. Most important, he doesn't feel like a victim of economic circumstances beyond his control. While he might dip into savings for a period of time, his lifestyle need not change. He is in control.

To some, constantly cruising along at a spending level that's near the bottom of the family's cyclical income level sounds like a life of permanent deprivation. But if there is one thing I would like to hammer home, it is a *new* definition of deprivation. True deprivation has nothing to do with a lack of stereos, restaurant meals, flashy toys, Caribbean vacations, and similar consumer items. To me, a worse kind of deprivation is a lack of security—the constant nagging feeling that the tiniest downturn in one's income, or the smallest domestic disaster such as a blown engine or broken window, can wipe you out.

We don't place much value on this feeling of security in our culture because it doesn't have an ad campaign on TV, it's not promoted by our political leaders, and it doesn't surround us with lots of visible stuff with which we can easily impress our neighbors. But anyone who has lived without security and then slowly, patiently acquired it knows that it's more satisfying to own than any consumer gadget.

If you feel your economic circumstance is good now—possibly it has improved with the economy—this is not the time to abandon frugality. It may be a good time to fix the roof or replace the dying car, but it isn't a good time to raise everyone's expectations. If there's anything we know for sure, it's that there'll be bad times again.

A BOOK REVIEW

Even black-belt tightwads can go all squishy and overspend when it comes to car repair. If the guy in the greasy overalls says your venturi is cracked, and you have no idea what a venturi is, you'll hand over the credit card rather than display your ignorance by asking, "My what?"

But take heart. Catherine McClintock of Fort Collins, Colorado, says *Auto Repair for Dummies* by Deanna Sclar (Ten Speed Press, $17.95) has lifted the veil surrounding automotive ailments. We obtained a copy and were also impressed. It contains over 400 pages of car-repair and maintenance information written specifically for people who "have never held a wrench." You'll want to read it cover to cover, as you would a mystery novel. It'll be fascinating to finally understand the purpose of weirdly named car parts.

This book includes everything from "How to Open the Hood of Your Car" to the location of the idle stop solenoid. "The what?" you ask. That's the point. This is explained in everyday language. You are guided through basic maintenance such as changing the oil and flushing the radiator, up through minor repairs such as replacing radiator hoses, all the way to fairly difficult tasks such as tune-ups and repacking wheel bearings.

There are tons of excellent illustrations, and it's even spiral-bound so it'll lie flat next to you while you're under your car. Catherine wrote, "So far, I've changed my oil and spark plugs, flushed my radiator, checked my hoses, belts, and fluid levels, and cleaned my battery terminals. And I've learned an awful lot about how my car works."

Our only criticism is that the book was last updated in 1988, and automotive technology changes quickly. But if you're driving an older car, even the small percentage of dated information would still be relevant.

Try to get the book through interlibrary loan before you buy. It's still in print, but you'll probably have to have a bookstore order it for you.

MUSIC FOR A SONG

One of my favorite nuggets of tightwad wisdom came from Darrell Schweitzer of Strafford, Pennsylvania. He said, "Make friends with compulsive upgraders." He was referring to computer buying, but the concept applies broadly.

New technologies are often underdeveloped and expensive, so if you wait a few years, the quality improves as the price drops. But technology junkies stampede to buy the newest high-priced gizmos—and dump their old equipment for ridiculously low prices. So, if you're patient, you can either buy new stuff once it is better and cheaper, or buy used stuff from compulsive upgraders.

Stereo equipment typifies this basic concept. CD players were first marketed ten years ago by Sony for $900. Today, a CD player with superior sound (but that is less durable) costs $100. Similarly, the earliest CDs were of low quality just when LP quality reached its peak.

Unlike turntables, CD players offer convenient operation and are nearly maintenance-free. The CDs themselves are "unscratchable" and should last forever. Because most people didn't replace their needles and balance their turntables to achieve optimum sound, early CD players did seem like a vast improvement. Consequently, CDs have almost completely snuffed out the LP market, which now comprises less than 2 percent of music sales.

But are CDs always better? Richard Lenhert, assistant editor of *Stereophile* magazine, told me that if you plan to spend less than $1,000, a new CD player will probably sound better than a new turntable. But if money is no object, a high-quality turntable will unquestionably deliver superior sound.

Further, some purists in the music industry feel that CD technology is flawed. They say that because the CD reproduces music through a digitizing process, it doesn't capture the subtleties of the LP. It's similar to the difference between a photograph, which has gray tones, and a magazine reproduction of a photograph, which is comprised of tiny black dots. Singer Neil Young, the most vocal critic of CDs, calls the last decade "the darkest time ever for recorded music." Many musicians and nearly all grunge bands insist that their music be available on LP.

Realistically, CD technology probably does suit the average ear and the average budget. And given that so little new music is available on LP, it's also a practical choice for those who desire the newest recordings.

So if you've already made the transition to CDs, look for bargains. Used CDs cost $8 to $10. If you want state-of-the-art CD quality, consider mail order. Our business manager, Elaine, joined BMG Music Service and buys only during buy-one-get-two-free sales. This brings the price of each CD down to $7.50. Be very sure to read all of the fine print in any mail-order club's literature.

But if you haven't made the jump—and here's the real point of this article—you can take advantage of one of the best yard-sale opportunities of our time, as compulsive upgraders are dumping their LP's. Duane Corpe of Mount Vernon, Iowa, reports that he bought a half-dozen for a total of $1.50. My uncle, a 45-ish baby boomer, finds records from his favorite artists of the sixties and seventies for 25¢. To preserve these LPs, he records the music on a cassette and then listens to that. (For a thorough discussion of LP- and cassette-preservation methods, read "Fair Play," published in *Stereo Review* magazine, July 1992.)

But note that the unbelievably low-priced LP may be a short-lived phenomenon. Due to increasing scarcity, many LPs are becoming collectors' items and some in mint condition can be worth hundreds of dollars. (For a thorough discussion of collectible LPs, read "Where's the Value in Vinyl?" published in *U.S. News & World Report,* December 1993.)

Aside from the cheap LP, used turntables are a bargain, especially if you already own one. If you're unhappy with the sound quality, try a little maintenance before you decide to heave it. If your needs are modest, yard sales may also offer some bargains. A friend failed to

sell a clean, new-looking turntable at his yard sale for $10. Since our turntable died at the hands of reckless toddlers, he traded his to us for five bags of our frozen berries. Although purists would shudder at our acquisition (because lower-quality turntables can be hard on LPs), it suits our needs. Our music-listening experience consists largely of breaking out old Doris Day and/or Bing Crosby Christmas music once a year. Otherwise, *quiet* is music to our ears.

The yard-sale LP strategy can be either a way to postpone your entry into the world of CDs or a permanent solution. If you do plan to switch to CDs, there's a good argument to be made for waiting to pick up used CDs and CD players as upgraders dump these within a few years. But be cautious. While some people set prices realistically, others try to recover part of their inflated purchase price. If a seller argues a ten-year-old CD player "is worth $250 because it cost $900 new," be aware that the sound quality may be worse than that of a new player costing the same amount.

In short, if you're resisting the expense of those space-age-looking disks, you're not "out of it." Many people continue to listen to LPs for reasons of a nostalgic preference for vinyl, because their favorite oldies are not available on CDs, because they believe the sound quality is better, or because they can listen to really good music for a fraction of the price.

Music is like movies, books, magazines, and fashion: It's much cheaper if you wait a couple of years. So if anyone laughs at you for being hopelessly behind the times, don't get mad, get friendly.

SAFETY-PIN UPHOLSTERY

If you have mediocre sewing skills or little time, sewing cushion covers with zippers seems like a daunting challenge.

One solution is safety-pin upholstery. I have never tried it for a six-cushion couch, but it works well for furniture with only one or two cushions. It can be used as either a temporary or permanent solution.

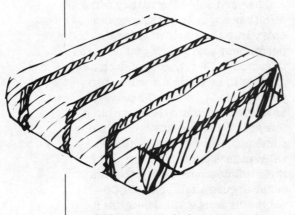

Safety-pin upholstery requires medium-size safety pins (a minimum of six per large cushion) and a piece of heavy fabric. Very simply, you wrap your cushion with the fabric in the same way that you would wrap a box with wrapping paper.

Ideally, the fabric should be large enough to overlap as you wrap from front to back, but if you happen to have material that isn't quite large enough to overlap and the old cushion covers are sturdy, you can fold it under and pin it to the old cover. The side-to-side dimension needs to be only large enough so that it can be wrapped under and securely pinned. In any case, wrap and pin front to back first, so that the folds are concealed on the sides. Using this technique, there will be no visible raw edges.

If you use this as a temporary solution, use the same fabric you hope to sew into real cushion covers someday. While waiting for something nicer to turn up, I have also used temporary fabrics: a surplus scrap of lightweight canvas, old drapes, and a torn bedspread.

Like real cushion covers, this pinned fabric can be removed for washing and quickly replaced.

Safety-pin upholstery has one final advantage. If I change my mind about the cushion fabric (as may happen when I find a better bargain rug) I can reuse this material elsewhere.

INSTANT ANALYSIS

When, back in 1990, I first wrote about our family's use of instant powdered milk, whole milk was very expensive in much of the country: $2.50 or more per gallon. At the same time, store-brand powdered milk in the 20-quart-size box was as low as $1.20 per gallon. But in more recent years, due to government regulations, whole milk prices have dropped to as low as $2.00 per gallon in many parts of the country, while powdered milk has climbed to $1.80 per gallon. With these skimpy savings, I wouldn't fault any tightwads for drinking whole rather than powdered milk.

But a couple of years ago Claudia Tomkiel of Carlisle, Pennsylvania, mentioned a third alternative: noninstant powdered milk, purchased in 50-pound-sack size, which she claimed tasted better than the instant variety. I promptly called local bulk-food sources and found it cost about the same as instant at that time, about $1.60 per gallon. Unimpressed, I disregarded the idea. More recently two other readers including Jane Moran of Meadville, Pennsylvania, wrote with similar information, only these readers also listed their per-gallon prices: from $1.00 (picked up at the factory) to $1.54 (from a bakery-supply company) per gallon. With the recent price increases of instant powdered milk, this became more interesting. Additionally, Jane maintained it tasted far better than instant (which she felt had a "burnt" taste) and was only slightly less rich than 2 percent milk. We made some and we agree: It does taste better than instant powdered milk.

Noninstant powdered milk comes in low-heat and high-heat varieties. This refers to the processing method. Low-heat is slightly more nutritious and slightly more expensive, but the taste is the same.

While noninstant milk is harder to mix, it *can* be done successfully in a blender or with a mixer. Mix 2¾ cups of powder (about 1 pound) to 2 cups of water, let the bubbles evaporate, and then add enough water to equal a gallon.

Like instant, noninstant tastes better if it sits overnight. So keep one jug of newly mixed in the back of the refrigerator while drinking from yesterday's mixed.

Many people wouldn't want to keep a 50-pound sack of anything around, but families who drink a lot of milk might. If this intrigues you, first buy a small quantity of non-instant milk from your local health-food store. (Purchased in small quantities, it will probably have a higher per-gallon cost than whole milk.) If you like it, try to find a cheaper source. A 50-pound sack for $75 equals $1.50 per gallon.

Our local price for noninstant milk is still about $1.60 per gallon. But people who live in the West and Midwest will do better because that's where most of the milk is produced. Contact large producers of dairy products near you to see whether they make noninstant milk and whether you can buy direct. If not, contact bulk-food sources: food coops, health-food stores, and bakery suppliers.

Finally, remember that powdered milk of either kind isn't just for large families. Singles, couples, and small families tend to buy milk in quarts because gallons go bad before they can drink them, so they pay even higher prices for milk. Powdered milk is also a good choice for people whose milk consumption is very limited and for those who primarily use milk for cooking, on cereal, and in hot drinks.

GIZMOS AND GIMMICKS FOR THE NOUVEAU FRUGAL

In the spring of 1991, just after we were featured in *Parade* magazine and on the Donahue show, over 200 feet of mail was delivered to our house. In June of that year, I delivered a set of twins (with, to be precise, exactly four feet). Even with additional help, months would transpire before we began to make a dent in the reader mail.

Along with these letters came a mountain of promotional materials for all sorts of money-saving enterprises: how-to videos, financial-freedom cassettes, vegetarian cookbooks, budget planners, haircutting kits, shop-at-home services, frequent-flyer promotions, toilet-tank water savers, multilevel-marketed everything, computer financial organizers, powdered-milk substitutes (hmmm . . .), toothpaste-tube squishers, flavoring and extract samples, fuel-economizer doohickeys, superinsulated water-heater wraps, coupon pouches, and, perhaps the most unusual, a toilet-to-bidet conversion kit.

I piled all of this stuff in boxes, planning to sort through it someday. I thought if I ever ran out of ideas for the newsletter, this stuff would make handy subject matter. Over time the pile grew . . . and grew . . . and finally it just grew dusty.

Occasionally, I tried to dig through it, but found that much of the promotional literature was too tiresome for a mother of infant twins to absorb on four hours of sleep. I developed an aversion to anything that rolled frequent-flyer miles, phone services, and credit cards into one promise-to-save-you-a-fortune program.

Well, the twins got bigger, and I got more sleep. With my new alertness, I began to spot some of these same products and services in the mass media. When a reader asked about one, I would tack the letter to my bulletin board, making it a priority to research. In most cases, when I overcame my aversion to tiresome literature, I found the analysis interesting. Sometimes I saw that readers could have learned the answers on their own. Other times researching the value of a $100 product required $200 worth of phone calls. Much of what I was able to learn could not have been obtained had I not been with "the media."

As I complete four years of publishing, I've begun to understand that along with increased interest in saving money, the 1990s have seen whole industries spring up to satisfy the newly frugal, many of whom have yet to kick their old habit of buying stuff. Now they can buy money-saving stuff to satisfy the craving without guilt.

The $12 Banana Hanger

They're attracted to easy ways to save money that require only that they sign up for a new gimmick or buy a new gizmo.

Thrift and environmentalism go hand-in-hand. Along with the money-saving gimmicks and gizmos, there's a whole mail-order line of "environmentally responsible" products. Some products are sound but come with a higher price tag than equivalent products you can purchase locally (a push mower is a push mower). Other products you don't need at all, like a rubber necktie made from an old tire (no kidding). These products, like those marketed to the frugal, satisfy our craving to consume without the guilt; we can feel good about buying anything with "Save the whales" silkscreened on it.

The media has recognized the interest of the newly frugal and that there's a huge collection of new products and services to bring to their attention. And indiscriminate product plugs are an easy way to fill airtime or column space. With all of this careless plugging of products, a scam or two is bound to slip through. Unfortunately, people believe "If it weren't true, they wouldn't be allowed to say it on television."

Albeit clunky, let me take a literary detour here and give you an inside view of the media.

I've made dozens of television appearances, and no one ever asked me to verify anything I planned to say. Most talk shows and news spots are hastily assembled. In some cases, I've arrived with barely enough time to catch my breath and clip on a mike.

As both the subject and writer of many articles, I can offer a unique perspective on the print medium. Most of the stories written about me have contained at least one error or misrepresentation. Even when reporters are extremely careful, mistakes happen. Often when I research questionable money-saving offers, I call reporters who previously wrote favorably of them to learn whether they had received any complaints. Invariably, they admit having had too little research time and say they simply trusted what was told to them—or they presumed that, since the gizmo had been plugged elsewhere, *someone* had done the necessary homework. And sometimes they weren't too concerned about letting their readers know they had goofed.

So you shouldn't blindly trust any media report you hear or read anywhere—including in *The Tightwad Gazette*. End of detour.

With the proliferation of talk shows, books, magazines, and newsletters, and these sources all interviewing each other, there has been far too much slipshod product and service promotion geared to the nineties money-conscious consumer.

There's also been a sort of subtle subversion in the thrift publishing business, a kind of "I promoted you in my book, you should promote me in your newsletter" feeling. I feel like a heel for not cooperating, but I didn't ask for their plug, and their book contains the same information that can be found in free library books.

Sometimes the product is given a blanket endorsement even though it isn't good for everyone in every circumstance. There's a lack of effort to analyze and quantify the benefit. In other cases the product might have some possible benefit—like a $12 banana hanger (a gizmo to hang a bunch of bananas on so they won't spot). But often people could improvise: Why not screw a cuphook into the underside of your cabinets?

A lot of this stuff you don't need at all. One birthday, Jim had a *Tightwad Gazette* coffee mug made for me. We realized there would be a market for such mugs among our most enthusiastic readers. Similarly, marketing whizzes have told me I'm missing out by not selling *Tightwad Gazette* buttons, decals, bumper stickers, and T-shirts. It's been suggested that I should sell *Tightwad Gazette* price books with blank pages (even though mine is a scavenged insurance-rate notebook). There was even a lucrative offer from a well-known calendar company that wanted to sell *Tightwad Gazette* tear-off thrifty-tip-a-day calendars. We never debated; all of these things were counter to our philosophy.

I could easily devote every issue to the promotion of semi-good products, although I personally get excited by little of this stuff. I could likewise devote each issue to debunking dubious products and services. I limit my efforts to ones that seem to be taken seriously by the media.

But in both cases, see this for what it is. This is America, the land of the entrepreneur, and there is nothing wrong with people spotting a trend and trying to make money. Just be aware that some of this stuff is useful.

Most of it is not.

DON'T PUT ALL YOUR CONFETTI EGGS IN ONE PAPER-SACK EASTER BASKET

So far, I've managed to collect only three long-handled FTD flower baskets from yard sales to use for permanent Easter baskets, but I seem to be acquiring children faster than I can acquire baskets. When you have six kids, every basket must be identical so that everyone is happy. Hence, I'm still making "disposable" baskets. But I enjoy surprising the kids with something new each year.

As my family has grown, the baskets have had to be quicker to make. So when Cheryl Tomski of Littleton, Colorado, sent in directions to make Christmas baskets using standard grocery sacks, I saw easy Easter-basket possibilities.

Cheryl's baskets were made from large grocery bags. I used lunch-size bags to make Easter baskets.

To make one, roll down the rim of a bag to within 2 inches of the bottom. Roll down a second bag to within 3 inches of the bottom, and tuck it into the first bag, so that its rim rests on the first rim. (To make the larger baskets, you would repeat this procedure until you've combined three to four bags.)

For a handle, cut 6 inches off the top of a standard grocery sack to form a paper circle, and fold in fourths to make a band 1½ inches wide. Glue the raw edge down. Put the basket inside this circle as shown.

To attach the nested bags together and the handle to the bags,

I used small dabs of hot glue because this was quick and easy. But if you have a bit more time—or aren't producing six baskets—you can enhance the "baskety" look with yarn. Lace it in and out of the rims and around the handle by poking holes in the bags with an embroidery needle. The basket can be spray-painted or otherwise decorated.

As for what to put in your paper-sack baskets, try confetti eggs. They're used in Mexican Independence Day celebrations but are great for other holidays. These colorfully dyed, confetti-filled eggs are free to make, won't cause cavities, and take up lots of space in sparse Easter baskets. When a child smashes an egg on his or someone else's head, it explodes (the egg, not the head) in a surprisingly dramatic shower of colored shell and confetti.

Obviously, confetti eggs require less time to smash than to make and clean up. (Pick an easy-to-vacuum place for this activity.) But it's fun to surprise kids with these at least once.

To make the eggs, first poke a tiny hole in one end and a ½-inch-diameter hole in the other end of a raw egg. Blow the egg out (saving the yolk and white for tomorrow's scrambled-egg breakfast).

Rinse the egg shells, and dye them as you would regular Easter eggs. (You don't need to purchase egg-dying kits. Add food coloring

and a teaspoon of vinegar to a cup of boiling water.)

While the dye dries, make confetti by cutting up colorful paper or magazine pages into ¼-inch squares. Or ask a copy shop for paper punches from its hole puncher. Use a funnel (make one from a roll of paper) to put the confetti in the eggs. Glue a piece of tissue paper over the large hole in the egg.

I used this idea when I needed wacky and dramatic props for an appearance on the David Letterman show. Dave loved it.

AVOIDING THE PRICE-BOOK HASSLE

In my first book, I wrote about the price book, a small, loose-leaf binder in which you record the lowest prices at various stores in your area, so you'll know which store generally has the best price on a particular item, and when a sale price really is a bargain.

While scores of readers have told me that the price book led to major savings, several have said they were hassled by management as they wrote in their books. Lisa-Anne French of Yarmouth, Maine, recorded prices in ten stores and at five of them was confronted by angry managers; some accused her of working for competing stores. She asked what one should do in this situation.

Curious, we called two Maine assistant attorneys general. They theorized that stores do have a legal right to ask people to leave; after all, the stores are private property. But, they said, if you explain what you're doing, refuse to leave, and are physically ejected, you might go to a private attorney to see whether you have a case.

We also called two local supermarket chains. Neither had any policy regarding customers writing down prices. A representative suggested telling the store's manager what you'll be doing *before* you begin.

In any case, I never had this problem. I think it's because I never went to every store in my area and jotted hundreds of prices in one intensive effort. I spent almost *no* time standing in aisles, conspicuously scribbling.

• First, I gleaned prices from my sales slips and from products in my cupboards with prices marked on them. I jotted down prices from sale flyers for a month. *Then* I went to the supermarket to fill in the gaps resulting from the few products that never went on sale. I did make a special trip to record prices from the

warehouse club, but there was a limited range of items to record. Because I gathered prices as I shopped, I probably didn't look like an undercover supermarket spy.

• I buy few convenience foods, paper goods, or cleaners, so I need to keep track of fewer than 100 items. I didn't record prices of items I don't buy.

• Some items need not be included in the price book, either because I've memorized the best price or because I have developed a price guideline for an entire product group. For example, I won't pay more than 7¢ an ounce for cold cereal. So I don't have a cold-cereal page at all, much less a separate page of prices for each type of cereal.

• I generally record only the lowest sale prices at the supermarkets. The only regular retail prices I record are for items that seldom go on sale, such as flour, and the few store brands we buy.

• Because we primarily buy only sale items from supermarkets, and because sale prices are similar from one supermarket to another, I was less interested in comparing supermarkets. I focused on comparing supermarket sales to the prices at other places that have few or no sales: warehouse clubs, the military commissary, farmer's markets, "damaged-goods" stores, discount department stores, U-pick farms, food coops, and health-food stores.

• After I gathered several prices, I would record a new price only if it was lower than what I had seen before.

As a final note, remember that through keeping a price book you gain a general sense of where you should shop for each item, but far more important, you learn the bottom price. It doesn't matter where you buy it, what matters is the price you pay.

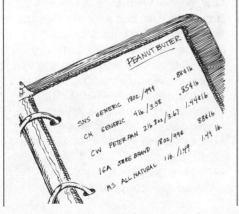

COPY CAT-ALOG

Dear Amy,

I use all of the gift catalogs that come in the mail to study to see what I can copy cheaply. A microwave bacon "fryer" that cost $35 and could be used only for that purpose was recreated with a package of wooden chopsticks that cost 99¢ and one of my microwavable bowls. I have made fun chocolate pizzas that looked even better than the ones in the catalogs (and I found that pizza stores will sell, very cheaply, or even give you the box to put it in). My next year's grandkid project is to copy a catalog's "doorway puppet stage" ($39.95) made from some fabric and a tension rod.

—Gail Jackson
 Blue Springs, Missouri

TOYS FROM TEENS

Dear Amy,

Looking for toys but don't want to spend a fortune? Try the local junior high or high school. These kids have outgrown their "baby" toys and are on the prowl for real money. Ask to put a note on the bulletin board or in the school paper, and be specific. I have gotten: 20 GI Joes for 25¢ to 50¢ each, an entire set of Castle Legos (retail $60) for $10, and a Little Tykes sink, stove, refrigerator, plus a huge box of play food for $25. Be sure to get the parents' permission.

—Julie Edgar
 Manassas, Virginia

IGNORE THE STORE

Dear Amy,

Here's a neat technique used for a wedding shower given for a fellow tightwad. We knew that many guests would be unable to spend much for shower gifts, but that other guests would prefer spending a lot more than necessary. So we issued an invitation with the following request: "Please bring a gift that cannot be purchased in a store." This encouraged homemade gifts and provided noncrafty guests with the possibility of buying gifts in creative places. The bride-to-be received many personal gifts made especially for her as well as a few garage sale items, plants, and other unique gifts. We didn't force frugality on the guests, we simply encouraged it along with encouraging creativity.

—Jill Tammen
  Lakeland, Minnesota

SAND SAVER

Dear Amy,

For years, in late spring or early summer, I've gathered road sand spread by the town during the winter. I scoop it from along the side of the road and put it in 5-gallon plastic buckets. I recycle it by spreading it where necessary during the following winter months. Three buckets full of sand have been sufficient for my 40-foot, double-width driveway and walk for one winter.

—Rudi Smith
  Brunswick, Maine

DOUBLE BUBBLE

Dear Amy,

Our local florist will reinflate those mylar balloons for about 75¢, so I get several uses from the same balloon for family occasions.

—Carolyn Pollock
  Hunt, New York

PHRASES, NOT PHOTOS

Dear Amy,

Neither my husband nor I particularly enjoy taking pictures on vacation . . . and we often forget the camera. His habitual note-taking (he's a reporter) has ended up reducing our desire for photos. At the end of each day of our trip, he makes concise notes about what we did . . . places we ate, sites we saw, people we met, etc. Once home, he rewrites and clarifies the notes and puts them with our other travel diaries. Periodically, we pull them out and relive the vacations, the notes reminding us of silly incidents we never thought to photograph. It gives us great memories, with much less film to buy and develop.

—Colleen Cooper Russell
  Broadview Heights, Ohio

HOW TO MOVE INEXPENSIVELY

Moving can cost thousands of dollars. How cheaply you can move depends on how much advance notice you have, how far you're moving, how much stuff you have, how healthy and strong you are, and how resourceful you're willing to be. If all of those factors are in your favor, a move can be almost free.

The following ideas are from over 250 letters from newsletter readers about their experiences with inexpensive moves.

LIGHTEN THE LOAD

By far the most common suggestion was to get rid of possessions. Scrutinize your belongings as to whether you need them at all, and if so, how easily they can be replaced. A professional mover can charge up to $1 per pound to move items, so you don't want to pay $1 to have a 50¢ can of beans moved. Lighten the load by hav-

ing a yard sale, taking books and magazines to libraries, and taking clothes to consignment shops. You might be better off giving an old piano to a piano dealer. Eat up your food during the months prior to your move. If you're moving locally, this is a good time to have your TV repaired, rugs cleaned, and furniture recovered. Have the stuff delivered to your new home.

PACKING MATERIALS

A professional moving company would charge you over $500 just for packing materials, yet this is the one part of your move that can be achieved almost for free. You will need to buy only packing tape and felt markers.

Free boxes can be found in abundance at a variety of places. Check liquor stores for boxes with compartments, copy shops for photocopy-paper boxes, supermarkets for fruit, egg, and gallon-water boxes, schools in late summer for book boxes, paint stores for paint boxes, and hospital loading docks for supply boxes. Dumpsters behind furniture stores are good sources of cardboard corners for large furniture and boxes for pictures and mirrors. Appliance stores have large pieces of cardboard to tape to furniture. And you saved the box and packing your computer or stereo came in, right?

Having boxes of a uniform size is helpful for longer moves, because you can pack the truck more tightly. You can buy new boxes and resell them to the moving company when you're done, or buy used ones from moving companies. Keep your eyes open for people just moving into your neighborhood, and ask them for their boxes. Trash piles in military housing are good places to look. Put out the word to your friends and coworkers. Another source is Paper Mart (800-745-8800).

Don't use newspaper for packing, as the print will come off on your stuff. Get an end roll of unprinted stock from your local newspaper. You'll also want to scavenge Styrofoam peanuts, Styrofoam blocks from office-equipment stores, and bubble wrap and shredded paper from hospitals and offices. Use your towels, sheets, and blankets. If you don't have enough, it might be cheaper to buy thrift-shop blankets than to rent blankets. Padded envelopes are good for small pictures.

Some items don't require boxes during shorter moves. Leave clothing in bureau drawers. Pack soft unbreakables in trash bags. Tie books in bundles. Remember to pack stuff in stuff—like in your washer.

PACKING TIPS

Pick up free brochures on packing tips from moving companies. Some companies even offer free packing classes.

In the weeks before your move, gradually begin packing the stuff you don't use every day. Certain items should be packed last—like the microwave and vacuum cleaner (so you can vacuum your old house last and your new house first). Don't fill large boxes with very heavy items. Pack dishes upright for less breakage. Mark all boxes with the contents and room destination. If disassembling anything, put small parts in a Baggie and tape to the larger item.

SPECIAL EQUIPMENT

If you're moving yourself, rent a hand-truck or borrow one from a supermarket, a lumberyard, or an employer. If you're moving with a trailer or pickup, you'll need a tarp and rope. Also consider renting a back brace.

THE MOVING-DAY LABOR

The second most common suggestion from readers was to get your friends to help you actually carry the stuff. To ensure their willingness, volunteer to help when they move in the years prior to your move. When they help you, be considerate. Have all of your packing accomplished before they arrive. Give them plants, food, and other items you can't take with you. To avoid overworking them, consider rounding up both a packing crew and unpacking crew. Provide a meal and beverages as a thank-you.

If you can't find friends, consider sources of inexpensive labor: workers through temporary and unemployment agencies, college or high school students, and teens from local youth groups or Scouts. One reader successfully hired men from a halfway house for recovering alcoholics.

THE WHEELS

If you're moving yourself, try to borrow a pickup, van, or truck, and/or a utility or horse trailer. Be sure to fill the gas tanks before returning borrowed vehicles. For longer moves, readers bought trucks, trailers, and even school buses. If you shop carefully, these can be resold after the move so you can at least break even.

TRUCK RENTALS

If you're renting a truck, do some research and compare many options. It's generally cheaper to rent midweek, midmonth, and not during the summer. It'll probably be cheaper to get a larger truck to make one trip than to rent a smaller truck and make several trips.

Because of seasonal "gluts" of trucks all going in the same direction, you'll save if you go in the reverse direction. So if everyone goes south in the winter, you could save half the rental cost if you move north at this time. If you're moving "against the glut," you have negotiating power. Get prices from several rental companies, and see if you can get one to bid lower. Also check with the national and local offices of the same company; sometimes prices are different.

It may be cheaper to return the truck to the point of origin or to pay a friend to come with you and drive the truck

back. You may save by dropping the truck off in a larger distant city rather than a small nearby town.

You might be able to get an AAA discount if you're a member, and you may save a little if you rent a manual-transmission truck. Remember to verify the odometer reading with the company before leaving and to fill the gas tank before dropping the truck off.

HIRING A MOVING COMPANY

This is your most expensive option, and the one that requires the most research. Moving companies vary in how they charge; it's usually some combination of distance, weight, and labor. Get a firm quote in writing, and ask about any hidden charges, deductibles, or deposits. Make sure that their insurance is for full replacement value.

You can save if you pack your own stuff, but the mover probably won't insure it. The stuff might be insured anyway under your homeowner's policy. Either way, it'll probably be cheaper to pack yourself and replace a few damaged items. Transport your most valuable breakables with you in the car. If the movers pack, watch them: Without supervision, they'll pack up your trash. Break down your furniture in advance. But avoid companies that insist on breaking *everything* down; some furniture, particularly any antiques, will never be the same again.

If you need just a few items moved a long distance, see if you can get your stuff on a truck going the same way.

If you're moving locally, small local movers will probably be cheaper. These "three guys and a truck" outfits often charge solely by the hour, so make sure that you have everything completely ready to go before they come.

Be sure the moving company knows the fastest route.

UNCONVENTIONAL OPTIONS

If you're moving a long distance, it can be cheaper to move some things through the post office—especially books that go book rate. Get prices from UPS and bus companies too. In this case, someone will need to be at the destination to pick up the packages.

Some readers were successful in finding independent truck drivers with empty loads who were willing to move stuff.

Some realtors offer discounts with certain moving companies and may even provide free use of the realtor's van. When choosing a realtor, be sure to inquire about this.

IF YOUR EMPLOYER IS PAYING

See if it will pay you to move yourself. The military has such provisions, and we found we could "earn" a little by moving ourselves. Many large companies may have similar policies. Save all your paperwork to be sure you get reimbursed.

MISCELLANEOUS TIPS

Baby-sitters are cheaper than movers, so find a place for your children away from the moving-day hustle.

If you're driving a long distance with a pet, it's worth the 50¢ to get a pet tranquilizer from your vet.

Before you move, get a credit history from your utility companies so that you won't need a deposit at your new destination.

Remember to make provisions to save during lengthy trips. Pack a cooler of food and drinks. Camp or stay with friends and relatives whenever possible.

Keep all receipts together if these would be applicable for income-tax deductions.

A great advantage of moving yourself is that you can afford to leave a full rented or borrowed truck in the driveway for several days while you do messy work such as replacing the carpet, sanding and refinishing the floors, repainting the whole interior, or simply a major cleaning. It's tiring, but these things are much more efficiently done in an empty house.

And remember the "Natural Law of Moving." The number of things you lose while moving is directly proportional to the number of things you find that you had thought you lost in the last move.

THE TWILIGHT PHONE ZONE

Although it seems like a worthy subject for my books, I've hesitated to tackle long-distance telephone service for several reasons:

• Virtually every one of the hundreds of long-distance companies that has sprung up since the 1984 AT&T breakup uses a different billing method.

• Virtually every customer has a different calling pattern.

• Whatever conclusions I publish could be obsolete within months, as rates change and new plans are offered frequently.

• If you bounce around from plan to plan to get the cheapest rates, switching fees could eat up any savings (unless you are taking advantage of a special).

• The few dollars you save by switching to a small company may not be worth the tradeoff in poorer service.

• It's easier for me to predict that you'll save money by making a touch-up paintbrush out of a carpet scrap and a clothespin than by switching phone services.

However, the subject of long-distance phone rates isn't completely hopeless either. An organization called the Telecommunications Research and Action Center (TRAC) has taken on the daunting task of monitoring the ever-shifting world of long-distance calling plans.

The TRAC periodically produces charts that compare the monthly cost of different plans for different usage patterns.

Studying the chart, we came to these conclusions:

• The companies that offered "friends and family" type plans were the cheapest if you made most of your calls to other plan customers, but I personally feel this is impractical, and the savings were not great.

• AT&T was never the cheapest in any category, but the extra expense was not great.

• This is an area of your budget in which you can legitimately throw up your hands and stick with whatever you have now, especially if you don't spend a lot on long-distance calls. But if such calls are a splurge you work into your budget, and you spend as much as $50 per month, it's possible that the information in the TRAC chart could save you as much as $10 a month. To get one, send a long SASE and $2 for the residential information chart or $5 for the business chart to:

TRAC
P.O. Box 12038
Washington, DC 20005.

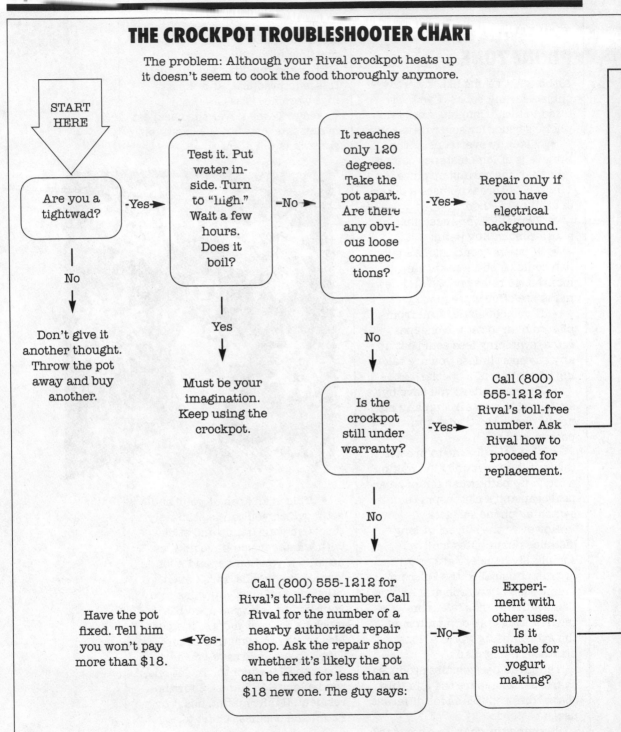

THE CROCKPOT TROUBLESHOOTER CHART

The problem: Although your Rival crockpot heats up it doesn't seem to cook the food thoroughly anymore.

START HERE

Are you a tightwad? —Yes→ Test it. Put water inside. Turn to "high." Wait a few hours. Does it boil? —No→ It reaches only 120 degrees. Take the pot apart. Are there any obvious loose connections? —Yes→ Repair only if you have electrical background.

No ↓

Don't give it another thought. Throw the pot away and buy another.

Yes ↓

Must be your imagination. Keep using the crockpot.

No ↓

Is the crockpot still under warranty? —Yes→ Call (800) 555-1212 for Rival's toll-free number. Ask Rival how to proceed for replacement.

No ↓

Have the pot fixed. Tell him you won't pay more than $18. ←Yes— Call (800) 555-1212 for Rival's toll-free number. Call Rival for the number of a nearby authorized repair shop. Ask the repair shop whether it's likely the pot can be fixed for less than an $18 new one. The guy says: —No→ Experiment with other uses. Is it suitable for yogurt making?

Yes→ Use as a yogurt maker until the pot dies completely.

No→ Use failed yogurt in cooking or popsicles. Disassemble the crock-pot for any reusable parts before discarding.

Save ceramic pot and glass lid. Can be used in combination as a bean pot or sauerkraut crock. Or save glass lid as a see-through cover (fits 3-quart saucepan perfectly). Ceramic pot could be used as a planter by the aesthetically tolerant.

Throw away the crockpot shell and other parts for which you can't imagine any possible future use.

Save the sheet-metal screws, electrical cord, plastic handles, rubber feet, and two-way switch in your "miscellaneous electrical junk" box for future electrical resuscitations.

Toss copper wire in your scrap metal box to be taken to scrap metal dealer in the future.

EXEMPLARY AUXILIARY

Dear Amy,

Many times women's auxiliary organizations to hospitals, churches, synagogues, etc., have once-a-year sales of clothing. The organization's members, who donate most of the clothing, are often well off . . . and what they give reflects this. The resulting bargains are often nothing less than phenomenal. If the sale lasts several days, the remaining merchandise is heavily discounted. Watch the local papers for these sales.

—Reader name withheld by
    request
    Pittsburgh, Pennsylvania

GET A DISH-COUNT

Dear Amy,

After two years of daily use in a household with several small children, we lost some pieces of our country-pattern dishes through breakage and chipping. My husband got a lead on a place that sold individual replacement pieces, but the prices were outrageous! A soup bowl was $15, a creamer was $22! But their list did name the maker of the pattern. We called 800 directory assistance (800-555-1212) and found that the maker had an 800 number. Direct from them, a soup bowl was $4, a creamer was $8! It pays to do some investigating!

—Kimberly Frodelius
    Solvay, New York

BOIL, DON'T TOIL

Dear Amy,

Here's a cleaning tip for pots with burned-on gook: Put enough water in the pot to cover the stain. Add 2 tablespoons of any brand of powdered dishwashing detergent. Boil for 15 to 30 minutes. This also works for dirty burner plates if boiled in a pot of water.

—Anna Johnson
    Kingfield, Maine

A CRAW DEAL

Dear Amy,

Instead of stocking our aquarium with exotic (and often expensive) tropical fish from the pet store and running an energy-consuming heater to keep them alive, my husband caught some crawfish from a nearby river. They are fascinating to watch, can live in an unheated tank, and are easily and cheaply replaced if they meet an untimely end.

—Amy Berrier
    Tamworth, New Hampshire

STORM THE DORMS

Dear Amy,

If you live near a university that has family/student housing, you can find excellent deals at yard sales there at the end of every semester, especially in May. Student families sell off much of their households very cheaply, or even leave hard-to-sell items out for the taking. (After all, you can't take everything back to Korea very easily!) Check it out!

—Frank and Shoshonah Dietz
  Austin, Texas

IT MUST BE SPRIG

Dear Amy,

When a recipe calls for parsley, just use the leaves from celery. It works great.

—Emile Taylor
  St. Louis, Missouri

MANURE MANEUVER

Dear Amy,

We live in a city with a very active fairgrounds and horse track. When fertilizing time comes for our gardens, we just load up some boxes and bags and a couple of shovels and head for the barns. The hands are more than happy to get rid of the piled manure. I compost it to make sure it doesn't burn the vegetation. Even in the city, a person can find manure for the taking.

—Mary Beth Frampton
  Tulsa, Oklahoma

NO MORE TEARS

Dear Amy,

We've made the switch to cloth diapers. It's been much more doable since we began to use nylon pants instead of vinyl ones. The nylon ones are nearly indestructible. The vinyl ones often got holes after just a few uses. We also found out that the larger-size nylon pants still did not leak. We skipped medium and went right to large, thus reducing the investment.

—Dorothy Miller
  Eaton, Colorado

BOOKS IN BULK

Dear Amy,

I live in the New York metropolitan area, and there are quite a number of publishing companies here. Many have company stores open to the public for brief periods during the month. In the case of one children's publisher, the prices are 25¢ to $2 per item, or a savings of about 75 percent. Sometimes the items are not just books, there are board games, household utensils, and school supplies. Readers in other parts of the country could check their Yellow Pages to see what's available.

—Ellen Peixoto
  Waldwick, New Jersey

TUNA-CHEDDAR CHOWDER

A soup called "tuna-cheddar chowder" may not sound particularly tempting, but this is actually one of the best soups I know. It is delicious and has an appealing orange-gold color.

2 carrots, shredded
1 onion, chopped
¼ cup butter or margarine
¼ cup all-purpose flour
2 cups chicken broth
2 cups milk
1 6½-ounce can tuna, drained and flaked
½ teaspoon celery seed
½ teaspoon Worcestershire sauce
¼ teaspoon salt
1 cup cheddar cheese

In a large saucepan, sauté the carrots and onion in the butter until the onion is transparent. Mix in the flour. Add the chicken broth and milk. Heat and stir constantly until thick and bubbling. Add the tuna, celery seed, Worcestershire sauce, and salt, and heat through. Add the cheese and stir until it melts. Serves 4.

REFUNDER BLUNDER

On December 28, 1993, NBC's *Today* show aired a segment called "The Great Coupon/Rebate Scam." It showed a November police and postal-inspection raid of a refund swap meet in New York State. Thirty-six people were detained, and authorities confiscated enough evidence to fill a 2-ton and a 20-ton truck. Arrests are anticipated pending further investigation.

As I watched this, I was disturbed. When I researched refunding for an article that appeared in my first book, I focused solely on whether refunders saved as much as they thought. This story indicated that some aspects of refunding commonly believed to be legal may not be.

To research this I spoke to postal inspectors; the IRS; assistant district attorney David Nutter, who had successfully prosecuted a refund fraud case; and the Coupon Information Center, which represents 25 major manufacturers and gathers data for prosecutions.

Bud Miller, the CIC operations manager, said that based on his organization's 1991 study of 250,000 refunds in a three-state area, he estimated $324 million worth of refunds, about one third of all refunds submitted annually, are fraudulent in some way. He said that all of the people arrested so far owned stacks of refund newsletters, and that he believes most of the fraud occurs through newsletter transactions. Although refund newsletters have been around for more than 15 years, it's only been in the last 2 years that manufacturers have learned how extensive fraud is.

Although no one knows exactly how many newsletters exist, one recent refund book listed 24 of them. The largest has 23,000 subscribers. The newsletters inform their readers of refund offers available and publish ads for people to buy, sell, and trade coupons and refund materials (proofs-of-purchase, receipts, refund forms, and combinations of these three things called "complete deals.")

Refunders typically buy only

name-brand products and save all proofs-of-purchase (POP's) and receipts in organized filing systems. In the future, when a refund is offered, they already have the necessary POP and receipt. In addition, they trade their surplus complete deals or individual refund materials through ads in newsletters, at swap meets, in local clubs, and with "refund pen pals." Theoretically, a group of ten refunders who all buy different products could trade their surplus and increase their refund income tenfold.

Because this refund activity had occurred openly and has been promoted in books, newsletters, and videos for 15 years, most refunders believe it's perfectly legal. But is it?

In December 1993, refund-newsletter publisher Ellen Biles of Norcross, Georgia, was convicted on four counts of refund fraud and later sentenced to 21 months in prison. Two counts of fraud involved the submission of three refunds for the same offer. She was entitled to only one refund. The other submissions were fraudulent because she violated the one-refund-per-household rule and because she submitted refunds for products she didn't actually purchase herself. The third and fourth counts on which she was convicted were for selling complete deals to an undercover postal inspector. This was fraud for several reasons, including that this was simply a way to evade the one-refund-per-household rule, and the purchaser couldn't honestly represent to the manufacturer that she knew the product had actually been purchased.

The trading of proofs-of-pur-chase and complete deals is generally illegal because most refund forms state or imply that you must buy the product to be entitled to the refund. Of the 138 forms we collected locally, 119 indicated you must buy the product yourself.

What if the form doesn't require that you be the original purchaser? An attorney for the postal service said he didn't think submitting this refund would be illegal. But Nutter said the manufacturer's intent is still clear, and he believed such a case could be successfully prosecuted. Unless you're certain you could pick your own prosecuting attorney, it might be wise to avoid this activity.

Trading through newsletters presents other problems: You could be trading with others involved in blatant fraud, and you could be receiving counterfeit materials.

Further, refunders have been led to believe that all refund income is tax-free. Refund income is generally tax-free because you're getting back part of the money you paid. However, if you're obtaining refunds through trade, you're really making a profit. If fraud is involved, the IRS wouldn't allow you to deduct any business expenses. Income from selling coupons and refund forms would also be subject to income tax. Coupons and refund forms sold to others within your state might be subject to sales tax.

Understanding refund fraud is important for two reasons.

First, many people who've never read a refund newsletter also have their extra refunds sent to friends and relatives. Technically, this would be mail fraud.

Second, with Biles's conviction, much of what we've seen or read about the methodology and benefits of coupons and refunds is in question. This includes my analysis of one refunder's grocery bills in my first book; I now realize that the figures I used included income from traded complete deals.

Most large libraries and bookstores have pre-1994 library books on coupons and refunds that indicate that trading complete deals is legal, that all refund income is tax-free, and that you can save up to 80 percent on your grocery bill by using this system.

Further, over the years, most of us have read magazine articles or seen programs on TV demonstrating "the amazing shopping trip": A coupon queen buys $200 worth of groceries for $10. In most cases, the coupon queens were also re-

funders, and because some of the most valuable coupons can be obtained through refunds, some of the coupons used on these trips were probably obtained through complete-deal trading. Unfortunately, these demonstrations contributed to a widespread belief that grocery-shopping magic can be worked with coupons.

In April 1994, the Postal Inspection Service declared war on refund fraud. They began an intensive effort to educate manufacturers on the magnitude of this practice and consumers on the legal consequences of engaging in it.

Refunding itself is not illegal, but ever-increasing form limitations and the 1994 legal understanding will make refunding more time-consuming and considerably less profitable.

I don't want to discourage anyone from sending in refunds. Many people consistently get certain products for free by combining sales, coupons, and refunds. I want people to do the math, as very often I find combining these three things does *not* result in a good deal. Most important, when you send in a refund, scrupulously adhere to the limitations on the refund forms.

OUTLET GASKET UPDATE

In my first book, I published an unattributed reader tip to use Styrofoam, or polystyrene, meat trays to make outlet gaskets that are similar to the ones you can buy at hardware stores. Installed under outlet covers, these seal out drafts. Some 2½ years after the idea was published in my newsletter, the criticism has been raised that this could be a fire hazard.

Before originally publishing this idea, I consulted my husband, Jim, who was a Navy electrician for 20 years. He reasoned that it would be safe because you can buy similar foam gaskets. After extensive research, I am not convinced he was wrong. But it does fall into a gray area. If you read my first book and used this idea, it's important that you have all the information to make an informed choice.

Store-bought gaskets are made of a variety of foam materials, although we found none that were of meat-tray-like polystyrene. Some, but not all, store-bought gaskets have the Underwriters' Laboratories approval seal, which indicates they meet safety standards.

Both polystyrene and UL-approved gaskets smoke, melt, and burn when exposed to heat. Unlike paper, polystyrene tends to melt and shrink away from a heat source; we could not get it to burn with a hot soldering iron. We put four different brands of UL-approved gaskets to a match test. One burned but went out when I removed the match. Two burned independently after three seconds of match time. One brand and the polystyrene burned independently after one second of match time.

This did not surprise UL communications director Holly Schubert. "We don't test to see if they'll withstand the heat from a match flame," she told me. "We test to see if they'll perform well under circumstances they would be exposed to in an outlet."

It's important to note that a UL approval indicates only that a product meets a safety guideline, but products that have not been tested could be equal or superior. Some electrical products don't require approval, but the manufacturers have them tested anyway for marketing purposes.

I asked William King, director of the Electrical Engineering Division of the Consumer Product Safety Commission, whether homemade polystyrene gaskets violated the National Electrical Code. Because the wording is so vague and because gaskets aren't addressed, King believes the interpretation would be up to local authorities. (UL agreed with this assessment.) If there had been many fires associated with any kind of gasket, it would have come to his attention. Thus, the CPSC has no official position on polystyrene gaskets.

While there are flammable materials in electrical boxes, King prefers that consumers don't add more. He was surprised to learn that some UL-approved gaskets were flammable. King personally believes that it's better to have ample air circulation in electrical boxes, since faulty wiring would heat up more in a tightly sealed space. Thus he had concerns not only about gaskets, but about child safety caps, which also block air flow.

Homemade polystyrene gaskets have not been tested by UL, and my flammability test is far from scientific. But it seems to me that polystyrene gaskets aren't dangerous as compared to some UL-approved gaskets.

So should you use gaskets at all? We end up with two "expert" opinions: the UL stance that even flammable gaskets are safe enough to earn its approval, and King's belief that putting anything flammable behind the switch plate or restricting air circulation within an electrical box may not be a good idea. In cases where experts disagree, I can only present their opinions and let you decide.

WEALTH, POVERTY, AND FRUGALITY

I was 11 years old when I began to understand wealth.

Our family had just moved into our third home in my brief memory. It was a large, Cape-style house with outbuildings on 74 acres. The homes I had known be-

fore were also large. Our family had a garden, drank either powdered milk or farm milk, took box lunches to school, ate oatmeal for breakfast, and wore secondhand clothes. For a brief time, I felt some discomfort about not having white go-go boots like some of my classmates. But then I noticed that kids who always had the latest, new clothes frequently lived in

small houses. I concluded that people who lived in small houses had new clothes, and people who lived in big houses had secondhand clothes.

My simplistic view of the world had plenty of exceptions. I knew a few families who lived in large houses and also had new clothes, and people who lived in small houses who had secondhand clothes. But the general idea is true. People who put their surplus money into short-term extravagances rarely build the same wealth as those who put their money in things with lasting value.

Although I figured this out at 11 years of age, the majority of American adults don't understand this basic idea. We still think that frugality has to do with being "poor," and that wealth and frugality are mutually exclusive terms. Overcoming this misconception is crucial to achieving a successful frugal life.

The fact is that income level has very little to do with whether a person chooses frugality. Many poor people aren't frugal, and a surprising number of wealthy people are.

Although this idea for an article has been kicking around in my brain for some time, two recent pieces of mail prompted me to write it.

A nonsubscriber wrote the following in reference to her occasional purchase of junk food: "I found if I try to be too thrifty or too cheap, my kids have a 'poor mentality' . . . in other words, thinking of themselves as being poor instead of thrifty. So I do make allowances once in a while for 'comfort food.' "

Grrrr! In her view, she has to give her kids the occasional Twinkie, like the other kids have, instead of an inexpensive alternative, or they'll have low self-esteem.

About the same time, I came across an article entitled "Why You're Not As Wealthy As You Should Be" by Thomas J. Stanley, Ph.D., who is the chairman of a research firm called Affluent Market Institute. The author began to study wealthy people 20 years ago and made an amazing discovery: People who live an affluent lifestyle are seldom wealthy. Affluent-lifestyle people spend all of their money on extravagances and have nothing left over.

Wealth, on the other hand, is not how much you earn, it's how much you accumulate. Stanley discovered that the typical wealthy person lives in a middle-class house, marries once and stays married, owns a small factory, chain of stores, or service company, and lives his entire life in one town. His money is seldom inherited. Dr. Stanley estimated that 80 percent of American millionaires are first-generation rich. Instead, the wealthy person typically acquires money through hard work and self-discipline. And he is a compulsive saver and investor. It simply isn't his nature to spend money frivolously because it wouldn't be a good investment.

He is someone like the late Sam Walton, the founder of Wal-Mart, who was a billionaire and well known for owning an old pickup and ancient office furniture.

A financial advisor I know confirms this distinction between affluence and wealth. Referring to her wealthiest clients, she says,

"You couldn't pick most of them out of a crowd."

This makes it clear how the confusion between affluence and wealth arises. We see the behaviors of affluent people, and this becomes our only clue as to how the "rich" behave. We don't see the behaviors of the truly wealthy. A goose-egg diamond ring stands out. A ten-year-old suit and a healthy bank balance don't.

Dr. Stanley observed, as I have, that most Americans are confused about the relationship between frugality and wealth. This confusion has a profound impact on how Americans spend. Because we think frugality has to do with being poor, we see it as an admission of economic failure. We think only poor people go to thrift shops, only poor people bring home a good find from the dump, and only poor people cut their kids' hair.

Because we don't want to be seen as economic failures, we spend our money the way we mistakenly think the wealthy do—usually on day-to-day extravagances. We feel good because, briefly, we've made people think we are wealthier than we are. If we do it often enough, we may even fool ourselves along with our neighbors.

It is true that most wealthy people buy a few more luxuries than do poor people, but the total percentage of income they spend on extravagances is extremely small. Consequently, a person with a low income and a wealthy attitude would live as modestly as possible to create a maximum surplus to save and invest.

Poor people often remain poor because they spend any surplus income on short-term gratification. Therefore, buying Twinkies is more likely to be the behavior of a person with a poor mentality than of a person with a wealthy attitude.

The point isn't that big houses are better than little ones (actually, little ones are usually more frugal), or that used clothing is always better than new, or that no one should ever buy Twinkies. Neither do I mean to imply that we should all strive to be wealthy. And certainly, many poor people are frugal and many wealthy people aren't.

What I do see is that many people are ashamed of being frugal. When we're pressured to spend on gifts at the office, we have a hard time saying no. When our relatives snicker at our thoughtful homemade gifts, we feel bad. When our up-to-the-eyeballs-in-hock obnoxious neighbor picks on us for owning an ancient car, we cower in embarrassment.

Likewise, when dealing with coworkers, neighbors, and relatives, I've found that if you explain your financial goals and the choices you must make to reach them, people seem more understanding. Who could object to your desire to save money to send your kid to college?

To be successful and happy in the frugal lifestyle, we have to be proud and confident in our choices. We must have a clear view of our goals, and we must understand the tradeoffs we're making. If we do this, we'll feel no shame about being frugal. Instead, we'll understand that we have a wealthy attitude.

The Tightwad Gazette
RRY Box 3570
Leeds, ME 04263

HOW TO SUBSCRIBE TO THE NEWSLETTER

The Tightwad Gazette is a monthly eight-page, black-and-white, no-frills newsletter. To receive a subscription send your name, address, and $12 to:

> *The Tightwad Gazette*
> RR1 Box 3570
> Leeds, ME 04263

To receive the newsletter for $1 per year, find eleven other tightwads to share a subscription with you.

   Back issues, starting from the June 1994 issue (#49), are available for $1 each. Sample issues are available for a self-addressed, stamped, business-size envelope.

   We'd love to read about your best tightwad strategy or favorite success story.

MONEY-BACK GUARANTEE

If *The Tightwad Gazette II* doesn't show you how to save more than you paid for it, return your copy with your cash register receipt to the following address for a full refund:

> *The Tightwad Gazette II*
> c/o Villard Books
> 201 East 50th Street
> 7th Floor
> New York, NY 10022

Index

ABOUT THE AUTHOR

AMY DACYCZYN started a newsletter called
The Tightwad Gazette in June of 1990.

Amy is a graduate of the Vesper George School
of Art in Boston. She did freelance work
for many design studios in the Boston area for
eight years before her marriage to Jim in 1982.
They and their six children live happily
and frugally in Leeds, Maine.